D1154104

The publisher and the University of California Press Foundation gratefully acknowledge the generous support of the Joan Palevsky Imprint in Classical Literature.

Cult of the Dead

Cult of the Dead

A BRIEF HISTORY OF CHRISTIANITY

Kyle Smith

UNIVERSITY OF CALIFORNIA PRESS

University of California Press
Oakland, California

© 2022 by Kyle Smith

Library of Congress Cataloging-in-Publication Data

Names: Smith, Kyle, author.
Title: Cult of the dead : a brief history of Christianity / Kyle Smith.
Description: Oakland, California : University of California Press,
[2022] | Includes bibliographical references and index.
Identifiers: LCCN 2021060187 (print) | LCCN 2021060188 (ebook) |
ISBN 9780520345164 (hardback) | ISBN 9780520975712 (ebook)
Subjects: LCSH: Christian saints—Cult—History. | Christian martyrs—
Cult—History. | Death—Religious aspects—History. | Church
history—Primitive and early church, ca. 30–600.
Classification: LCC BX2333 .S65 2022 (print) | LCC BX2333 (ebook) |
DDC 235/.2—dc23/eng/20220128
LC record available at https://lccn.loc.gov/2021060187
LC ebook record available at https://lccn.loc.gov/2021060188

Manufactured in the United States of America

28 27 26 25 24 23 22
10 9 8 7 6 5 4 3 2 1

For Dom Bertolph

The past is never dead. It's not even past.

WILLIAM FAULKNER, *Requiem for a Nun*

Contents

Illustrations

PLATES

Preface

A few years ago, at a friend's dinner party, I was introduced to the proprietor of an antiquarian bookshop in Toronto called the Monkey's Paw. Specializing in what its owner deems arcane and absurd, the Monkey's Paw is a curious place. Many around town know it as the home of the Biblio-Mat: a used-book vending machine reminiscent of a 1950s-era refrigerator. Drop a toonie (a Canadian two-dollar coin) into its slot, and the Biblio-Mat starts to buzz. Then a bell dings and out pops a random book on some obscure subject.

I had browsed around in the Monkey's Paw before and had even chatted with its owner—both of us unaware we had a mutual friend—but I never bought anything from him. As much as I admired his strange books, an ingrained backpacker's ethos of minimalism kept me from acquiring any of them. So when small talk over cocktails at the dinner party inevitably pivoted to the "And-what-do-you-do?" question and I told the bookseller that I'm a religion professor who studies the ancient Christian martyrs, I was only politely interested when he clapped his hands together in delight and announced that he had just the book for me. But as it happened, he did. His book was the impetus for this one.

On display in his storefront window was a weathered English reprint of an elaborately illustrated volume that had first been published in Italian in the sixteenth century. Its dun-colored pages were propped open to an image of a man tied to a wheel that is about to be rolled down a road of iron spikes (see fig. 1). The book's other illustrations—dozens of facsimiles of the original copperplate engravings—are just as grisly. One man is about to be crushed in an olive press. Another stands as a human brazier forced into offering red-hot coals of incense to a pagan idol with his bare hands. A third cowers on one knee as the schoolboys gathered around him prepare to stab him with, of all things, their *pens*—the pointy styli that Roman students used to employ to scratch letters onto wax-covered tablets.

Despite all these theatrical and innovative forms of violence, the book's engravings lack blood and gore. Their violence is instructive, not gratuitous. Various augers, cauldrons, wheels, chains, pulleys, and hacksaws are shown in action but usually frozen in the immediate moment before their use. This does not make these images any easier to see. Anticipated horrors can be more cringe inducing than already completed scenes.

Set as they are against a generic backdrop of porticoes and archways in an otherwise empty classical city, the horrors I found displayed in the bookseller's window unfold in an imagined world. The men and women about to be on the receiving end of a torturer's tool are anonymous. Clad in identical loincloths, they gaze off impassively toward some distant horizon. They could be anyone. And they are almost never pictured alone. Those being tortured are presented together, either in pairs or in threes or fours, with others who are undergoing similar sorts of trials. Those steeling themselves to have a limb chopped off are on one page, those being stretched or hung are on another, and those about to be branded or burned are yet elsewhere.

Across twelve systematically organized chapters, the book collects, classifies, divides, and subdivides every conceivable way that early Christian martyrs might have had their flesh torn, butchered, or burned. In celebrating the hardware that won the martyrs their

FIGURE 1. Martyrs being tortured on wheels, designed by Giovanni Guerra with engraving by Antonio Tempesta for Antonio Gallonio's *Trattato de gli instrumenti di martirio, e delle varie maniere di martoriare usate da' gentili contro christiani* (Rome, 1591).

FIGURE 2. Arrangement celebrating some of the tools used to torture and kill Christian martyrs, designed by Guerra with engraving by Tempesta for Gallonio's *Trattato de gli instrumenti di martirio.*

paradoxical victory over death, a few of the engravings present just the tools of torture alone—no martyr in sight. At first glance, one especially well-curated ensemble looks like a floral motif ready to be replicated on a roll of wallpaper (see fig. 2). But look more closely at its frilly ribbons and palm fronds and see that they adorn a collection of cudgels, ropes, and blades. I took the book straight to the register without checking its price.

Once I got my new prize back to my office, it took little sleuthing to figure out what it was. The *Treatise on the Instruments of Martyrdom, and the Various Manners of Martyrdom Used by Gentiles against Christians* was originally published in Rome in 1591. Its text was written by Father Antonio Gallonio, a Catholic priest and scholar of ancient Christian martyrdom, while its engravings were designed and executed by artists from Florence and Modena. What I had bought was a 1903 English translation, competently done by a British academic. Yet oddly, there was not much in the book's front matter to explain why it had been written. No translator's preface, no scholarly introduction, nothing except for a publisher's note cryptically signed with the initials "C.C." And this is where things got weird.

The initials, I soon discovered, were those of Charles Carrington, the pseudonym of a Paris-based publisher better known for books like the Beautiful Flagellants trilogy by Lord Drialys, a fictional English aristocrat who supposedly traveled to Boston, New York, and Chicago in search of American women eager to be spanked by a peer of the realm. In other words, Charles Carrington was a publisher of late Victorian porn. But even though sadomasochistic and other erotic fiction was his bread and butter, it seems that Carrington occasionally dabbled in somewhat more pensive pursuits to lend his publishing house a veneer of respectability—and given the constraints of the age, perhaps legality too.

Carrington's note on Gallonio's *Treatise* (which he published under the abbreviated title *Tortures and Torments of the Christian*

Martyrs) starts out soberly enough. He is quick to remind his readers that Gallonio's book was issued with the full approval of the church. No introduction to it is needed, he says, because it "speaks for itself." Christians of all stripes, Catholics and Protestants alike, already know and celebrate the "moral grandeur" of the early Christian martyrs. Soon enough, Carrington's piety fades. The "prodigious vogue" that Gallonio's book once enjoyed in early modern Europe was, he alleges, thanks less to the sanctity of the martyrs and more to the "morbid love of horrors" that lurks "deep down in our poor human nature." Our collective fascination with martyrs might be due to something else too, he says, something beyond our love of blood. Lest any confusion remain about why someone like Carrington would want to republish Gallonio's book, he clears it up when—veiling his most explosive thesis behind the words of a nineteenth-century French historian—he begins to speculate about the nature of the "unions" between Christian men and women on "the last night they spent together in prison," knowing their deaths would come with the dawn.

With his real interest in Gallonio's *Treatise* now communicated to those in the know, for the sake of the usual customers more interested in the latest from Lord Drialys, Carrington offers reassurance to those who might be scandalized by such insinuations: "Needless to say, not a word of this appears in the good Gallonio."

Carrington understood the persistent allure of blood and spectacle but, needless to say, failed to grasp either the circumstances of the ancient Christian martyrs or the motives of the "good Gallonio," who wrote about them more than a millennium after their deaths. In fact, Carrington missed the point entirely—but not because of his salacious union of sex and death in the moldering recesses of a Roman prison. The real violence Carrington did to Gallonio's work were with the cuts of his editorial scissors.

In his publisher's note, Carrington explains that while he has, of course, kept all the illustrations of the martyrs' suffering, he has trimmed away the priest's many tiresome prayers and his "meticulous parade of names," which is to say the "long lists of perfectly obscure and entirely unknown Saints whom Gallonio scrupulously records as having perished under such-and-such a form of martyrdom." Such long-winded list making does nothing for the book, according to Carrington, and droning through all those forgotten names would "only be a weariness of the flesh to the modern reader."

What Carrington failed to comprehend—or simply did not care to—is how crucial that collection of names was for Gallonio and for any of his early modern readers who still remained devoted to the sainted martyrs of the ancient Christian past. For Carrington, the dreadful images were the book's selling point. (They sold me.) But for Gallonio the images were secondary. They were useful only as visual aids, as a sort of early modern stock photography, that a faithful Catholic could use to better see and sympathize with the particular pains of a particular martyr on the particular day of their death.

That wheel? That's how the virgin martyr Saint Catherine of Alexandria was tortured on November 25, even if she miraculously broke the "Catherine wheel" to which she was bound and had to be beheaded instead. The professor stabbed with the pens of his students? That was Saint Cassian of Imola, a Christian schoolmaster who was killed on August 13.

Gallonio's "parade of names" and the form of violence associated with each was his way of collecting and organizing saints like Catherine, Cassian, and so many thousands of others who were said to have followed Jesus in martyrdom in so many flamboyant ways. And by focusing on the *cult* of these martyrs—that is, by focusing on all the rituals, objects, calendars, lists, and tales with which centuries of Christians have cared for and remembered their saints—this book tells the story of how Christianity became (and how it still remains) a cult of the dead.

Introduction

Christianity is a cult of the dead. And the story of its obsession with martyrdom and the remains of the dead begins with the cross. The cross has been an instantly recognizable symbol for centuries, but what is often forgotten is how this tool of Roman torture became more than a reminder of a single event in the past. It was a model for imitation again and again. According to early Christian tradition, all but one of Jesus's faithful apostles were martyred. Some were crucified, others beheaded, stabbed, flayed, or sawn in half.

The centrality of martyrdom to Christianity has profoundly affected the development of its cultural expression and devotion, from its art and architecture to its liturgy and literature—even its conception of time. The Christian calendar is a cycle of saints, a daily celebration of the martyrs who walked in the footsteps of the apostles. Martyrs' shrines are places of pilgrimage where miracles have occurred. Martyrs' relics are material manifestations of the holy, where heaven meets earth. Martyrs' stories—hundreds of lurid legends of unimaginable suffering and endurance—have been copied and recopied, translated and rewritten. The most rustic villagers of medieval Europe heard about the martyrs from itinerant preachers who carried condensed accounts of their deaths, while the most illustrious work in Middle English is a salty collection of travelers' tales told en route to a martyr's shrine in Canterbury.

Though the Christian martyr cult peaked in the Middle Ages, interest in martyrs did not wane with the rise of Protestantism or even the scientific skepticism of the Renaissance and the early modern age. Catholic scholars eager to justify the cult of the martyrs excavated the catacombs and scoured the monastic libraries of Europe in a grand attempt to replace lost relics and collect every saint's life that had ever been written, reasoning that this would help separate holy fact from pious fiction. Meanwhile, Bible-based reformers promoted their own martyrs—not as saints to be venerated but as the newest links in a monumental chain of Christian suffering that joined contemporary witnesses to the gospel with those of the ancient past.

The Christian cult of the dead owes a lot to the unique perspective of Luke-Acts, the New Testament's two-volume history of Jesus and his earliest followers better known to most as the Gospel of Luke and, by the same author, the Acts of the Apostles. Luke's Jesus (as opposed to Matthew's, for instance, who is a second Moses and the fulfillment of Israel's history) is a second Socrates. He is an innocent and impassive martyr in the mold of that most self-assured of the ancient Greek philosophers. For Luke, who writes with evident knowledge of the Greco-Roman tradition of noble death, Jesus is a template—a model for emulation. And the first to follow Jesus in martyrdom was the deacon Stephen. According to Acts, Stephen was stoned to death in Jerusalem for his bold testimony on Jesus's behalf.

Stephen's story soon jumped from the page. His life and death, retold over several centuries in many literary elaborations, itself became a model of Christian martyrdom. Stephen's place in the Christian calendar, the movement of his relics, the sermons preached in his honor, the construction of his shrines, and the books that meticulously cata-logued his miracles—a litany of healings that Saint Augustine of Hippo once read aloud to his North African congregation—offer an entryway into several chapters of this book, about martyrs' stories, martyrs' rel-ics, martyrs' calendars, the many sermons preached about martyrs, and the lists of martyrs' miracles that were kept at their pilgrimage shrines.

This flourishing of Christian culture around the martyrs acceler-ated tremendously after the conversion of the Roman emperor Con-stantine in the early fourth century. With a Christian on the throne, other Christians were emboldened to tell the history of the Roman Empire anew. For one of Constantine's advisors, this meant combin-ing a chronicle of Roman persecution with an almost gleeful account of the deaths of those persecutors: all those anti-Christian emperors who had reigned before Constantine. For other classically educated Christians, such as Eusebius of Caesarea, the bishop of the eastern Mediterranean port city where Pontius Pilate once served as prefect, Constantine's rise to power demanded an altogether new form of history: the ecclesiastical, or "church," history.

As Eusebius saw it, narrative accounts of the martyrs were central to the story of the church. Several martyrdom narratives existed be-fore Eusebius began writing, but he was the first to systematically gather and transmit them as a collection, thus helping to establish a recognizable genre of Christian death literature. Eusebius's example of this new form of Christian history quickly became the model for many heirs and imitators, both those who wrote in Greek, as he did, and those who wrote in other important literary languages of late antiquity, like Latin, Armenian, and Syriac (a Christian dialect of Aramaic).

Heroic stories were not the only mementos of the saints that cir-culated throughout the Christian world. Martyrs' bones, fragmented remains of the dead still pulsing with holiness, traveled just as widely.

Many of these relics were thought to belong to those who were killed during the persecutions about which Eusebius wrote; others, to much earlier witnesses for the gospel, such as Stephen and the apostles. Though Christians believe that Jesus's body was assumed into heaven after his death and resurrection, this was no obstacle to having a thriving trade in his relics too. Princely collectors from Byzantine emperors to crusading kings went to great effort and tremendous expense to acquire bits and pieces of anything that might have touched Jesus in his life and, more important, in his death. The most revered of these "contact" relics were thorns from his crown, splinters from his cross, and burial sheets from his tomb. Many centuries before the Shroud of Turin captivated Christian pilgrims, several other scraps of cloth were said to have been miraculously imprinted with a perfect likeness of Jesus's face.

While it is Jesus's life that continues to dominate the Christian calendar (notably in the long, penitential seasons of Advent and Lent and the more festive seasons of Christmas and Easter which they respectively precede), scores of other martyrs have participated in this annual cycle of fasts and feasts. Thanks to Usuard, a ninth-century Parisian monk, many Christian liturgical calendars are still, to this day, just expansive lists of saints. Usuard was not the first to collect and collate the martyrs (the Venerable Bede's attempt was widely influential, as were others before his), but his especially well-organized list became the calendar against which all others were measured. It was the Medieval Standard Time by which Christians kept pace with the seasons and their lives.

Any saint with a day in Usuard's calendar was sure to be found in Jacopo de Voragine's immense, thirteenth-century compendium, known as *The Golden Legend*. Many of Jacopo's more fabulous stories are indeed legends (which is to say, popular stories of rather dubious authenticity), but the Latin term for them is less freighted: *legendaria* were simply collections of "readings" about the lives of the saints.

Jacopo's collection, which is written in silvery but unadorned Latin, is a reader's digest of saints, an encyclopedia of martyrs that was originally intended to aid traveling mendicants such as the Dominicans—that most famous of the medieval preaching orders. Perhaps inadvertently, the Dominicans afforded a wide exposure to Jacopo's book, turning what had begun as a reference work into an unexpected best seller. Many hundreds of complete manuscript copies of *The Golden Legend* still survive, and with the arrival of print in the fifteenth century, Jacopo's book initially outpaced even the Bible in its number of editions and translations.

So popular were saints' lives that even tales about fictional travelers to a saint's shrine were a hit. Geoffrey Chaucer's *Canterbury Tales* is not a compendium of saints' lives, but the stories his characters tell along the way from London to Canterbury at once honor the traditional medieval pilgrimage and bawdily critique its follies and excesses. By the end of the fourteenth century, when Chaucer was writing, Canterbury Cathedral was well known as the house of an especially competent wonder-worker, Saint Thomas Becket. This beloved bishop-martyr was officially elevated to the ranks of the saints in the late twelfth century, scarcely more than two years after he was killed by knights acting on the orders of King Henry II. The books collecting and describing Becket's posthumous miracles are as important for understanding medieval piety as is the cathedral that was the terminus for the thousands of pilgrimages he once inspired.

Despite its massive popularity, even Becket's shrine was imperiled by the time of King Henry VIII. In this case, the disagreement between church and crown was not confined to two men. Henry's fury over the pope's refusal to annul his marriage to Catherine of Aragon led to a permanent schism between the Church of England and the one in Rome. Years later, when Henry's eldest daughter, and the only fruit of his contested marriage, briefly reestablished Catholicism in England, she inaugurated a new age of martyrs. "Bloody"

Mary burned hundreds of Protestants at the stake, including Thomas Cranmer, the formerly Catholic archbishop of Canterbury, spurring the composition of yet another new form of ecclesiastical history. Not surprisingly, martyrs were again at its center, just as they had been for Eusebius centuries earlier during an altogether different leadership transition. After Mary's death, Queen Elizabeth's ministers, seeking to solidify their new, national church, built upon the three literary pillars of the English Reformation: the Bible, the revisions of Thomas Cranmer's *Book of Common Prayer,* and the wonderfully illustrated monument of Protestant church history that had come to be known as *Foxe's Book of Martyrs.*

At the same time, the response of the Catholic Counter-Reformation, both in England and on the Continent, was one of entrenchment. Over and against the Protestant call of *sola scriptura,* "by scripture alone," Catholics reasserted the importance of scripture and tradition. In Rome, a circle of scholarly priests and lay brothers dove deep into the past with the goal of reaffirming the long history of the Christian cult of the dead. They plumbed the newly rediscovered catacombs for martyrs' relics. They reread their Livy and Tacitus, seeking clues about ancient Roman methods of torture that might enliven, in gruesomely specific ways, their devotional readings on the sufferings of the saints. And they composed new ecclesiastical annals while simultaneously revising the liturgical calendar, purging it of saints of local or more recent interest in favor of a universal list more thoroughly grounded in tradition.

In the seventeenth century, a group of priests from the Southern Netherlands known as the Bollandists responded to increasing skepticism toward the stories of the saints by committing themselves to a preposterously difficult task: they would track down, analyze, critically edit, and then publish every saint's life that had ever been written. In the process, they would question legendary accretions and seek to clarify truths. Their scholarly and "scientific" approach to the saints was not without controversy. When the Bollandists challenged the founding myth of the Carmelite order, which claimed a connection to the Hebrew prophet Elijah, they attracted the rather unwanted attention of the Spanish Inquisition. After decades of suppression, the Bollandists reemerged to carry on their work. It continues today.

North Sea

NORTHUMBRIA
✝ Rievaulx Abbey

Norwich

Oxford
London
Canterbury

FLANDERS

Elbe River

Wittenberg

Cologne
✝ Heisterbach Abbey

NORMANDY

Paris

Seine River

Via Francigena

Rhine River

Danube River

Tours
Loire River

Basel
Zürich

Atlantic Ocean

Lyon
Vienne

Rhône River

ALPS

Trent
Milan
Venice

Turin
Pavia
Piacenza

Montpellier
Narbonne

Genoa

Bologna
Florence

Adriatic

Zara

Roncesvalles
PYRENEES

Santiago de
Compostela

Acquapendente

Rome

Saragossa
Lleida

MINORCA

Bari

Almería

Strait of Gibraltar

Mediterranean Sea

Hippo
Carthage

Strait of Messina
Messina
SICILY
Cata

THE LAND OF THE DEAD

Danube River

CRIMEA
Caffa

Black Sea

CAUCASUS MOUNTAINS

Constantinople

Nicaea

ARMENIA

CAPPADOCIA

Aegean Sea

Athens

Smyrna

Cyrrhus

Edessa Nisibis

Mosul

Myra

Antioch

Tigris River

PERSIA

SYRIA

Euphrates River

Beirut

Mediterranean Sea

Baghdad

Nazareth
Caesarea
Jerusalem
Bethlehem

Jordan River

Judean Desert

Alexandria

Dead Sea

Desert of Scetis
Monastery of the Syrians ✝

EGYPT

Nile River

△ Mount Sinai

Red Sea

1   *The First of the Dead*

When my children were younger, I would walk them to school. Along the way, our dog would invariably stop to pee on the same signpost in Saint Alban's Square, a small park in central Toronto. There is nothing remarkable about Saint Alban's Square. A rectangle about the size of a football field, it boasts a few benches, some modest trees, and a city bike-share depot. A paved walkway (not always plowed during the winter) runs lengthwise across its center from west to east.

Saint Alban's Square is so named because it sits in the shadow of the former Anglican Cathedral of Saint Alban-the-Martyr, a nineteenth-century church built of rose-colored Ontario sandstone. Although it now serves as the private chapel of an all-boys school named for Saint George, Saint Alban's once competed for prominence with the more established Cathedral Church of Saint James, downtown and closer to Toronto's business district and lakeshore. Indeed, in the early twentieth century, as the city continued its northward march to further encompass what was formerly forested countryside, Saint Alban's was important enough that the archbishop of Canterbury and the American financier J.P. Morgan each visited once for evening prayer.

Toronto, to its great credit, is now arguably the most multicultural city in the world. More than half its citizens claim Korean,

Tagalog, Portuguese, Amharic, or any one of several dozen other languages as a primary tongue before English. But the city is still marked with traces of its Anglo-Christian colonizers, many of which, like Saint Alban's Square, remain hidden in plain sight. I often wonder how many dog walkers or bench sitters in my neighborhood know that Saint Alban was supposedly the first Christian martyred in Britain.

Know it or not, Toronto is filled with saints. Martyrs' names are plastered everywhere throughout the city—whether on signs in parks like Saint Alban's or on those that identify scores of streets, schools, and subway stops. Such sanctified signage is hardly unique to Toronto. Just head down the Saint Lawrence River to French Catholic Montréal, and it is nearly impossible to stand out of sight of at least one road named for a saint, even if several were christened not for beheaded martyrs of old but for more recent residents: for example, Rue Saint-Paul's Paul de Chomedey de Maisonneuve, who founded the city, and Rue Saint-Denis's Denis-Benjamin Viger, a nineteenth-century *patriote* and newspaper publisher who railed against British control of it.

In 1834, when the provincial outpost disparagingly known as Muddy York was incorporated and rebaptized as Toronto, a name of Mohawk or Huron-Wendat origin, the city was divided into five administrative wards. Four were named for the patron saints of the British Isles: Saint George of England, Saint Andrew of Scotland, Saint Patrick of Ireland, and Saint David of Wales. (Among other British colonies, the Caribbean island of Saint Vincent was similarly drawn and quartered.) Toronto's fifth original ward was dedicated to the unflappable Saint Lawrence, later a patron saint of Canada. Like Vincent, Lawrence was a deacon who was roasted alive on a gridiron. But Lawrence remains more famous, for his unsolicited grilling advice: "Flip me over!" he is said to have shouted to his executioners. "I'm done on this side." The patron saint of chefs and comedians still lends his name to Toronto's culinary hub, Saint Lawrence Market.

Alban's martyrdom was no less lurid. The Venerable Bede offers the fullest account of his death. Writing from his monastery in eighth-century Northumbria, Bede set his tale much earlier, during a time of strife for Christians in Roman Britain, explaining that Alban must have been swept up in one of the third- or maybe fourth-century persecutions in Verulamium, now the commuter city of St Albans just beyond the M25 ring road that encircles Greater London. In Bede's telling, which is preserved in his *Ecclesiastical History of the English People*, Alban was not born a Christian, but he was inspired to become one after kindly sheltering a haggard priest who sought refuge with him. Alban kept the man hidden for days, watching him closely as he performed his prayers. Inevitably, the two were betrayed. Alerted that Alban was harboring a Christian, Roman soldiers arrived to search his house. Thinking fast, Alban swapped his clothes for those of the priest and promptly offered himself to the soldiers instead. His haphazard scheme was quickly uncovered.

Later, standing before a judge, Alban was given multiple opportunities to recant. But neither cajoling nor torture could shake him. The convert remained steadfast and refused to renounce his new faith. Like so many other ancient Christian martyrs in story after story, Alban would not deny Christ by making the customary offering of incense to Rome's emperor or the city's pagan idols. For this, he was sentenced to death.

Alban did not flinch. Far from fearing death, he was eager to reach the place where he could bend his neck to the sword. Bede says that in his haste to bypass a crowded bridge over the Ver River, one clogged with onlookers hoping for a glimpse of the bloody spectacle to come, Alban turned his face to the heavens and prayed for the flow of the waters to stop so that he and his executioner could cross to the far bank unhindered. The miracle happened at once, and it came with an unintended effect. Upon seeing the suddenly dry riverbed, the astounded executioner dropped his sword and fell at Alban's feet, further slowing the saint's rush to martyrdom. Once a replacement executioner was found, the first gladly joined Alban in death. Alban's next miracle, his second on the day, was posthumous— barely. Before Alban's freshly decapitated head had even hit the ground, the second executioner's eyes leaped from their sockets to prevent him from gloating over his gruesome handiwork. Matthew of Paris, a thirteenth-century monk and manuscript illuminator who lived in an English abbey dedicated to Saint Alban, presented the scene complete with the martyr's head suspended in foliage and the second executioner lurching forward to catch his own eyeballs with his gauntleted hand (see fig. 3).

I told my children Bede's tale about Alban so many times that they will no doubt be able to recount it word for word someday to an unsuspecting therapist. Still, as familiar as they are with the legend of Britain's first martyr, their questions about the story when they were younger never changed. The general historical circumstances of Christian persecution and Roman emperor worship were too abstract to concern them, and they had surprisingly little interest in either of Alban's miracles. True, the specter of someone's eyes falling out was sufficiently disturbing to occasionally warrant some brief assurances about its unlikelihood, but this was a passing concern. Instead, they usually wanted to talk about what was clearly (at least to them) the most baffling part of the whole horrid story: Alban's eagerness to die and the sudden willingness of the first executioner to join him. That, not Alban's miracles, was what made the story so unbelievable. Why—they always wanted to know—would anyone be in a *hurry* to have his head chopped off?

For those unfamiliar with the tales of the ancient Christian martyrs, their apparent zeal for death may be more unsettling than any description of their executions, no matter how graphic or grisly. Time and again the story is the same: never do the martyrs resist the chopping block; at worst, they are unruffled by it, and sometimes even pleased. Whether it is Lawrence mocking his executioners while they grill him alive, Alban refusing to let his death be delayed by a crowd, or—most notorious of all—Saint Ignatius, the bishop of Antioch, ordering his friends to let lions crunch his bones, the martyrs in these stories and so many others do not avoid dying for Christ but rather embrace it.

A number of letters attributed to Ignatius of Antioch still survive, most of them written to budding Christian communities as the bishop was being hauled from Antioch to Rome across Asia Minor. Several of these letters are undoubtedly spurious, written or heavily embellished by others long after the fact, but some are quite likely to be genuine epistles from the second century. This always amazes me. I have studied and taught the history of Christianity for years, but I am still astonished that we can reach across the centuries to directly encounter the words of a long-dead someone who lived in a time so radically different from our own.

In one of the most frequently cited passages from Ignatius's *Letter to the Romans,* the bishop implores his readers not to intercede on his behalf. He tells them that they would be doing him a grave disservice were they to stop him from being killed: "Let me be the food of wild beasts," he pleads, "through whom it is possible to attain God." In describing his body as "God's wheat," Ignatius fashions his flesh into grist to be ground in the mill of martyrdom and then baked into "Christ's pure bread." For Ignatius, the conclusion is clear: willingly dying for Christ is simply what it means to be, as he calls it, a "true disciple."

The idea that Jesus's violent and painful death should be celebrated as a model for Christians to follow might strike many today as

FIGURE 3. "The Martyrdom of Saint Alban," detail from the *Life of Saint Alban* by Matthew of Paris, thirteenth century. Trinity College Library, MS 177, f. 38r, Dublin.

e au farrazin. du marcir clarte fanz fin.
yn cstien ki ; ueisin: la cir fuc conce eu fac rostir

1.7

absurd. Narrow though the road that leads to life may be, surely Jesus did not intend for it to wend its way through a lion's colon? But for many of the earliest Christians, if much more in theory than ever in actual fact, sanctity was to be found in following Jesus down just such a tapered path. If his life was to be imitated, why not his death? We obscure this fundamental fact about the history of Christianity when we allow the word *saint* to conjure up the image of a pious and peaceful person, some sort of garden-variety Saint Francis with a bird on his shoulder. Historically speaking, it's not the sun-wrinkled smile on Mother Teresa that is the icon of Christian holiness—it's the char-grilled one on Lawrence. Any clearheaded study of the stories of the ancient Christian martyrs and the vast religious culture that arose around them must inevitably lead to "the inescapable but repugnant conclusion," as Candida Moss once put it, "that dying for Christ may be a central, rather than peripheral, part of the Christian experience."

How central? Consider again Toronto's first five patron saints: George, Andrew, Patrick, David, and Lawrence. Lawrence, as we have seen, was grilled. George, a soldier in the emperor Diocletian's elite Praetorian Guard, is said to have been beheaded in fourth-century Palestine after refusing to renounce his faith. Despite George's later reincarnation as a dragon-slaying crusader, he is still revered throughout the Middle East among both Christians and Muslims alike. Andrew, one of the twelve apostles, is thought to have succumbed in Greece after being bound to an X-shaped cross. His saltire, Scotland's white X on a blue field, was later merged with George's red cross on white to form the original Union Jack. While it is true that neither Patrick nor David—the bishop-evangelists of Ireland and Wales—was martyred, both lived under the constant threat of death by devoting their lives to preaching the gospel to those who were not always so keen to hear it. According to one legend, Ireland's first martyr (a carriage driver named Odran) was killed by a lance intended for Patrick.

Alban is not nearly so well known as some of Toronto's other martyrs, but fortunately for him, the city's custom of naming its wards for Christian saints persisted until the end of the nineteenth century. As Toronto grew and annexed its surrounding towns and villages, Alban eventually earned a ward of his own, in what was then the leafy suburb of Parkdale. By that time, plenty of other saints had been added to the initial list of five—namely, seven: John, James, Stephen, Matthew, Thomas, Mark, and Paul, known for appearing in or writing parts of the New Testament. According to one early Christian tradition or another, *all* of them (save John) were martyred. Remarkably, of the thirteen saints on Toronto's final municipal roster, only Patrick, David, and John are thought to have died as old men.

It is worth noting how these New Testament martyrs met their ends.

The Acts of the Apostles narrates the deaths of both James and Stephen. According to Acts, James, the son of Zebedee and the brother of John the apostle, was beheaded in the first century by Herod Agrippa, the grandson of King Herod the Great. According to the Armenians, James's head is still in Jerusalem, buried in the cathedral named for him in the Old City's Armenian Quarter. His cathedral in northwestern Spain, at the end of the most famous Christian pilgrimage route in the world, was built in Santiago de Compostela over the spot where the rest of him is believed to be buried. A later tradition about James (one reminiscent of Alban's martyrdom) holds that his accuser repented, fell at the apostle's feet, and was killed alongside him. Meanwhile, according to Acts, Stephen was killed in Jerusalem too—not beheaded by a king but stoned to death by a vigilante mob.

One tradition about Matthew, one that presumes an impossibly fast acceleration of the institutional and liturgical development of Christianity, holds that he was stabbed in Ethiopia while saying Mass. It seems that Matthew had angered the Ethiopian king by scolding him for pursuing his own niece. Besides being a blood relative of the king, the young woman was a virgin and a nun. Thomas was speared even farther afield, also thanks to his preaching about sexual ethics. One early story puts his death in Persia, but the most enduring tradition about this apostle claims that he died in India after convincing many women there (including the married ones) to convert to Christianity and pursue lives of chastity. Apparently, their husbands were less smitten with this plan.

In Egypt, the Alexandrians dragged Mark through their city with a rope around his neck. Generations of Egyptian Christians treasured his bones until some Venetian merchants stole them from his sarcophagus and sailed out of Alexandria's harbor under cover of night. Rather belatedly, Pope Paul VI returned most of Mark's relics to Egypt in 1968, on what was said to have been the nineteen hundredth anniversary of the apostle's death.

Finally, we come to Paul. The New Testament does not record where and how he died, but it has several passages that imply he expected to die violently. In the Acts of the Apostles, a man named Agabus examines Paul's belt and prophesies that he will be bound hand and foot and "handed over to the Gentiles" in Jerusalem. Dismissing the protests of his friends, Paul declares his willingness to die "for the name of the Lord Jesus." The early consensus tradition holds that Agabus got it half right: Paul was handed over to the gentiles, but in Rome—not Jerusalem. It seems he was then beheaded during the reign of the infamous emperor Nero. According to one interpretation of the book of Revelation, which was composed several decades after Paul's death, the three-digit mark of the beast is a simple code: 666 is just the sum of the numeric values of the letters in the name Nero Caesar.

What is especially noteworthy about Toronto's ward-namesake martyrs is how many on the list are believed to have known Jesus or, at one step removed, known those who knew him. Matthew and

Mark are credited with writing two of the four Gospels included in the New Testament; Andrew, James, and Thomas are consistently numbered among those closest to Jesus, three of his twelve apostles. Paul did not know Jesus during his life, but (again according to Acts) not only was he present in Jerusalem when Stephen was stoned, he even held the coats of those who killed him. After receiving a blinding vision of the resurrected Jesus while on the road to Damascus, Paul was transformed from an ardent persecutor of Jesus's followers into far and away their most influential promoter. The bulk of the New Testament is a series of letters attributed to him. Most were written to encourage the emerging Jesus-following communities throughout the eastern Mediterranean, in places like Corinth, Galatia, Philippi, Thessalonica, Ephesus, Colossae, and Rome.

Had those who named Toronto's wards chosen to honor other apostles, the story would have been the same: ten of the twelve were martyred. Only John, as we have seen, is believed to have died of old age. Even the unfaithful disciple, Judas Iscariot, although most certainly not remembered as a martyr, also died violently. How is less clear. There are several traditions about his death, including two conflicting accounts in the New Testament alone. According to the Gospel of Matthew, Judas hung himself. In Acts, however, he is said to have died after falling in a field—fittingly, land he purchased with the money he was awarded for betraying Jesus. Peter adds that Judas "burst open" after his fall, then "his bowels gushed out."

With John and Judas the only exceptions, all of Jesus's apostles died as martyrs. Or at least they did according to the many ancient and medieval legends that narrate their deaths. Like Stephen, James the Less (often called the brother of Jesus) was stoned to death in Jerusalem. Other traditions have it that this James—there are a confusing many in the Bible—was thrown from the pinnacle of the Jewish Temple in Jerusalem. Somehow he survived the fall, but he was soon finished off with a fuller's club.

Like Andrew, at least three other apostles may have been crucified. The consensus about Peter (Andrew's brother) is that he was crucified in Rome around the time when Paul was beheaded there. In the Gospel of John, Jesus tells Peter that he will be made to "stretch out" his hands, a turn of phrase often interpreted as a prediction of Peter's crucifixion. According to the most widely known story about Peter, he was crucified upside down—apparently at his own request—so that no one would equate his death with that of Jesus. Some ancient sources claim that Philip and Jude (also known as Judas Thaddeus) were crucified too. Others say that Jude, like James the Less, was clubbed to death (or maybe axed?) and that Philip died after being suspended by his ankles on iron hooks like a slaughtered pig.

Simon the Zealot, the most obscure of the twelve, was either crucified alongside Jude in Persia or sawn in half there. Yet another tradition about Simon says that he was crucified in Britain (not Persia), which would make him (not Alban) that island's first martyr. Whatever the case, most Western renditions of Simon show him standing, in one piece, and jauntily leaning against a crosscut saw as long as he is tall. Depicting martyrs with the means of their martyrdom is a standard artistic practice.

The martyrdom of the apostle Bartholomew has to win the prize for most appalling. Depending on which ancient source one consults, he was crucified, flayed, or beheaded—or some combination of the three—in either India or Armenia. Michelangelo opted for an Armenian flaying in *The Last Judgment*. Visitors to Rome should be on the lookout for Bartholomew in this altar wall fresco in the Sistine Chapel. Hovering on a cloud at Jesus's feet, the nude and thickly bearded apostle holds a flensing knife in his right hand; in his left, he clutches the empty bag of his own skin (see fig. 4). Art historians have long surmised that the skin-bag Bartholomew's boneless and sagging face is a distorted self-portrait that Michelangelo quietly painted into the fresco.

FIGURE 4. The apostle Bartholomew holding his own skin, detail from *The Last Judgment* by Michelangelo, 1536–41. Sistine Chapel, Vatican City.

Whether any of these often contradictory and always gory traditions about the deaths of the apostles is true or not is a question that has important consequences for many Christians. Some recent apologists have argued that if the apostles were in fact killed for their faith, then the resurrection of Jesus must also be true, since surely no one would die for a myth. Setting such head-scratching logic aside, it is clear that parsing fact from fiction at a remove of so many centuries is an exercise more of faith than of history. Some small particles of historical fact may lie buried beneath layer upon layer of literary accretions, but if our goal is to understand how Christianity developed into a cult of the dead, then the most valuable pearl we can glean from these tales about the deaths of the apostles is already in hand: *they exist.* Their long endurance from one generation to the next (how else would Michelangelo know to render Bartholomew skinless?) tells us what we need to know. For nearly two millennia, Christians from Britain to India have believed that many of those who followed Jesus in life must have followed him in death. Dying for Christ was not extraordinary. To quote Ignatius again, it was simply what was expected of a "true disciple."

For many Christian communities in the ancient world, it was a matter of great pride to be able to claim a martyred apostle as their own. It still is. With reference to the one said to have evangelized their forebears, Christians in southern India still call themselves Saint Thomas Christians. A gleaming basilica in the city of Chennai, on the Bay of Bengal, is believed to house his remains. Meanwhile, nearly every Coptic church from Cairo to Chicago is named for Saint Mark.

According to the Gospels, we should have anticipated this great outpouring of blood among Jesus's followers. Jesus told them they would be persecuted, imprisoned, and hauled before kings and governors—all for the sake of his name. If the many stories about the deaths of the apostles are to be believed, that is what happened. Of course, there is also the story of Jesus's own death.

Though casual observers might assume that the four canonical Gospels—the four quasi-biographical narratives about Jesus in the New Testament—all tell the same story about Jesus's death, Jesus the Martyr (the one whose death is to be imitated) is the literary creation of one Gospel writer in particular: Saint Luke. His description of Jesus's death and the way in which the first Christian martyr, Saint Stephen, sought to imitate it set the stage for the later surge of Christian culture around the martyrs.

To get a sense of Luke's contribution to the soon to emerge Christian cult of the dead, compare his portrait of Jesus with the one painted in the Gospel of Mark. Mark's Gospel is the oldest of the four preserved in the New Testament, but it was not written immediately after Jesus's death. In fact, biblical scholars agree that it is unlikely to have been composed until something like forty years after Jesus's crucifixion—and presumably not long after a Jewish uprising in Jerusalem in AD 70. This revolt against Roman rule, only the latest in a string of violent rebellions, led to the destruction of the city. Roman soldiers sacked and burned Jerusalem, including the majestic Temple of the Jews that King Herod the Great had built. The first-century Arch of Titus in Rome records the empire's triumph over Judea with its relief sculptures of the spoils that were carried off from the Temple and later melted down—loot that included the Temple's grand menorah, which was later adopted as a symbol of the modern State of Israel (see fig. 5).

When Luke says the twelve-year-old Jesus was accidentally left behind in the Temple after his parents visited the city for the feast of the Passover or when all four Gospel writers talk about Jesus overturning the tables of the money changers and trying to drive them from the Temple during a later Passover feast, it is Herod's Temple to

FIGURE 5. Arch of Titus, c. AD 81. Via Sacra, Rome.

which they refer. Today, the Dome of the Rock and al-Aqsa Mosque sit atop the platform where Herod's showpiece once stood, but the Temple plaza's Western Wall remains a place of prayer where Jerusalem's destruction in AD 70 is still remembered.

Perhaps because he was writing in the immediate aftermath of this traumatic event, Mark presents a fearful Jesus who goes to his death agitated and unwilling. On the evening of his arrest, when Jesus is just outside the city walls with his followers in the Garden of Gethsemane, he chastises his exhausted disciples (who keep falling asleep) and says to them, "I am deeply grieved." But the same scene in the Gospel of Luke, which was not composed until the early second century, explains that the disciples kept falling asleep because of *their* grief—Jesus's grief is not mentioned.

On its own, this apparently minor discrepancy over who was doing the grieving in the garden, whether Jesus or his disciples, may seem inconsequential. At least it does until Mark and Luke go on to tell the tale of Jesus's crucifixion and death. Mark's account is brief. It begins with Roman soldiers pressing a passerby into service, a man named Simon of Cyrene. They force him to help Jesus carry his cross out beyond Jerusalem's walls to Golgotha, "the place of the skull." Mimicking the soldiers, who mock Jesus as "the King of the Jews," the two thieves who are crucified on either side of him taunt Jesus too. Mark does not tell us what they said. Jesus keeps silent as well. But in the late afternoon, as Jesus breathes his last (death by crucifixion was a slow one of gradual asphyxiation), he finally does cry out. It is a plaintive lament taken straight from the Psalms: "My God, my God," Jesus moans, "why have you forsaken me?" This is not a triumphant conclusion. Jesus dies betrayed. His disciples are terrified and have no idea what to do.

Luke renders Jesus's death in an entirely different way. Though the main contours of his story mirror those in Mark, the details make the difference. Instead of narrating the tribulations of a passive man distraught by his fate, Luke recounts the death of a self-assured prophet who counsels others through their sorrow. In addition to Simon of Cyrene, who here again must help Jesus carry his cross, Luke explains that many women followed Jesus, all mourning and weeping, to the site of his execution. Throughout the commotion, Jesus is unperturbed. Seeming to foretell the destruction that would later befall Jerusalem, Jesus comforts the women. He says they should mourn not for him but for themselves and their children.

When Jesus arrives at Golgotha, the two thieves are again there. This time we hear them speak. The first mocks Jesus as a false messiah for his inability to save himself, but the other—who would come to be known as the good thief—rebukes the sneers of the first. Addressing the not-so-good thief, the good one admits to his crimes and acknowledges he has been justly condemned but, nodding at Jesus, says, "This man has done nothing wrong." When the good thief asks Jesus to remember him when he comes into his kingdom, Jesus reassures the man at once: "Truly I tell you," he says, "today you will be with me in Paradise."

Such prophetic tranquillity in Luke's Gospel is even more striking when Jesus yields to his cross. Again he dies in the late afternoon. And again his last words come straight from the Psalms. But it would be jarring, considering all that had happened, for Luke's Jesus to die bewildered and forsaken. So Luke finds another verse for Jesus to quote. In this one he offers himself up willingly: "Father," Jesus says in a resolute voice strong enough for all to hear, "into your hands I commend my spirit."

These two very different accounts of Jesus's final hours, both canonized in the New Testament alongside the two attributed to Matthew and John, underscore a crucial point about later Christian martyrdom narratives, one that the historian Daniel Boyarin once put in a memorably pithy way: "Being killed is an event. Martyrdom is a literary form, a genre."

What makes Jesus a martyr in Luke's Gospel is not *that* he died but *how* he died—which essentially is to say, how his death was narrated. Though there was never any set checklist of literary elements that, if present, would transform the event of a death into the narrative of a martyrdom, several of the most important hallmarks of later Christian martyrdom literature are right here in Luke: the martyr's brief trial on trumped-up charges, unjust condemnation to death, and most conspicuously, calm acceptance of death despite the laments of others.

Luke was an educated Greek, a physician, it seems—hence all the hospitals bearing his name—and he knew how the ancient philosophers died: they went to their ends stoically, giving comfort to others while needing none of their own. He also understood that for the true philosopher, dying was a public performance, part of a practical and embodied philosophy of life and death. The truest philosopher, he knew, dies nobly: in control and on their own terms.

In Jacques-Louis David's eighteenth-century painting *The Death of Socrates,* the philosopher of philosophers sits calmly on his prison bed and reaches for the cup of hemlock that he has been condemned to drink (see fig. 6). David frames the poisoned cup—the means of Socrates's martyrdom—in the center of the scene. Although Socrates is imprisoned in David's painting, as he is in Plato's dialogues that are set during the last days of the philosopher's life, he would have posed no risk of flight even if he hadn't been. David indicates this with undone shackles strewn across the floor. Socrates had wealthy friends who could have bribed the guards to let him escape or seen to it that he was exiled rather than executed for the crime of teaching the well-heeled sons of Athens to question their fathers' authority, but for him, fleeing would have been a cowardly affront to the Athenian Laws (with a capital *L*) which he held so dear. In David's vision of the scene, Socrates keeps philosophizing until the end, gesturing skyward with a still sculpted arm, his white hair and beard the only indications of his age. Meanwhile, his friends cover their eyes or turn away, unable to watch.

The wrongly executed philosopher was a character that Luke's audience, Greek-speaking gentiles, would have known well. It was also a literary model that Luke could reuse. His most important contribution to the Christian martyr cult was his presentation of Jesus's death, but his account of Stephen's stoning comes a close second. Although Stephen was not a Christian—like Jesus, he was a Jew who was killed in Roman-occupied Jerusalem—he is still remembered as the first Christian martyr. Luke recounts Stephen's death in his second volume, the Acts of the Apostles, which is a history of the Jesus movement's humble beginnings and slow spread throughout the Mediterranean world. It is the only book in the New Testament that mentions Stephen.

According to Acts, Stephen often spoke with great wisdom, but, like Jesus, he stood falsely accused. Those who testified against him claimed that they had heard him say Jesus would destroy the Temple and "change the customs" passed down through all the generations stretching back to Moses. When the high priest calls for Stephen to answer these charges, the soon-to-be martyr launches into a jeremiad that invokes the Jewish patriarchs. His speech ends with an unforgivable insult. He accuses those who have spoken against him of being willful persecutors of the prophets, including the most recently crucified "Righteous One." Moments later, when Stephen gazes to the heavens and tells the crowd around him that he can see "the Son of Man standing at the right hand of God," his blasphemy becomes too much to bear. They drag him beyond the city walls and stone him to death (see fig. 7).

Just three short verses narrate Stephen's end, but they are packed with meaning. We read that the "witnesses" against him gave their coats to Paul to hold, and that Stephen, as he was being stoned, repeated Jesus's final words from the cross—the ones from *Luke's*

FIGURE 6. *The Death of Socrates* by Jacques-Louis David, 1787. Metropolitan Museum of Art, New York.

FIGURE 7. *The Stoning of Saint Stephen* by Rembrandt van Rijn, 1635. Metropolitan Museum of Art, New York.

Gospel, of course, not Mark's. But there is a change too: whereas Jesus had commended his spirit to his Father, here Stephen commends his spirit to Jesus.

Some chapters later in Acts we hear from Paul. In describing his conversion from a persecutor of what he calls "the Way" into a fervent acolyte of that same path, Paul speaks in Hebrew to his listeners and touts his Jewish bona fides as one who was brought up in Jerusalem and "educated strictly" at the feet of the rabbi Gamaliel "according to our ancestral law." Paul's account of his conversion while on the road to Damascus—his tale of a blinding vision of Jesus, who rebukes him for his persecuting ways—is an impassioned one. But when he recalls for his audience his own role in Stephen's stoning, he nearly finds himself facing a similar fate.

Intriguingly, the story that Paul relates about "keeping the coats" of those who killed Stephen is not a direct account of the stoning itself. Instead, he tells his audience about another vision of Jesus he had, this one after falling "into a trance" while praying in the Temple. In this vision, Jesus tells Paul to flee Jerusalem, saying that the Jews "will not accept your testimony about me." Paul tries to convince Jesus that they will listen to him, since they know that he used to beat and imprison Jesus's followers and they even saw him standing there while they shed "the blood of your martyr Stephen." But Jesus ignores Paul. Again, he insists that Paul must leave, saying, "Go, for I will send you far away to the Gentiles."

Clearly, Luke is not writing for Jews. Wrongly accused philosophers of the Way are at the center of the cult of the dead that he unwittingly helped to establish. It is no coincidence that Jesus, Stephen, and Paul are all falsely accused, that Jesus appears to Stephen in a vision before Stephen's death, that Stephen dies repeating Jesus's words on the cross, or that Jesus appears to Paul first to stop him from persecuting Jesus's followers and then again to implore him to leave Jerusalem to find a more receptive audience among the gentiles. Although the Christian cult of the dead did emerge from this intricate matrix of anti-Judaism, it was the rabbi Gamaliel, Paul's teacher, who—in a very strange way—played a major part in the spread of Stephen's cult throughout the Mediterranean world.

Stephen's cult, like the Gospels written about Jesus, did not arise immediately after his death. In fact, the first literary reference to him besides the one in Acts did not appear until the late second century.

Acts connects Paul to Stephen's death, but Paul himself never mentions Stephen once in any of his letters. We do know that some form of a cult dedicated to Stephen was flourishing by the fourth century, since plenty of sermons in the martyr's honor survive from that time, usually preached on the annual celebration of his death. But the real explosion of Stephen's cult occurred in the early fifth century, when his long-lost bones were fortuitously rediscovered.

The story of the finding of Stephen's relics is set in rural Palestine, at some distance from Jerusalem. The year is 415, and the tale begins with a priest named Lucian, who always sleeps in the baptistery of his church so as to closely guard its sacred vessels. As Lucian snores, an old man wearing a cross-fringed garment as white as his beard appears to him in a dream. The priest is understandably startled when the old man calls to him three times and then tells him to visit Bishop John of Jerusalem so that together they might go and investigate the mortal remains in some nearby tombs. When Lucian inquires after the old man's name, he declares, "I am Gamaliel, who instructed Paul the apostle in the law." The old rabbi in Lucian's dream then explains that, like Paul, he was in Jerusalem when Stephen was stoned. Although Stephen's body was left exposed, outside the northern gate of the city on the road to Damascus, Gamaliel says that he personally arranged for it to be carried away at night. The rabbi had it taken to his country house, near the site of what later became the very church where Lucian was sleeping.

Eventually, as the story progresses, Stephen's tomb is identified. The earth shakes when the tomb is reopened, and from Stephen's sarcophagus seeps an odor so sweet that no one there to smell it had ever scented anything so sublime. In the grammar of Christian martyr stories, this was a sure sign of success, an olfactory X marking the spot. But a sweet smell was not the only proof that Stephen's tomb had been found. Many who were present at the exhumation—all of these witnesses tormented with tumors or fevers, headaches or hemorrhages—were cured as soon as the martyr's relics emerged. Later, Stephen's bones were formally enshrined in a church built in his honor just steps from Jerusalem's northern wall.

The portability of bones and stories meant that Stephen's cult could not be confined to Jerusalem. Some of his relics were given to a visiting Spaniard. When they arrived on the island of Minorca, the wonder-working bones converted the Jews there. In Roman North Africa, Saint Augustine urged his congregation to keep detailed records of the miracles that Christ wrought through his martyr Stephen. Whole books of Stephen's miracles were collected, and Augustine would regularly read them aloud to his flock. For them, these were a natural extension of the miracle stories they knew from the Gospels, and evidence of the power of saints who—though dead—remained alive in the world.

2 *The Names of the Dead*

In the summer of 598, Pope Gregory I sent a letter to Bishop Eulogius of Alexandria. This was not an uncommon thing for Gregory to do. The pope was a prolific and learned writer whose life's work includes scores of sermons, several biblical commentaries, a four-volume collection of miracles attributed to the saints, and hundreds upon hundreds of letters—each of which was meticulously copied down by a scribe before being dispatched to its recipient (see fig. 8). Records of Gregory's correspondence were prized. Copies of his scribes' copies, most made centuries after the pope's death, are still kept in the Vatican Library.

Though Gregory and Eulogius exchanged several letters during their tenures as the spiritual leaders of two of the historically most important Christian cities, this particular letter from Rome to Alexandria is especially interesting. Part of it helps us understand the development of the cult of the saints. Another part is mundane. But in combining the ordinary with the extraordinary, Gregory's letter gives us a glimpse into the full range of issues that concerned two bishops who dwelt on opposite shores of the Mediterranean more than fourteen hundred years ago.

What is immediately evident from Gregory's letter is that it is a response. Eulogius had already written to the pope—in part to com-

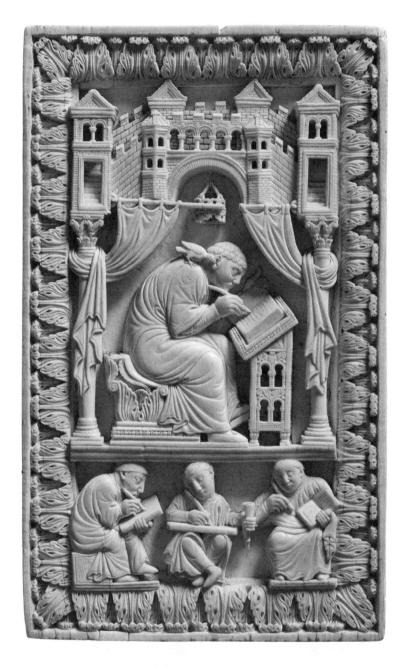

FIGURE 8. Saint Gregory (*center*) with scribes (*bottom register*), ivory relief carving for the cover of a liturgical book, late tenth century. Kunsthistorisches Museum, Vienna. © KHM-Museumverband.

plain about a shipment of Roman lumber that had recently arrived at Alexandria's port. It seems the logs were shorter than Eulogius was expecting. But instead of apologizing for the mismeasured lumber, Gregory defends himself and tells Eulogius that had the Alexandrians taken care to send a larger ship, the Romans would have gladly loaded it with longer lumber. Still, the pope is magnanimous: "Next year," he promises Eulogius, "should it please Almighty God, we will prepare larger pieces" and send them free of charge. That was the practical part of Gregory's letter. But Eulogius had written to him about an altogether different matter too. He had an urgent question for the pope about a commodity much more precious than lumber. He was in search of a lost collection of stories: violent tales of persecution, torture, and the last hours of the ancient Christian martyrs. Had Gregory ever heard of such a collection? Did he know which martyrs' stories it included? And was it possible that an overlooked copy might, by chance, be hiding somewhere on a shelf in Rome?

Three centuries before Gregory and Eulogius exchanged their letters about this lost collection of martyrs, the emperor Diocletian was hard at work creating them. Diocletian's "Great Persecution" officially lasted for a decade, from 303 to 313, but it was preceded by a purge of Christians from the Roman army.

Rivaled only by Saint George, Saint Sebastian was the most famous soldier-martyr to die under Diocletian. A favorite subject of the Italian Renaissance—with Sebastians by Botticelli, Perugino, Titian, Mantegna, Giovanni Bellini, and others—the martyr is usually depicted bound to a tree, wearing nothing but a loincloth or a short tunic pulled down around his waist to expose his muscled torso and the multiple arrows protruding from it (see fig. 9). But this is not how Sebastian died. Somehow, the arrows missed his vital organs. After

FIGURE 9. *Saint Sebastian* by Sandro Botticelli,
1474. Staatliche Museum, Berlin.

they were extracted and Sebastian was nursed back to health, he waited for Diocletian at a place where he knew that the emperor and his army would soon come marching. When Sebastian spotted Diocletian, he shouted at him and cursed him for all the suffering he had brought upon Christians. After the emperor recovered from his momentary shock at the apparent resurrection of one deemed dead, he ordered that Sebastian be clubbed to death on the spot and tossed into Rome's main sewer, the Cloaca Maxima. One can hardly blame the artists who decided that a nude soldier bound to a tree would make a more appealing visual subject.

Not long after Sebastian's martyrdom, once Diocletian's persecution was over, the great church historian Eusebius of Caesarea began drafting his *Ecclesiastical History,* or *History of the Church.* Eusebius was enthralled with those Christians who had stared down imperial violence unafraid, and he often invoked the martyrs' heroic deeds, weaving in references to or extended quotations from the stories about Christians who died decades before Diocletian's reign.

Eusebius never mentions Sebastian—it seems that Saint Ambrose, the bishop of Milan in the late fourth century, was the first to preach about this former soldier's martyrdom—but does have plenty to say about Diocletian and all the other pagan emperors who had treated Christians so poorly. In ambling over the three hundred years from the time of the apostles to the victorious reign of Constantine, Eusebius describes persecution and martyrdom as frequent threats for Christians. He duly celebrates Constantine, the first Christian emperor, but as for those who challenged Constantine for control of the Roman Empire, these men Eusebius makes out to be drunkards, rapists, and thieves: unrepentant murderers upon whom the god of the Christians had finally inflicted a long overdue vengeance.

Take Galerius, the emperor whose edict helped end Diocletian's persecution. As Eusebius tells it, Galerius did not issue this edict out of any sympathy for Christians or because he believed they had suffered enough. No, Eusebius explains, Galerius was concerned about Christians for personal reasons. He hoped that his edict of toleration might relieve him of the horrific ailments that the Christian god had sent upon him. Far from glossing over Galerius's divinely inflicted suffering, Eusebius wallows in it. First, he says, lesions appeared on the emperor's genitals. Then "an incurable fistula developed in his bowels and spread throughout his innards. From his insides, an unspeakable mass of worms burst out, and a deathly stench wafted up. The whole mass of his body had already been turned into lard through his gluttony before the illness, and then it rotted, offering an unbearable and disgusting sight to those who visited him."

Despite (or perhaps because of) his rhetorical excess, Eusebius was quickly anointed a master of his craft. And, as he had endured Diocletian's persecution himself and even witnessed the murder of Christians in Palestine, Eusebius was trusted as an unparalleled historical authority. For a time, he was the only Christian historical authority. He less than humbly acknowledges this role at the outset of his *Ecclesiastical History*, begging his readers' pardon for what he calls its imperfect and incomplete nature, owing to a lack of any guidance in how to write it. "Since I am the first" to write a history of the church, Eusebius says, it is "a lonely and untrodden path." Others—many others—would soon follow him down this path, imitating and expanding on the model he created, but Eusebius would forever remain both pioneer and pinnacle of this new historiographical genre: the church history.

Eulogius, in other words, did not need to remind Gregory who Eusebius was. While Eulogius was reading (or rereading) Eusebius's *Ecclesiastical History*, he had noticed more than one reference to

Eusebius's own collection of stories about the earliest Christian martyrs. But why, Eulogius wondered, had he never encountered this collection of stories himself? Surely copies must have been made? Yet insofar as Eulogius could tell, not a single manuscript of any collection of martyrs' tales was circulating among Alexandria's cosmopolitan Christian elite. Hence his request that Gregory please look in Rome's libraries.

Eulogius knew that Eusebius was a trusted historical source and an exceedingly careful documentarian. While Eusebius did compile and interpret his sources in ways that advanced a distinctly Christian point of view, he never lied about them or invented his quotations. We know that Eusebius compiled at least one collection of martyrs' stories, because he wrote them himself. Initially, he included this collection, known as *Martyrs of Palestine,* in his *Ecclesiastical History.* Later he spun it off as a stand-alone collection of tales. Lost in the original Greek, *Martyrs of Palestine* survives in an early translation into Syriac—the Christian dialect of Aramaic that became such an important literary language throughout much of Syria, Mesopotamia, and Persia. But Eulogius was not interested in the *Martyrs of Palestine.* The collection he sought from Gregory was the unabridged stories of those whom Eusebius calls "the ancients," the earliest martyrs, who, like Ignatius of Antioch, followed in the footsteps of the apostles.

In seeking this apparently lost collection of stories, Eulogius had definitely written to the right person. Soon after his death, Pope Gregory became *Saint* Gregory the Great, one of the four honorary doctors of the Latin Church along with Saint Ambrose, Saint Augustine, and Saint Jerome. Almost single-handedly, Gregory revised the practice of Roman worship to further incorporate the daily celebration of saints and martyrs. So influential were his changes that the most important style of Latin plainsong—the one used throughout the Middle Ages and still heard today—was named in his honor, even though

"Gregorian" chant was not standardized until centuries after the pope's death. If anyone in the sixth-century Roman world should have known about Eusebius's lost collection of martyrs' stories, it was Gregory. But the pope was flummoxed. He wrote back to Eulogius not only to explain that his search of Roman libraries had come up empty handed but also to admit that he had never heard of *any* collection of martyrs' stories, beyond just a handful gathered in a slim volume, until he had received the bishop of Alexandria's letter.

Gregory's ignorance of this collection is perplexing. If persecution and martyrdom were so central to the story of Christianity, as they most certainly were for Eusebius and all those historians who followed his model, then how is it that one of the most important intellectuals of the early Middle Ages (to say nothing of one who also happened to be a renowned proponent of the cult of the saints) could have had no knowledge of any collection of martyrdom stories?

A good explanation lies in what Gregory says next. The pope tells Eulogius that although he has never encountered a book filled with martyrs' tales, he is quite familiar with a volume in which "the names of almost all the martyrs" are written. This book of necronyms, so the pope explains, is simple: it is just a list of martyrs that also notes where and when each died. The pope continues, "We celebrate the solemnities of Mass on such days in commemoration of them."

The book that Gregory describes for Eulogius—a list of names, dates, and places invoked in worship—is clear evidence for a cult of the dead. It provides, as one famous twentieth-century scholar put it, the "hagiographic coordinates" of the martyrs. It tells us who they were and where they were located in space and time. And the spot where all these personal, geographical, and temporal coordinates meet is the point from which a holy story, or "hagiography," can begin.

The annual memorials of the martyrs, those solemn commemorations that Gregory mentions, were a form of communal storytelling—one that, at least in Gregory's day, was more practically useful than a codified anthology of long-winded tales copied down in a book.

Still, some of those long-winded tales were worth their time in telling. One of the most widely celebrated martyrs that Eusebius lists among "the ancients" is Polycarp, the bishop of Smyrna in the middle of the second century. Now the seaside city of İzmir on Turkey's Aegean shore, Smyrna has a thoroughly ancient history. The book of Revelation mentions it as one of the Seven Churches of the Apocalypse—which were expected to endure persecution—and some claim that Greek history itself began in Smyrna with Homer's birth there in the eighth century BC. For Eusebius, Smyrna's long history had become part of a cosmically important epic because the city was the home of Polycarp the martyr. The Christians of Smyrna, Eusebius tells us, had written a letter about Polycarp, addressed to all the "communities of the holy universal church in every location." Eusebius says that he incorporated the complete narrative of Polycarp's death in his collection of the "martyrdoms of the ancients," so what we get in his *Ecclesiastical History* must be a summary version. In it, Eusebius mixes paraphrase with direct quotation of the letter supposedly written by the Smyrnaeans.

Eusebius begins his recitation of the letter by explaining that Polycarp was not even the first Christian in his city to suffer. Others had already been "dragged over seashells and sharp stones," had their entrails and organs "exposed to view," and been given over "as food to savage animals." But, Eusebius explains, the pagan crowd in the city's arena was still hungry for blood. They called for Polycarp, but their cry was a strange one: "Seize the *atheists!*" they shouted. "Find Polycarp!" It was Polycarp, they bellowed, "the father of the Christians," who had taught his spiritual children to reject the gods of the Romans and to refuse to sacrifice to the image of Caesar—a god incarnate.

When Polycarp heard about the violence in his city and the crowd that was lowing for his blood, Eusebius says, "he remained undisturbed" and made no plans to flee. But those closest to their bishop were terrified and bundled him away to a country estate until tempers could calm. While there, Polycarp spent his days in prayer, meditating on his approaching end. Three days before he was arrested, he dreamed that his pillow had burst into flames. Polycarp interpreted this (correctly) as a sign that he would burn for Christ.

This early disclosure of Polycarp's death does nothing to spoil the story. Readers in Eusebius's day already had a good understanding of the martyrdom genre, and they knew their Christian heroes would die. The literary pleasure in the tales told about the saints is in the suspense over how they will meet their ends and what they will say in opposition to those in power before they do. These narratives, in any case, usually follow a generic arc. Similarities between the martyrs and Jesus are sometimes so obvious in late ancient Christian tales that they reach the point of ridiculousness. In Polycarp's case, both he and Jesus retire to a garden to pray, and then foretell their own deaths. Those sent to arrest Polycarp find him "reclining in an upper room." The Last Supper was celebrated in a similar domestic space. Accordingly, Polycarp greets those who have come for him and orders that someone give them a meal. Well fed, the imperial goons happily wait for Polycarp to finish his prayers. Like Luke's Jesus, Polycarp is placid in the face of death.

At this point in the story, Eusebius stops paraphrasing and starts to quote directly from the Smyrnaeans' letter. After Polycarp is led into Smyrna—like Jesus, on the back of a donkey—he is interrogated by a man named Herod. It is Herod who demands that Polycarp offer sacrifice to "Lord Caesar." But the bishop is unswayed. Neither Herod nor the terrible "din in the stadium" can frighten him. In fact, over the shouts of the crowd, Polycarp can hear words of encouragement coming from heaven: "Be strong, Polycarp," says the voice, "and play the man."

When threats to throw him to the beasts have no effect, Polycarp's vision of the flaming pillow proves true. He is to be burned alive. As is lamentably so often the case in these stories, Jews are described as "especially eager" to gather kindling for the fire. Once the wood is prepared, Polycarp stops those readying to nail him to the stake, explaining that God will grant him the power "to remain in the fire undisturbed, even without the security of your nails." Instead, Polycarp is bound with ropes, "just as a noble ram offered up," just "as a whole-burnt offering." Two biblical sacrifices have just become one: Polycarp is now Jesus and Isaac at once.

After Polycarp thanks God for deeming him worthy to share the cup of Christ with those who have been martyred before him, the fire is lit. But, like Daniel in the fiery furnace, Polycarp does not burn. The fire gracefully envelops him, "like a linen sail filled by the wind," and from within his flaming cocoon, Polycarp's body becomes "like gold and silver being refined in a furnace." From the fire wafts the sweet smell of frankincense: the sure sign of his holiness. Once it is clear to those present that the fire will not kill Polycarp, his persecutors run him through with a sword. A torrent of blood quenches the flames.

After Polycarp's death, the Christians of Smyrna set out to retrieve his remains. More than anything, they want "to have fellowship with his holy flesh." The Jews, however, already know that Christians venerate the remains of their martyrs, and they convince the governor of Smyrna not to hand over Polycarp's body, lest the Christians "abandon the crucified one and begin to worship this one." The story's narrator in the letter rejects this accusation, explaining that Christians worship Christ alone. Still, he admits, Christians do "love the martyrs as students and imitators of the Lord."

Once the pyre is relit and Polycarp's flesh is burned from his bones, the Christians swoop in to collect them, regarding such relics as "more dear than precious stones and more valuable than gold." What then became of Polycarp's relics we cannot say. We hear from the Smyrnaeans only that they were deposited "in a fitting place," where Christians still gathered "to celebrate the anniversary of his martyrdom with exultation and joy."

Soon after Eusebius tells this tale of Polycarp's death and the quick inauguration of the martyr's cult, he weaves another long story about martyrs into his *Ecclesiastical History*. This next one is set two decades later—during the reign of Marcus Aurelius in the last quarter of the second century—and at the opposite end of the Roman Empire, in the Gallic cities of Lyon and Vienne, on the banks of the Rhône. This time, Eusebius paraphrases little. Almost all of what he says is a direct quotation from his source, whose full account, he reminds us, "has been included in our *Collection of Martyrs*"—the book Eulogius could not find.

Before telling us what happened to the Christian martyrs of Lyon and Vienne, Eusebius turns the past on its head. Aware of his novel contributions to the historiographical arts, Eusebius explains that while earlier Roman historians may have focused on tales of military valor, "victories in war, trophies against enemies, the prowess of generals, and the manly courage of soldiers who have polluted themselves with blood and myriad murders for the sake of children, fatherland, or some other superfluity," he will do the opposite. He will not praise the flashing swords of the virile. He is more taken by the immortal crowns of old men. His stories are of the women and children who won "peaceful wars" contested for piety. Eusebius's victors are not killers; they are those who are killed. And in dying for Christ, their names have been inscribed upon "eternal plaques."

The story about the martyrs of Lyon and Vienne is again framed in the form of a letter. And again the Christians of the cities are accused of failing to uphold the social mores of the Roman Empire. This time, however, they are not maligned as atheists for failing to worship the Roman gods. Instead, they are accused of cannibalism and incest—or, as Eusebius says, quoting his classically minded source, of holding "Thyestean banquets" and having "Oedipean intercourse." Such sensationalist charges were very effective. Christians had already been banned from public places in Lyon and Vienne, including the baths and the markets, but now, even if some non-Christians in the city "had previously acted in a more measured way on account of friendship," the accusations of cannibalism and incest were two steps too far, so the pagans "became exceptionally harsh and gnashed their teeth at us." Not all Christians could endure the social exclusion, much less the threat of torture. The letter writer dismisses those who faltered as "untrained," weaklings who were "unable to bear the strain of a great competition." They had been offered the opportunity to be born again in martyrdom, but they "aborted" their chance for new life in Christ.

Unlike the story of Polycarp, which barely mentions the other martyrs of Smyrna, the tale about the Christians of Lyon and Vienne has many heroes. One is a priest, an old man "over ninety years old and very feeble in body." Others include a female slave and a boy of only fifteen. All were killed for Christ.

The story about the slave Blandina is especially striking. Her Christian master faltered and offered incense to the emperor, unable to bear the strain of torture, but Blandina was so powerful in her resolve that the men who took their turns with her, each trying every "type of torture in succession, from morning till evening," gave up and conceded defeat, admitting that they "no longer had anything they could do." Through the testimony of her ravaged body, Blandina "was rejuvenated like a noble athlete." But her trial was not over. Soon she would be dragged into the arena and "hung on a wooden stake," offered up "as food for the beasts." With arms outstretched in prayer, Blandina took on "the form of a cross." For a while, no beast would come near. Eventually, an old bull decided to gore her.

Blandina's multiple rounds against "the Adversary" made her victory over death all the more stirring. That an old man, a boy, and this "small, weak, and despised woman" could robe themselves in the triumph of Christ, "the invincible athlete," made clear that martyrdom, unlike the combat of old, was a contest open to all.

If culture, as the anthropologist Clifford Geertz famously defined it, is merely "the stories we tell ourselves about ourselves," then the culture of ancient and medieval Christianity grew out of twinned storytelling traditions about the martyrs. On the one hand, the church ritually remembered the names and deaths of the saints, annually celebrating those like Polycarp as icons of Christian perseverance; on the other, church historians in the mold of Eusebius wove narratives about these martyrs into grander accounts of endurance and the eventual triumph of the now-Christian Roman Empire.

In the early 440s, when he was about forty himself, one of Eusebius's most well-known intellectual heirs was living in Constantinople. The scion of a prosperous Christian family from Gaza, the church historian known as Sozomen was worldly and well educated. He had trained as a lawyer in Beirut before moving to Constantinople (now the Roman Empire's administrative capital), and he would have witnessed his adopted city's explosive growth firsthand. Relatively speaking, Constantinople was new. Constantine had established it only a century earlier, on the site of the former town of Byzantium, but by the time of Sozomen's arrival in "New Rome" on the Bosporus, the metropolis was outgrowing itself.

Strategically located on a small, eastward-jutting peninsula at the mouth of the Black Sea, Constantinople was protected on three sides by water (and, by the sixth century, the formidable Byzantine navy). Constantine had ringed the coastal parts of his city with seawalls and added another bulwark stretching overland, across its western side, to protect against invaders arriving on horse and by foot. These were customary defensive measures given the dangers of the age, but Constantine's land wall constrained the city's growth. Soon a new one was needed, set well to the west of the emperor's original fortifications.

Begun in the early fifth century and completed during the reign of the pious Christian emperor Theodosius II, the engineering marvel that is the Theodosian wall system more than doubled the enclosed area of Constantinople and rendered it almost impervious to attack. Now the nomadic Huns or any other would-be aggressor arriving by land would encounter a moat and beyond that a low wall. Nothing terribly impressive yet. But should invaders manage to cross the moat and scale the wall, they would find themselves trapped on a paved terrace beneath the city's outer wall, a substantial barrier of mortared brick and smooth-cut limestone blocks. Still, the defenses did not stop there.

Inside the outer wall was yet another terrace, this one useful for the protected movement of the city's troops and armaments, and above it rose the final impediment: Constantinople's massive *inner* wall. An average of twenty feet thick and forty high, with even taller towers and turrets stationed at regular intervals along its three-and-a-half-mile-long course, the largest of the city's ramparts repelled every invader for a thousand years (see fig. 10). It was only an onslaught from Ottoman cannons in 1453 that finally battered down parts of Constantinople's undermanned and (by then) ancient and dilapidated defenses. By the mid-fifteenth century, the city was an island anyway, about the only thing left of the once grand Byzantine Empire.

Back in the mid-fifth century, however, Sozomen had no way of knowing that he was living on the cusp of a full millennium of Byzantine glory. No matter. He was more focused on the past than on the

FIGURE 10. Constantinople's Theodosian Walls, partially reconstructed.

future. From Sozomen's vantage point, one that was especially well protected behind the city's new walls, Constantinople was the hub of Roman power. From it radiated an increasingly global network of Christian culture and influence. Sozomen's writings suggest just as much.

Sozomen had already completed one history of Christianity. Following Eusebius, his first history of the church began with Jesus and ended three hundred years later with Constantine's victory over his co-emperor Licinius in 324. The emperor's triumph put a Christian alone atop the Roman Empire for the first time. Regrettably, we know little else about Sozomen's account of the first three Christian centuries. Like so many other works from antiquity, even those from the pens of widely celebrated authors, it has not survived. Thankfully, Sozomen's other historical project has enjoyed a longer life.

Completed in 443, his extant *Ecclesiastical History* begins where his first left off: with Constantine's inauguration of a newly Christian Roman Empire. The story continues through the emperor's founding of Constantinople in 330 and, a century later, the reign of Theodosius II, whose walls protecting Constantine's city visibly cemented its status as the epicenter of a muscular Christendom.

In Sozomen's telling, after his victory, Constantine was soon secure enough in his rule that he could afford to spend time on nonmilitary matters. It was he, the Christian emperor, who convened the first of several councils of the church's bishops, thus officially beginning a centuries-long argument over the nature of Christ—that paradoxical combination of humanity and divinity in one person—and the nature of the relationship between Father and Son. At the first ecumenical gathering of bishops, held across the Bosporus from Constantinople in the town of Nicaea, a single vowel made a lot more than an *iota* of difference. With the emperor's support, most bishops decreed that the Son of God is the "same in essence" (*homoousios* in Greek) as God the Father, not merely "similar in essence," or *homoiousios,* as others had argued, adding an *i,* and thus some sort of lesser divinity. The Nicene Creed, that formal statement of Christian belief first promulgated at the Council of Nicaea and subsequently revised at later synods, preserves the term *homoousios* in its reference to the Son as "*one in being* with the Father."

While debates over arcane theological terms may have appealed to bishops and the church's educated elite, the discovery of ancient relics did more to capture the general public's interest in the emperor's new cult. Sozomen explains to his readers that Constantine, grateful to the Christian god for his victories on the battlefield, had resolved to build a church in Jerusalem. It was to be a heavenly dome protecting and glorifying the place of Jesus's death and resurrection.

During the reconnaissance phase, the emperor sent his own mother, Helena, on an archaeological expedition to the Holy Land.

Sozomen describes some of the fabulous things that she discovered, including her grand prize: what she believed was the very cross upon which Jesus had been crucified. Constantine's Church of the Holy Sepulchre was built over the spot where she found it. To this day, the church remains a major tourist attraction in Jerusalem and the site of endless bickering among the Roman Catholic, Greek, Armenian, Coptic, Syrian, and Ethiopian clerics who contest its control. Moving a chair or a rug just inches from where the status quo says it is supposed to remain has been enough to provoke fistfights.

Meanwhile, back in Constantinople, Sozomen tells us, Constantine worked feverishly to construct the new and destroy the old. Within his city and beyond, he endowed dozens of other Christian churches, building up temples to the new god while pulling down those that had been erected in honor of the old ones. Then, abruptly, Sozomen's story shifts.

Lest his readers see Constantine as a mere mason, just a builder of walls and churches, Sozomen balloons the emperor's importance far beyond civic concerns. It was Constantine, he says, who not only convened the Council of Nicaea but also spread the name of Christ throughout the whole of the known world: north over the Danube, west across the Rhine, to the Goths and the Gauls and even the fearsome Celts at the ocean's distant shore. The Caucasian mountain kingdoms, up the Bosporus and out at the eastern edge of the Black Sea, had already fallen to Christ. The Armenians and the "barbaric Iberians," as Sozomen calls those who would later name themselves for Saint George, were among the very first peoples to convert to Christianity. But the gospel of Christ had traveled farther than Armenia and Georgia. In fact, it had already spread beyond the Roman frontier, down the Tigris and deep into Persia. This was said to be a land still wet with the blood of martyrs.

According to Sozomen, the Jews of the Persian Empire had acted in concert with the Zoroastrian magi, a priestly caste who charted the stars and served the sacred fire, to charge the Christians of Persia with treason. Making their case before the Persian king, the Jews accused Christians of being Roman spies, secret agents of their new friend and ally in the west: Constantine. Some Christians in Persia, they said, had even written letters to the Roman emperor, a clandestine correspondence that he received with glee. Thanks to these letters, so the charges went, Constantine now had inside information about the domestic affairs of his most powerful imperial rival.

As a result of these accusations, a high-ranking eunuch who had faithfully served the Persian king for decades and even tutored him in his youth was killed for converting to Christianity. So was the chief of the artisans' guild. But it was the humble son of cloth dyers, a bishop named Simeon, who was heralded as the first Christian martyr in the East. He, along with scores of his companions, was beheaded around 340, just a few short years after Constantine's death.

The initial allegation against Simeon seems to have had more to do with loyalty than with whatever god he chose to worship. Sozomen explains that the Persian king imposed heavy taxes upon Christians as a first punishment for their perceived betrayal. As a prominent bishop, Simeon was charged with collecting these taxes. He refused. Sozomen goes on to recount the final moments in the life of the bishop, the eunuch, and the chief of the artisans and tells us tales about many others who were killed too. Some of these stories he narrates at length and with evident knowledge of their important details. In particular, Sozomen quotes extensively from the martyrs' last words: all the speeches and prayers they offered right before they were killed.

Just how Sozomen learned so much about the martyred Christians of Persia is not entirely clear, but it is unlikely that he could have known about them through word of mouth alone. He must have had access to translations of the sophisticated literary histories that narrated the martyrs' deaths. But, like Eusebius, Sozomen wrote in Greek. He does not seem to have known the Aramaic dialect of Syriac, but plenty of people, especially those who lived in the northern Mesopotamian cities along the trade routes that stretched between Rome and Persia, were conversant in both Greek and Syriac. Important texts were regularly translated from one language to the other as monks, merchants, and missionaries moved back and forth across the porous and frequently shifting frontier between the two empires.

Even with all he had learned, Sozomen admits to his readers, with a clear sense of frustration, that the most basic facts about many of the Persian martyrs—their names, where they were from, how they were killed—could never be known. He claims that his ignorance of these hagiographic coordinates was thanks to an especially morbid form of Persian ingenuity: those who persecuted the Christians, Sozomen says, deployed such an extravagant variety of novel forms of torture that no one could remember just what had happened to whom. So many Christians had been murdered in such a short span of time that there was not even a reliable tally of the dead, much less an accurate record of their names and when, where, and how they had given their lives for Christ.

Despite his avowed difficulty in securing the facts, Sozomen claims that at least sixteen thousand Christians were killed in Persia. Most are "beyond enumeration," he despairs, martyrs unnumbered and unnamed. Sozomen is pained that so many names have been forgotten, despite the best efforts of the Persian and Syrian Christians—and, he adds, the good people of Edessa, the most important city of Roman Mesopotamia, who "devoted much care to this matter."

Sozomen's gall at the anonymity of the martyrs reflects his interest in recording their names, a key to understanding his conception of Christian history and the broader importance of the Christian martyr cult in late antiquity. Undoubtedly, Sozomen wanted to impress his Roman readers with the sheer volume of blood their fellow Christians had spilled in Persia. But this was not his primary concern. He was skilled enough as a narrator to know that specific stories about specific martyrs would always move people in ways that an abstract account of the dead (no matter how overwhelming in number) simply could not. Not every martyr could have their story told, but each merited an enduring record of their name and where, when, and how they had been killed.

We confer the same upon our dead. Though they rarely report the where and how of a death, every tombstone in every cemetery declares the name of the person buried below and the date when they died. A cemetery is not a monument to death; it is a collection of memorials to individual dead. Likewise, for Sozomen, it is not martyrdom in general but the names and stories of individual martyrs that are so important for Christian history.

Even at modern military memorials, such as Arlington National Cemetery or the Vietnam Veterans Memorial in Washington, DC, the individual soldier is never wholly subsumed to the collective. At Arlington, hundreds of thousands of identical white headstones extend for row after manicured row, but inscribed upon each is an individual name. As for that famous wall of polished black stone that rises and recedes "as a rift in the earth," its architect, Maya Lin, wrote that its chronologically ordered list of more than fifty-eight thousand American dead is intended to "convey the sense of overwhelming numbers, while unifying these individuals into a whole." Even as it leaves all the Vietnamese, Laotians, and Cambodians killed in the Vietnam War unnumbered and unnamed, this wall offers a piercing nationalist appeal by expressing an overwhelming number as a walkable litany of individual names.

Naming is Adam's first act in the book of Genesis. Before Adam is "Adam" he is tasked with naming the animals as God creates them. This is a sacred and intimate act of knowing. As each animal crosses beneath Adam's gaze and receives its name, it passes from nonbeing into being. Naming is just as fundamental in the Orthodox theology of icons. A true icon must be inscribed with the name of the person depicted, who, by name and by visage, becomes a mirror of Christ—the holy prototype. Elsewhere in Genesis, a change in name accompanies a change in mandate: Abram becomes Abraham when God tells him that he is to father many nations. Likewise, in the New Testament, Simon becomes Peter ("Petros" in Greek) when Jesus tells him that he is the "rock" (*petra*) upon whom he will found his church. A similar transition occurs with the bestowal of a baptismal name, that sacramental entry into new life in Christ. When a monk commits to his vows and leaves his old life behind, he takes another new name, to begin yet another new life in Christ.

Martyrdom too is such a transition, one consistently described by ancient Christians as a second baptism, but this time in blood. Remembering the martyrs' names is a sacred duty. Still, given the gendered power dynamics of the Roman world, it is all the more remarkable that Eusebius willingly equated the name of a female slave with that of a bishop. Blandina, Polycarp, and the rest—all their names were recorded together, Eusebius says, on "eternal plaques." In expressing his interest in the names of the later martyrs killed in the East, Sozomen hints at a list compiled by the Christians of Roman Edessa, who, recall that he said, were among those who "devoted much care" to recording the names of the dead. Somehow, their list has survived. And it can still be read today—if one knows where to look.

In 1843, William Cureton, an assistant librarian and the keeper of Oriental manuscripts at the British Museum, finally had a chance to examine a parchment codex—a book written on pages of animal skin—that had recently been acquired from a monastery in Egypt. Another scholar had been hogging it, using the manuscript to prepare a printed edition of a text written by Eusebius on the manifestation of the divine. Eusebius's *Theophany* was lost in the original Greek, but here it survived in an early Syriac translation from Roman Edessa. By many odd twists of fate, the manuscript had made its way first to Egypt and then, centuries later, onward to England.

Cureton noted that the manuscript also included Syriac translations of two other texts attributed to Eusebius: the long version of his *Martyrs of Palestine* (also lost in Greek) and a brief encomium, or speech of praise, in honor of the martyrs. But what attracted Cureton's interest was not the sudden reemergence of several ancient Christian texts that had long been lost to scholars. No—he was more interested in a brief note scribbled in a margin near the end of the *Martyrs of Palestine*. According to the date in the note, it had been added by a reader many centuries after the manuscript was made. In fact, the marginal note claimed to reproduce the original scribe's colophon—which is to say, the original scribe's concluding remarks at the end of the manuscript in which he explained to readers where and when he had completed his work.

Colophons are often found at the end of ancient and medieval manuscripts. In addition to recording vital information about the manuscript's production, they frequently include pious requests that the reader pray for the humble scribe who completed his work at such and such a place on such and such a date. In this case, it seems that the manuscript which Cureton had before him at the British Museum had long ago suffered the ravages of age and that, centuries earlier, its final page—where the original scribe had written his colophon— was already in danger of falling off. To preserve the colophon, some later reader had kindly recopied it in a margin on an earlier page.

By the time Cureton had an opportunity to examine the ancient manuscript, its final page with the original colophon had, indeed, fallen off and been lost. In Cureton's translation from the Syriac, this is what the note said: "Behold, my brethren, if it should happen that the end of this ancient book should be torn off and lost, together with the writer's subscription and termination, it was written at the end of it thus: viz., that this book was written at Edessa, a city of Mesopotamia, by the hands of a man called Jacob. In the year 723 in the month Tishri the latter it was completed. And agreeable to what was written there, I have written also here, without addition. And what is here, I wrote in the year 1398 of the era of the Greeks."

These odd dates, especially the reference to "the era of the Greeks," demand some unpacking. According to the note writer, who says he added nothing to the "subscription and termination" (the colophon) of "a man called Jacob" (the scribe), the manuscript was produced in the city of Edessa "in the year 723 in the month Tishri the latter." Second Tishri, or "Tishri the latter," is an Assyrian lunar month corresponding to November. But the year was not AD 723. The BC/AD dating system familiar to us did not emerge until the sixth century and was not in common use until long after that. So instead of calculating the years since the birth of Christ, both the original scribe (Jacob) and the anonymous writer of the later note counted from the beginning of "the era of the Greeks"—which is to say, the beginning of the Seleucid Persian Empire, in 312 BC, after the death of Alexander the Great.

If we subtract 312 from 723, we arrive at a more intelligible date of 411. Likewise, if we subtract 312 from 1398 (the year when the later note writer says he is writing), we learn that he copied Jacob's colophon of 411 from the back of the book into an earlier margin in 1086, more than six hundred years after Jacob completed his work and nearly eight hundred before Cureton had a chance to read any of it at his desk in the British Museum.

These dates explain the librarian's keen interest in the marginal note. Cureton knew that fifth-century manuscripts were exceedingly rare (they still are), but to find one that was dated by a scribe to a *specific* month in a *specific* year at the very beginning of the fifth century? Well, that was simply unprecedented. Cureton could tell by the distinctive handwriting, by the scribe's polished turn of the Syriac script, that he was holding a very old manuscript. But if the original colophon could be found and confirmed, then he had before him the very oldest dated book known to still exist in the world (see fig. 11).

For some, what made this manuscript even more valuable than its great antiquity was the list of martyrs' names on its final pages. They are divided between East and West, with the newest Christian dead from Persia in one column and an older roster of apostles and martyr-saints from the Roman Empire in the other. Dying for Christ was important for all Christians, geographic and linguistic divides notwithstanding, and the martyrs of Persia were only then (in the early fifth century, that is) having their stories told. Among them, Simeon—the son of cloth dyers, who refused to collect the Persian king's taxes—is the first to be named in the manuscript's register of bishop-martyrs from the East. Many others follow. In the list of the earliest martyrs from the Roman Empire, those saints whose cults were already established, the names are organized by month and by date, just as in the book of martyrs about which Gregory had told Eulogius.

Appropriately, the ancient Syriac manuscript's list of Roman martyrs begins on the twenty-sixth day of the former Kanun, December 26, with the feast of Saint Stephen. Playing with his name, Eusebius refers to Stephen as "the first to bear the 'crown' [*stephanos*] of the victorious martyrs of Christ." Death did not defeat the Christian martyr; death, so we have seen, was an athletic triumph that merited a metaphorical crown: the *stephanos* of laurel leaves won by Olympic victors.

From yet another note written in the manuscript, we know that in the early tenth century it was moved from Edessa to a Syrian monastery in Egypt. Nearly a thousand years later, it was moved again—this

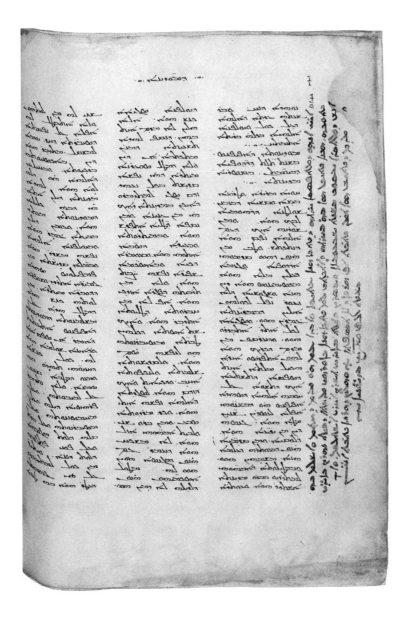

FIGURE 11. Marginal note recopying the scribe Jacob's colophon in the oldest dated book in the world, Edessa, 411. British Library, Add. MS 12150, f. 239v, London.

time to England. As Cureton says about "this matchless volume," its fate is one of the most remarkable "among all the curiosities of literature." And we can trace its travels thanks to the notes of an abbot and a young woman's diary.

The desert of Lower Egypt, and specifically a small depression just west of the Nile delta between Alexandria and Cairo, has been an important center of Christian monasticism since the time of Constantine. Known today as the Wadi al-Natrun for its salt deposits and alkaline lakes that once provided the raw materials used in mummification, the Desert of Scetis was never the most welcoming land for living humans. This helps explain why Christian ascetics seeking a life of solitude chose to inhabit it as a place of retreat. Inhospitable as its arid climate may be for humans, however, it is excellent for the preservation of manuscripts.

Egypt never had a native Syriac-speaking population, but the desert's monasticism was so renowned as a model of communal Christian asceticism that it attracted people from all over the Mediterranean world, including the formerly Roman Near East. In the early ninth century, a number of Syrian Orthodox monks from Mesopotamia helped repopulate an abandoned monastery in the Desert of Scetis. A hundred years later, in 925, a vizier of the Abbasid caliph arrived in Egypt and presented himself at what had by then become known as the Monastery of the Syrians. He was a tax collector, and he had come to claim what the monks owed their Muslim rulers. His demand came as a shock to the monks, since they had long been spared taxation and in any case could not afford to pay what he said they must. The monastery's wise abbot, Moses of Nisibis, knew he had one hope: he could travel from Egypt to Baghdad, the capital of the caliphate, to appeal to the Muslim ruler himself. He set out in 927. It would be five years before he returned.

After an interminable wait, Moses was eventually granted an audience in Baghdad. Perhaps surprisingly, he was successful in his appeal. Contrary to the vizier's imperious demand, the monks of the Monastery of the Syrians would remain tax-exempt subjects of the caliph. But this welcome news was not the only souvenir that Moses brought back to his brothers in Egypt. He had spent the better part of his long wait to see the caliph visiting other Syriac-speaking monks in monasteries throughout Mesopotamia. From them, Moses bought (or was given) some 250 Syriac manuscripts. In many, he inscribed personal acquisition notes explaining where and when he had gotten them. Moses's handwritten comments offer the sorts of warnings that monastic readers were accustomed to encountering: curses upon those who would dare harm or alter any of the books or, worse still, attempt to take them from the monastery's library.

The many nineteenth-century Europeans who sought to acquire ancient Christian manuscripts for their growing libraries in London, Paris, Rome, Berlin, Saint Petersburg, and other important centers of learning did not pay much heed to such threats of ancient monks. Then again, neither did the nineteenth-century monks who sold the manuscripts to European book hunters. In the monks' defense, no one in Egypt—at least no one at what had become the inaptly named Monastery of the Syrians—could read Syriac anymore. For centuries, this monastery had been the preserve of Coptic Orthodox monks. The unintelligible Syriac books of its former inhabitants had thus remained virtually untouched, if in various states of disrepair, for hundreds of years. Some sat upon shelves, but many dismembered others were housed in a vaulted room that one visitor who arrived at the Monastery of the Syrians in 1837 described as a chamber "filled to the depth of two feet or more with the loose leaves of Syriac manuscripts."

In December of the following year, the Reverend Henry Tattam, a Coptic scholar from Bedfordshire, England, set out for Egypt with his stepdaughter, Miss Eliza Platt. Miss Platt kept a diary of her exotic travels so as to amuse her mother upon their return. Her entry for Sunday, January 13, 1839, describes how she awoke in a tent that had been pitched beneath the walls of the Monastery of the Syrians. "Mr. Tattam," she writes, referring to her stepfather, "immediately entered the convent, where pipes and coffee were brought him; after which the priests conducted him to their churches, and showed him the books used in them. They then desired to know his object in visiting them; upon which he cautiously opened his commission by saying that he wished to see their books. They replied that they had no more than what he had seen in the church; upon which he told them plainly that he knew they had."

Tattam, it seems, was familiar with the reports of the visitors who preceded him and knew the story of the chamber filled with loose manuscript pages. The monks "laughed on being detected," Platt continues in her diary, "and after a short conference said that he should see [the books]. The bell soon rang for prayers." According to Platt's entry for the following day, the monks conducted Tattam to the vaulted room after breakfast, "where he found a great quantity of very old and valuable Syriac manuscripts."

Three weeks later, after perambulating around the Desert of Scetis to examine the holdings of other monastic libraries, many of which had Coptic manuscripts that Tattam acquired, he and Miss Platt returned to the Monastery of the Syrians in the company of their intrepid guide, a man identified simply as Mohamed. Other manuscript hunters—as we learn from an observer writing in the 1870s— plied the monks with a sweet Italian cordial exuding notes of clove, rose petal, and cinnamon, and Tattam and Mohamed "had recourse to the same means of negotiation . . . and applied them with similar success, only substituting raki for rosoglio." For his efforts, Tattam returned to England toting forty-nine Syriac manuscripts, including the one that Cureton later found with the note dating its production to November 411. It was eventually cataloged as British Library Syriac Additional Manuscript 12150.

More visitors went to the Monastery of the Syrians throughout the early 1840s, where the monks insisted each time that they had sold all the manuscripts they owned but eventually produced more to sell—and slowly came to appreciate just how much those they had already sold must have been worth. Hundreds of loose pages and fragments of pages made their way in bundles to the British Museum. Eagerly opening and examining each as it arrived, Cureton hoped upon hope that one might contain the lost page he was looking for: the one with Jacob's own colophon, which would confirm the date later transcribed in the margin of the manuscript.

"And now, Reader," Cureton writes of his eventual discovery,

> if thou hast any love for the records of antiquity; if thou feelest any kindred enthusiasm in such pursuits as these; if thou hast ever known the satisfaction of having a dim expectation gradually brightened into reality, and an anxious research rewarded with success— things that but rarely happen to us in this world of disappointment— I leave it to thine own imagination to paint the sensations which I experienced at that moment when the loosing of the cord of the seventh bundle disclosed to my sight a small fragment of beautiful vellum, in a well-known hand, upon which I read the following words:
>
> "There are completed in this volume three books—Titus, and Clement, and he [Eusebius] of Caesarea.
>
> "Glory to the Father, and to the Son, and to the Holy Ghost, now and at all times, and for ever.
>
> "This volume was completed in the month Tishri the latter, in the year 723, at Edessa, a city of Mesopotamia . . ."

These ancient words, Cureton concludes, were "enough to repay me for the labour of my research, and to confirm and verify the facts connected with it."

In his book *Sum: Forty Tales from the Afterlives,* the writer and neuroscientist David Eagleman posits that every human dies three deaths: "The first," he says, is the obvious one, "when the body ceases to function. The second is when the body is consigned to the grave. The third is that moment, sometime in the future, when your name is spoken for the last time." Of most of the thousands of Christians said to have been martyred in Persia, nothing remains. They are dead thrice over, according to Eagleman, with no body, no grave, not even a name. But when, in the early 2000s, four partially legible fragments of the ancient manuscript so dear to William Cureton were identified among the hundreds of manuscripts and fragments of manuscripts still at the Monastery of the Syrians, a few new entries were unceremoniously added to our sixteen-hundred-year-old list of Christian martyrs from Persia. All we can make out about one of these martyrs is that he was a monk "with a pierced ear." We do not know his name.

3   *The Remains of the Dead*

The Sainte-Chapelle still stands opposite the Cathedral of Notre-Dame on the western end of the Île de la Cité, the battleship-shaped island in the middle of the Seine in the heart of Paris. Completed in 1248—less than a decade after its patron, King Louis IX, first commissioned his architects, masons, and glaziers to begin their work—the Sainte-Chapelle exemplifies the sumptuous rayonnant style of French Gothic architecture. Medieval visitors to King Louis's "Holy Chapel" described it as a rival to some of the finest chambers in paradise. This is no exaggeration. As any tourist who has been there already knows, especially one who has had the good fortune to visit on a sunny Parisian day, to be in the Sainte-Chapelle is to be bathed in color and light. The fifteen stained-glass windows that enclose its nave and apse form an almost unbroken, fifty-foot-high wall of red and blue, glorifying a space that formerly housed dozens of sacred relics (see fig. 12).

The largest reliquary, or relic container, once kept inside the Sainte-Chapelle was a massive silver ark called the Grande Châsse. It sat at the church's focal point on an elevated platform in the apse. Three copper-gilt reliefs on its front and sides depicted Christ's flagellation, crucifixion, and resurrection. At the rear, double doors and multiple locks secured its sacred contents. And inside, like a Russian

FIGURE 12. Interior of Paris's Sainte-Chapelle, consecrated 1248.

nesting doll, were still smaller reliquaries, each containing an ancient relic. Most of these were thought to have touched Jesus himself. They included a stone from his tomb, the lance that pierced his side, the scarlet cloak draped on him in mockery by the Roman soldiers, and even some splinters from the very cross upon which he was crucified. But King Louis's most precious relic, and the Sainte-Chapelle's raison d'être, was the crown of thorns.

The Sainte-Chapelle was a private relic chapel and martyrs' shrine. Pilgrims and the public were welcomed inside on certain feast days—notably September 30, when the relics in the Grande Châsse were brought out and venerated—but the chapel's relatively small size and location within the Palais de la Cité's courtyard signaled that this was the preserve of the king.

The Sainte-Chapelle's decorative stonework and stained-glass windows still tell the story of why King Louis had it built. Dozens of painted quatrefoil medallions on its masonry graphically illustrate the deaths of saints—Stephen, Lucy, Sebastian, Thomas Becket, and others—all of whom won the crown of martyrdom in dying for Christ. The chapel's celebrated windows continue this twinned theme of martyrdom and crowning: lining the nave are scores of scenes that illustrate the crowning triumphs of Old Testament kings and queens; meanwhile, the apse windows visually narrate the New Testament, with the central one depicting the crucifixion of the King of Kings—the martyr upon whose head the crown of thorns once rested.

The final window in the nave's cycle of kings and queens ushers the biblical past into the mid-thirteenth-century present. Intended as the sum of those preceding it, this window commemorates a barefoot King Louis walking humbly among his subjects as they process the crown of thorns into Paris. It was taken to Saint-Denis for safekeeping until the Sainte-Chapelle could be built to house it. Such artistic publicization of Louis's piety and divine right to rule brought ancient Jerusalem to medieval Paris, put the French king in the line of David and Solomon, and signaled that Louis was the preeminent defender of Christendom.

Louis's presentation of himself as the ideal Christian king went beyond his collection of relics, his grand processional displays, and his patronage of artistic and architectural masterpieces. In 1244, when he was thirty years old and the Sainte-Chapelle was still being built, the temporarily enfeebled king took a vow from his sickbed. If, he promised, he recovered his health and his strength, then he would bring Paris to Jerusalem. He would travel to the Holy Land as a crusader and, God willing, die there as a martyr. Four years later, in June 1248, after six weeks of pomp and circumstance celebrating the consecration of the Sainte-Chapelle, Louis and an army of twenty-five thousand men and seventy-five hundred horses—one of the largest, best-equipped, and best-funded Christian armies ever to depart on crusade—finally set out.

Our English word *relic* comes from the Latin noun *reliquiae,* which refers to the remnants of something, and from the related verb *relinquere,* which means "to leave behind." In common usage, a relic can be any left-behind thing—from a floppy disk to the Whig Party, or a pair of corduroy bell-bottoms—but the Christian sense is usually the bodily remains of saints and martyrs. The word can also refer to a martyr's personal effects, such as clothes or shoes or other belongings. For one very obvious reason, it is such nonbodily "contact relics" that are the most closely associated with Jesus. According to Christian scripture and tradition, he ascended into heaven after his death and resurrection—just the weapons that killed him and the shroud used to bury him were left behind. Second only to the holy cross, the most renowned and symbolic of these sanctified instruments of torture was the crown of thorns.

The crown changed hands frequently over the centuries, from when it was first proclaimed an authentic relic, during the reign of Constantine, until King Louis acquired it from Baldwin II, his cousin and the last Latin emperor of Constantinople, nine hundred years later. Though Louis took pains to hide the commercial side of the transaction, he reportedly paid 135,000 French livres. This was a monumental sum. By some estimates, it was three times more than the cost of building the splendid chapel where the crown was housed. But even though Louis may have paid more for the crown than anyone else before him, his eagerness to possess relics of Jesus's passion was in no way novel. They were typically sought after and guarded by princely patrons. What drove Louis to acquire his, and to pay handsomely for ornamental and architectural reliquaries to hold them, was his desire to possess visible remains of the holy. In theory, this is also what motivated the Crusades. They were a series of papally sanctioned quests to reclaim the very land upon which Jesus and his disciples had once stood.

By Louis's day, pilgrims from throughout the Mediterranean and the Middle East had been traveling to the Holy Land for centuries. Many were poor, and they often returned home with little more than a rock, a pocketful of dirt, or maybe a palm frond as a souvenir. The imperial elite dug deeper—excavating, dismantling, and shipping off the Holy Land, piece by piece. Constantine's mother, Helena, claimed the staircase that Jesus was believed to have ascended before Pontius Pilate condemned him to death. She had the "Scala Sancta" sent to Rome, where it was reinstalled in her family's private relic chapel.

Although many of the relics that Helena found in Jerusalem were, like the Holy Stairs, kept under private, imperial control, her expedition to the Holy Land was a very public pilgrimage. It must have been quite the spectacle to watch as the emperor's own mother directed the digging at the presumed site of Jesus's execution. What long-buried treasures might be uncovered? After some effort and much suspense, eventually—according to later legend—Helena's excavators found not one but three crosses buried deep underground. To identify which one had belonged to Jesus and which were those of the two thieves who had been crucified alongside him, Helena summoned a gravely ill woman to the site, then had her led before each of the crosses in turn. Neither of the first two had any effect, but upon touching the third the woman was instantly healed.

Once again, Christians had inverted the old order of the Roman world: despite suffering death, martyrs won crowns of victory; despite killing Jesus, a wooden cross bloomed into a tree of life.

Helena sent much of what had now been tested and positively identified as the holy cross back to Rome, but she kept several of the holy nails she found embedded in it. These she dispatched directly to Constantine so they could be fitted into his helmet and his horse's bridle. In her motherly estimation, a rusty nail that had once been driven through Jesus's hand would do far more to protect her son than the finest steel.

Helena's success in finding the relics of Jesus's passion spurred widespread interest in pilgrimage to the Holy Land. Soon, fragments of the cross began appearing throughout the Roman world, thanks in no small part to the salesmanship of Bishop Cyril of Jerusalem, who encouraged both the distribution of relics and the visits of pilgrims to his city. He was famously quoted as saying that Christians outside the Holy Land could only hear the stories about Jesus and his apostles; those in Jerusalem could see, smell, and touch them too.

Cyril's efforts on behalf of Jerusalem coincided with a broader promotion of martyrs' relics and the materiality of the holy in fourth-century Christianity. In his sermons, Basil of Caesarea—a bishop from the mountainous region of Cappadocia in central Asia Minor—consistently emphasized that anyone who touched a martyr's relic would participate in that saint's holiness. Basil's younger brother, the renowned theologian Gregory of Nyssa, said the same about such talismans. In a long treatise extolling the pious life of their sister Macrina, who had organized a community of virginal and ascetic women on the family's sprawling estate, Gregory recounts his amazement when sitting with his sister's body soon after her death. One of Macrina's followers had revealed to Gregory that his sister always kept a relic of the cross pressed against her breast: the holy splinter, she explained, was hidden inside a signet ring that Macrina wore tucked beneath her clothes as a pendant on a necklace. For Gregory, the moral of the story was clear: the fragment of wood inside Macrina's ring had shaped his sister into the saint she was. The powerful relic had transformed her, guiding her life into one of unceasing participation in the holiness of the cross.

Following the lead of imperial and ecclesiastical elites such as Helena and Macrina, other Christians quickly took notice of the burgeoning cult of relics. One nun from Gaul, a woman named Egeria, wrote of traveling to Jerusalem for Easter in 386 and of her visit to the city's Church of the Holy Sepulchre—which stood over the spot where, over half a century earlier, Helena had uncovered the cross. Egeria was inside the Holy Sepulchre on Good Friday for the annual veneration of the cross, and she writes that its procession through the church caused such a commotion that deacons had to be posted around it as sentries. It seems that instead of kissing the relic, as one was supposed to do to honor it, at least one overzealous pilgrim had tried to bite off a chunk.

Not everyone could possess a fragment of the cross. Even wealthy and well-connected pilgrims often had to settle for something less. This usually meant a small pressed-metal ampulla containing a thimbleful of olive oil. These were often attached to strips of leather and, like Macrina's signet ring, worn around the neck (see fig. 13). No splinter of wood floated inside, but the oil was nearly as good. It was a contact relic of a contact relic. According to one sixth-century

FIGURE 13. Pilgrim's ampulla with remains of a leather strap and Greek inscription ("Oil of the wood of life from the holy places of Christ"), c. 600. Cleveland Museum of Art.

pilgrim from Piacenza, a town in northern Italy, once each flask had been filled, a deacon would touch it to the cross. Then the oil would start to bubble and fizz, and the ampulla would have to be capped quickly to prevent the now living liquid inside from spilling to the ground.

❖ ❖ ❖

For the average Christian without the stomach or opportunity to become a martyr, proximity to God meant proximity to the tombs of the saints. According to Saint Jerome, the famed biblical scholar and unrivaled polemicist of ascetic orthodoxy, by the late fourth century so many people had abandoned the pagan temples in the center of Rome in favor of the martyrs' shrines in the suburban cemeteries beyond its walls that the city had all but changed its address.

The relationship between a martyr's shrine and the tomb over which it was built has deeply colored our understanding of the cult of the saints. It is rather misleading, though. Outside Rome, especially in the Greek East, early martyrs' shrines tended to be architecturally and locationally distinct from the memorials to their honorees in civic cemeteries. Still, for those non-Christians in the Roman Empire who practiced more traditional means of caring for the gods, it was deeply unsettling to see repositories of bones (wherever they were kept) transformed into places of feasting. It was even more disturbing when the cult of martyr-heroes that centered on tombs and shrines became a cult of those same martyrs' relics—which could be fragmented, distributed, and kept in private chapels within the home. Being near the dead was disgusting enough, but to willingly touch, dismember, and venerate their remains as if life were still present in a desiccated bone?

Such revulsion over the Christian relic cult never fully disappeared. As the historian Peter Brown puts it in his classic account of the cult of the saints in Latin Christianity, "a common reticence and incomprehension" regarding the veneration of relics still runs through "our cultural bloodstream." This is, he surmises, due to our intellectual debt (whether we know it or not) to the thinkers of the European Enlightenment. For David Hume, Edward Gibbon, and other prominent philosophers and historians of the eighteenth century, the simple monotheism of the very earliest Jesus followers was bastardized by the irrational polytheism of the cult of the saints.

Gibbon, the author of the six-volume *History of the Decline and Fall of the Roman Empire,* especially looked down with contempt upon what he saw as the vulgar superstitions of the ignorant masses.

The idea of traveling to the Holy Land to acquire and export its relics seemed bizarre even to some later pilgrims who went there themselves. In his account of a voyage to the Holy Land aboard a steamship, published in 1869 as *The Innocents Abroad, or The New Pilgrims' Progress,* Mark Twain grumbles, "But isn't this relic matter a little overdone? We find a piece of the true cross in every old church we go into, and some of the nails that held it together. I would not like to be positive, but I think we have seen as much as a keg of these nails." Twain surely expected readers to find his quip funny, but this jibe at the ubiquity of relics in Catholic and Orthodox churches was well worn. The ire of those who fashioned themselves as more sophisticated religious observers had long been directed at those who would bow before splinters of wood and fragments of bone.

But is the cult of saints' relics really that hard to understand?

Human remains revolt us because of their inescapable connection to putridity and death, but the nonbodily remnants of our heroes do not summon such disgust. Undoubtedly, there is a difference between bodily relics and other material remains, but it is better understood as one of degree, not one of kind. Our fascination with the *things* associated with those most celebrated among us is universal, and to possess these objects is, in a way, to possess a bit of whoever once touched them. Gregory of Nyssa understood this with a new appreciation for his sister's holiness when her relic pendant was revealed: for much of her life, she had possessed a fragment of Christ.

Like people, objects can be transformed when their true histories are revealed. Take *Salvator Mundi,* an image of Christ as the Savior of the World. This painting changed hands not long ago for the price of a used car. Then, in 2017, it set the record as the most expensive painting ever sold. The *Salvator Mundi* had been professionally restored between the two sales, but it was not the restorers' physical labor that transformed it into an art object worth hundreds of millions of dollars. No, it was their realization that the painting was one of Leonardo da Vinci's (see fig. 14). But although the cleaning certainly hastened the *Salvator Mundi*'s new attribution, without broad agreement among a community of art historians that what was formerly believed to be a subpar product of Leonardo's school was painted by the hand of the master himself, no amount of stripping and scrubbing could have increased its value so exponentially. Only the collective testimony of Leonardo experts could do that.

Experts are unnecessary, however, for witnesses who are present themselves. In 1957, after the final out at Ebbets Field signaled that baseball's Brooklyn Dodgers were officially moving to Los Angeles, scores of children jumped from their seats, climbed over railings, and rushed on to the diamond. According to the great sportswriter Red Smith, some kids "clawed at the mound" while others "dug for home plate." All scooped dirt into empty paper bags. Lamenting the departure of their heroes but wanting some memento of the ground where they had played, the children had no need for a baseball historian to remind them that this dirt was different—that this was where Robinson and Hodges, Campanella and Snider had stood and spit and sweated.

The incarnation, that uncomfortable paradox at the heart of Christian theology, insists that the divine became flesh and that Jesus too once stood and spit and sweated. The fundamental corporeality of Christianity might have been lost on the likes of Gibbon and Twain, but for King Louis and every other ancient and medieval Christian, Christianity's materiality *was* the faith. This is what made the contents of the Sainte-Chapelle's Grande Châsse so valuable: that bit of John the Baptist's skull, that vial of Mary's milk, all those bones of the martyrs—none of these things was just a memento of an irretrievable past; all were timeless points of intersection where the

FIGURE 14. *Salvator Mundi* by Leonardo da Vinci, c. 1500. Restored in 2007; auctioned in 2017 for $450 million. Louvre Abu Dhabi.

holy and the human converged. Saints led a double existence through their relics: present on earth while being glorified in heaven. Relics were an earthly portal to paradise. It was therefore extremely important to ensure their authenticity. But this proved difficult when different objects told the same story about their pasts and all seemed endowed with the power to heal.

A keg of nails could pose a problem.

The many ancient scraps of cloth associated with Jesus tell some of the more intriguing tales about the medieval desire to possess material remains of the holy. They also highlight the difficulty of distinguishing authentic remains from fraudulent ones. The Grande Châsse contained several strips of linen that were believed to have swaddled the infant Jesus in the manger and others said to have wrapped his brutalized body in the tomb. Yet another piece of linen in the Grande Châsse was curiously described by one seventeenth-century cataloger as the "S. Toile enchaffée en une Table," or "Holy Towel affixed to a Board." The holy towel was a *sudarium,* this being the Latin term for "sweat cloth" or "handkerchief." The one in the Sainte-Chapelle had never belonged to Jesus but was thought to have touched him. Somehow, it had been imprinted with a perfect likeness of his face.

Remarkable as this may have been, the sudarium in Paris was not nearly so famous as another in northern Spain. That one, the Sudarium of Oviedo, was believed to have covered Jesus's head. John's Gospel mentions such a cloth. On the morning of the resurrection, when Jesus's mystified disciples arrived at his empty tomb, Peter is said to have noticed some "linen wrappings" on the ground and "the cloth that had been on Jesus' head." The headcloth was "not lying with the linen wrappings but rolled up in a place by itself." The anonymous pilgrim from Piacenza who wrote about the flasks of fizzing oil at the Holy Sepulchre mentions having seen what he was told was this same cloth, adding that it was stored in a cave not far from Jerusalem, guarded by the monks of a nearby monastery. Perhaps it later made its way across North Africa, from the Holy Land to Spain, staying just ahead of Persian, then Arab, then Moorish advances.

Of course, far and away the most illustrious cloth associated with Jesus today is neither a handkerchief nor a head covering but rather a shroud. Though its name suggests an Italian provenance, the first record of the Shroud of Turin comes from fourteenth-century France. Seven centuries later, it still captivates crowds. In 2010, when it was put out for display in the foothills of the Italian Alps, more than two million pilgrims, tourists, and otherwise curious onlookers went to see it. Despite the shroud's popularity, recent popes have avoided making any definitive statement about its authenticity. The Vatican promotes the shroud as a devotional tool, a visual aid for the prayerful contemplation of Jesus's suffering and death. Whether it is an actual contact relic that was once wrapped around Jesus's body is a question judiciously left to the faith of each individual believer.

The Shroud of Turin has long had its skeptics. Even before the age of radiocarbon dating and other means of scientific analysis, there were doubters. This is mainly a result of the shroud's spotty history. Relatively speaking, the stories about the shroud and those who miraculously benefited from venerating it just do not extend back that far. In 1543, when the shroud was still in France, the voluble reformer John Calvin used an argument from silence to rail against its authenticity: "How is it possible," he asked, his voice rising with incredulity from the page, "that those sacred historians, who carefully related all the miracles that took place at Christ's death, should have omitted to mention one so remarkable as the likeness of the body of our Lord remaining on its wrapping sheet?"

In the Byzantine Empire, any likeness of Jesus that was miraculously imprinted and preserved upon cloth was known as an *acheiropoiēton,* a technical term for an image "not made by human hands." In western Europe, the most famous of these supernatural images of Jesus was imprinted on a woman's veil. Long before anyone had ever heard of the Shroud of Turin, the Veil of Veronica was a sensation.

Each time the Veil of Veronica was removed from its reliquary and processed to the Santo Spirito hospital in Rome, there was a miracle. Those who traveled to the city to see it were awarded with indulgences, which typically meant a reduction of their time in purgatory by several years (and sometimes several centuries). Small reproductions of "the Veronica," known as vernicles, were struck on cheap metal and pinned to pilgrims' hats like Boy Scouts' merit badges. By the early fourteenth century, Jesus's image on Veronica's veil was so well known that Dante could offhandedly mention a Croatian pilgrim in *The Divine Comedy* who had traveled to Rome just to see "the Veronica." His readers needed no explanation.

One of the more famous Renaissance depictions of Veronica and her veil is that of the Flemish painter Hans Memling. His Veronica kneels by a roadside, at some distance from a walled city on the horizon, and holds out her veil by its corners to display a perfect image of Jesus's face (see plate 1). In a wonderful example of life imitating art, the iconic gesture of a matador waving his cape in front of a charging bull is still known as a veronica. But who was she?

No one by the name of Veronica appears in the New Testament. The later legend about her, though, claims that she was among the women who encountered Jesus as he carried his cross from Jerusalem to the place where he was crucified. Overcome with pity at the sight of the wounded Jesus dripping with sweat and blood, Veronica handed him her veil so that he might at least have the minor dignity of wiping his face. When Jesus returned the veil, it was impressed with his likeness. Fittingly, Veronica went on to become the patron saint of photographers (and rather less so, laundry workers).

Some early versions of her legend tell a different story. They say that Jesus, at some point prior to his crucifixion, gave Veronica a *portrait* of himself on cloth—not her own sweat-and-blood-stained veil. It was with this painted image that Veronica later traveled to Rome and cured the emperor Tiberius of his ailments. This version of the story helpfully accounts for the relic's antiquity and explains its presence in Rome within months of Jesus's death.

Although the Veronica legend is in no way biblical, elements of it—blood, a piece of cloth, the power to heal—are reminiscent of those that are. That the legend seems biblical helps explain the veil's popularity among pilgrims and the ancient history ascribed to it, even though there is no written record of its existence until 1199.

Perhaps the most apparent biblical connection to the Veronica legend is the story of Jesus healing the woman with the issue of blood. In Luke's telling, which is set during Jesus's public ministry and wedged between two other miracles, Jesus and his disciples are walking among a throng of eager followers when an unidentified woman who has been bleeding for a dozen years comes up behind him and reaches out for the hem of his cloak. She believed she would be healed if only she could touch the fringe of Jesus's garment. At once, Jesus senses that something has happened. Turning around, he demands, "Who touched me?" Peter, who is being jostled along with his Lord in the middle of the same mass of people, is baffled by Jesus's question. Tentatively, he points out the obvious: "Master, the crowds surround you and press in on you." To this Jesus responds, "Someone touched me; for I noticed that power had gone out from me." The power to which he refers is, of course, the power to heal.

As any reader of the New Testament already knows, Jesus was not the only one with such power: it was communicated to his followers, and it took on many forms. In the Acts of the Apostles, the sick are healed when nothing more than Peter's shadow passes over them. Similarly, we read elsewhere in Acts, continuing Luke's preoccupation with divinely infused textiles, that God wrought "extraordinary miracles" (or, more literally translated from the Greek, "no common works of power") through the apostle Paul, "so that when the hand-kerchiefs or aprons that had touched his skin were brought to the sick, their diseases left them, and the evil spirits came out of them."

In the mid-1800s, Sister Marie of Saint Peter, a French Carmelite nun, was instrumental in establishing a special devotion to the Holy Face of Jesus. In part, this was a result of popular interest in Sister Marie's own visions of the Lord. She was not alone. Experiencing visions of Jesus, especially those of his agony, has long been acknowledged as a particular hallmark of female piety and asceticism.

Just a few years before Sister Marie had her visions of Jesus's torture and death, Blessed Anne Catherine Emmerich—who, like so many other female visionaries, had spent much of her life ill and bedridden—reported her own. But unlike Sister Marie, Emmerich had a scribe, a published poet and novelist named Clemens Brentano, to whom she could recount what she had seen. Brentano saw firsthand that dreams were not the only thing of Emmerich's that were dominated by Jesus's suffering: she also bore the wounds of Jesus's passion on her body. Pricks from the crown of thorns dotted her scalp; the gash from the holy lance marred her side; the stigmata from the holy nails bled from her hands.

In 1833, about a decade after Emmerich's death, Brentano published his literary elaborations of the dead woman's visions as *The Dolorous Passion of Our Lord Jesus Christ*. Many more decades later, but just months before Emmerich's official beatification by Pope John Paul II, the actor and filmmaker Mel Gibson released *The*

Passion of the Christ. Elements of it, including a scene of Veronica's encounter with Jesus, borrow from Brentano's *Dolorous Passion,* and Gibson refers to Emmerich's visions of Jesus in the film's credits.

Perhaps the strangest scene in *The Passion of the Christ* is not the one in which Veronica hands her veil to Jesus but another quasi-biblical one, immediately after his scourging. It begins, biblically enough, with Pontius Pilate's wife. According to Matthew's Gospel, this unnamed Roman woman experienced her own vision of Jesus. It so disturbed her that she sent an urgent message to her husband, imploring him to spare the man's life. But the episode ends there. Matthew says nothing else about Pilate's wife—not even what she did after her request was ignored. Gibson eagerly filled in the blanks. In his cinematic adaptation of the biblical passion story, Pilate's wife personally delivers a bundle of fresh linen cloths to Mary and Mary Magdalene. Somehow, she knew that they would need them. Taking what can only be interpreted as the very first altar cloths, the two Marys lower themselves to their hands and knees and use what they have been given to soak up Jesus's blood as it pools in the hollows of the cobblestones on the street where he had just been whipped. This was the precious blood, as genuine a relic as there ever was.

As interest in the relics of Jesus's passion took hold among ordinary believers, so too did the desire to possess other relics—such as the bones of Jesus's apostles and the ancient Christian martyrs and saints. Soon enough, the bishops of many cities, large and small, had been enlisted as the impresarios of martyrs' relics and their cults.

Catering to the pilgrims who traveled to a martyr's shrine was big business. Pilgrims had to be fed, housed, and—if they were ill or injured—nursed back to health. In return, they offered cash donations, sometimes sizable ones, to the martyr's caretakers. They bought souvenirs too. Oil-filled ampullae were always popular, as were coin-size clay tokens and small loaves of bread impressed with the saint's image. As news of healing miracles and other blessings at a particular shrine spread, so did the popularity of that shrine's martyr. Growing streams of pilgrims to the shrine of an especially beloved saint had the potential to radically transform a local economy. It is no wonder, then, that bishops and local elites throughout the Mediterranean and Middle East wanted to acquire martyrs' relics—even if that meant breaking open tombs.

Yet as the profusion of sweat cloths, cross fragments, and other relics of Jesus's passion had already demonstrated, it was difficult for bishops to know which bones were the authentic relics of a martyr and which were not. Fortunately, templates soon emerged to authenticate the discovery of true relics and to properly transfer (or "translate") them from one place to another.

The first truly public redeposit of martyrs' bones in the West seems to have happened in Milan in 386—the same year that Egeria visited the Holy Sepulchre and mentioned seeing sentries stationed around the cross. At the time, Ambrose was the bishop of Milan. A brilliant rhetorician and later a saint himself, Ambrose profoundly influenced his more widely known protégé, Saint Augustine of Hippo. In a letter to his sister, Ambrose recounts that a chorus of voices dogged him after he dedicated Milan's new basilica. The Christians of his city, he explains, would not stop begging him to properly consecrate their new church by installing martyrs' relics inside. They understood that the bones of God's "very special dead," as Peter Brown has called them, would immediately render the place holy. Ambrose understood this too, so he promised his congregation that he would comply with their wishes and sanctify their new church with martyrs' bones—if only he could find some.

How Ambrose knew exactly where to look is not something he mentions in his letter, but he does tell his sister that a "prophetic ardor" entered his heart. Soon he found the telltale signs of two Christian martyrs and instructed some of his junior clerics to dig up the spot where the saints had been buried. Nervous at what they were being asked to do, they were overjoyed when they eventually discovered Saint Gervasius and Saint Protasius, both nearly intact despite the many years that they had been entombed. The authenticity of their relics was confirmed when the saints healed a sick man who had been brought to the site. The following day, as the relics were being processed to their new home inside Milan's basilica, a blind man in the crowd regained his sight.

Once the saints' bones were safely deposited, Ambrose rose to address his overjoyed congregation. He preached to them about the holy martyrs, who "declare the glory of God." He pointed to the miraculous healings that his flock had just witnessed and reminded them of the power of Jesus and the apostles. Then he asked his listeners to recall from scripture how many had been healed just by touching the robes or even handkerchiefs of the saints. Likewise, he foretold, any garment "laid on top of the holy relics" of Saint Gervasius and Saint Protasius would be imbued with the power to heal. Centuries later, Philippe de Champaigne still heard the message. In his seventeenth-century painting of the translation of the relics of Saint Gervasius and Saint Protasius, one eager man runs up to the martyrs, reaching out to touch their bier with his handkerchief in hand (see fig. 15).

The miracles performed by the relics of these saints and their procession to Milan's basilica quickly became models for authenticating and translating a martyr's bones. Like Helena's discovery of the cross, Ambrose's discovery of Saints Gervasius and Protasius answered a community's desire for the presence of the holy, aided by divine inspiration for where to look and properly confirmed by a healing miracle. Seeing what Ambrose had done, Christians in other cities were eager for their own churches to be sanctified with the bones of a martyr. The old connection between tomb and shrine was now replaced by one between tomb and altar, with newly acquired relics stored either in a crypt beneath the altar or directly inside it, within its plinth. Several church councils passed decrees requiring that a martyr's relic be embedded in all altars as a condition of their proper consecration. With its martyr always *there,* the altar was really the place where heaven met earth, echoing the book of Revelation's vision of the souls of the martyrs residing beneath the heavenly altar.

With their martyrs so nearby, Christian communities expected the blessings of their saint to be effective. But patronage was a two-way street. If a saint was somehow failing in the duty to bless and aid the community, then the saint was told so—in no uncertain terms. On occasion, an ineffective martyr's relics were humiliated—which is to say, they were removed from their reliquary and piled on the ground. With the church's candles snuffed out, there they were left— cold, alone, and exposed—as punishment for abandoning those who had prayed to the saint for help.

Clearly, martyrs' bones were not dead: saints were still present in their relics. As many Christian theologians have put it, how else could relics work their miracles if the saints and their divinely granted power were not still there?

The martyrs and saints who faithfully attended to those devoted to them made their relics a precious commodity. And in a world without the benefit of modern medicine, what could be more valuable than the power to heal? Martyrs' bones were precious, but they were also portable and not easily distinguishable from other bones. This was a fraught combination. Inevitably, martyrs' relics were illegally sold, counterfeited, smuggled, and stolen. Relics could be given away as gifts, typically as an act of patronage by the wealthy, but their sale— besides being legally prohibited by many civil and ecclesiastical

FIGURE 15. *Translation of the Relics of Saint Gervasius and Saint Protasius* by Philippe de Champaigne, 1661. Louvre Museum, Paris. © RMN-Grand Palais / Art Resource, New York.

codes—was widely regarded as especially distasteful, since commerce in material manifestations of the holy was assumed to be fraudulent, almost by definition.

Because an on-the-spot miracle could not always be counted on to verify the authenticity of any given relic, it was expected that some form of official seal or documentation, all the better if written in Greek, would accompany the relic—even if it was not being gifted or translated away. Appropriately, these letters of authenticity were known as *authenticae*. Of course, the florid handwriting and wax impressions of authentication documents could be counterfeited too, especially if there was money to be made—which there most certainly was.

The author of one twelfth-century treatise on saints' relics condemned those who peddled counterfeit bones and other remains. He wrote of one unscrupulous monk who had tried to sell a half-eaten crust of bread by stuffing it into a reliquary—the bite marks on the loaf, so the monk said, were from Jesus's teeth.

Because it was so difficult to authenticate the provenance of a piece of bone or a husk of bread, it was standard practice by the early medieval period to enclose relics within a container. These could be fabulously opulent. The gold, jewels, and fine craftsmanship of the most exquisite reliquaries were not easily faked. Such expensive containers thus confirmed the authenticity of the relics they held while advertising the objects' value. For one Benedictine abbot, reliquaries served an additional purpose: they disguised the earthly ordinariness of skin and bones. Just as Christ's flesh and blood are disguised as bread and wine in the Mass, so too, said the abbot, should relics be hidden within gold and jewels, so as not to horrify those who venerate them. Others were disgusted by such reasoning. Criticizing the fervor that lavish reliquaries inspired, Bernard of Clairvaux accused rich and poor alike of being more concerned with admiring the beautiful than venerating the sacred.

Though their approaches to the relic cult may have differed, Bernard and other medieval clerics were united in their anxiety over relics' authenticity. The problem was that relics were not always willing to speak up for themselves. Skin and bones, rocks and dirt, wood and bread—they all littered the world. It was not enough to take a traveling peddler at his word. A true relic required one of two things: some sort of visible sign of its authenticity (which meant a costly reliquary or the stamps and seals of bureaucratic *authenticae*) or, as the Veronica legend demonstrated, a compelling and widely accepted story about its provenance and many healing miracles. It was all the better if the relic had both a storied history and a fancy reliquary.

There is something uncannily familiar about this medieval authentication problem. We too need visible markers or a crowd of reliable witnesses to prove authenticity. The children who rushed on to Ebbets Field in 1957 knew that the dirt they had scratched from the ground with their own hands was authentic, but as they grew up and boxed it away with their Cracker Jack cards, their first-place ribbons, their school yearbooks, and all the other ephemera of childhood, how could they prove this to anyone else? How, for that matter, could any collector know that an expensively purchased series-winning home-run ball was not just another foul shagged from the stands at batting practice? Baseballs, like bones, are hard to tell apart.

Aware of fans' enthusiasm for memorabilia, the executives of Major League Baseball (MLB) understood that this concern with authenticity was far from frivolous, especially when an FBI investigation in the late 1990s revealed that thousands of autographed balls, game-worn uniforms, and pine-tarred bats circulating in the marketplace were almost assuredly fake. Even seemingly reputable sellers who packaged their merchandise in expensive display cases with official-looking "letters of authenticity" could not always be trusted. Sometimes their goods were counterfeit too.

So beginning in 2001, MLB sent a third-party authenticator to every game played by every team. Their job was (and is) straightforward: to observe—closely. If any ball, bat, base, jersey, glove, or other potentially valuable game-used item is of interest, whether because of a milestone hit, a winning strikeout, a stolen base, or any other reason, the authenticator will signal for it during or immediately after the game. Upon its delivery to the authenticator's seat near the dugout, half of a tamper-proof sticker is affixed to the item. The other half is scanned so the authenticator can log a description of the item in an online database. Only game-used memorabilia with a secure chain of custody directly witnessed by the authenticator can be certified. Balls that leave the field of play, including those involved in home runs, do not remain within the authenticator's continuous line of sight and thus cannot be authenticated.

The highly regulated process immediately did two things: it established a gold standard for determining the authenticity of any item being marketed as a piece of game-used memorabilia, and it kept these authentic items under the direct control of each of MLB's thirty clubs for them to monetize. Gone were the days of children tearing up Ebbets Field.

As Stephen Andon describes in his wonderful analysis of commodified sports memorabilia, in 2008, after the last out at the old Yankee Stadium, it was not young fans but the team's grounds crew that poured on to the field. Dirt from the infield was shoveled into white buckets that were then sealed and affixed with the official stickers of authenticity. Gallons upon gallons of infield dirt were later repackaged and sold to fans by the teaspoonful, netting the Yankees millions of dollars.

Other relics were similarly fragmented. Why sell an intact game-used baseball to one buyer when its cowhide covering could be removed, refashioned into multiple relics, and sold at different price points to several collectors? Tokens & Icons, an officially licensed memorabilia reseller, explains on its website that it "creates products from authenticated materials to celebrate their histories and those who value them." For just $95, it will sell you a sterling silver pendant (chain and gift packaging not included) crafted from a piece of an MLB-authenticated game-used baseball. The leather on the pendant's face, prospective buyers are assured, "features the unmistakable red stitching and the little scratches and scuffs that let you know it has seen game play."

The immense value and portability of relics and reliquaries proved too tempting for thieves—even those who professed to fear God. As Patrick Geary describes in his influential study of medieval relic thefts, the stealing and smuggling of martyrs' remains was hardly uncommon. In fact, it was usually accepted. Such acts may have enraged the communities that lost their relics, but they had the strong support of the communities that benefited from the furtive relocation of martyrs' bones.

Dozens of so-called *furta sacra* accounts survive from the Middle Ages. As Geary explains, these narratives tend to follow a pattern: first, a priest or a monk travels to a martyr's shrine; once there, he is impressed by its record of miracles; then he resolves to steal the saint's relics for the welfare of his community. One further element common to many of these stories helps rationalize why these thefts were accepted: a saint's relics could not be moved without consent of the saint. Sometimes relics really did speak for themselves. If mishandled, they could bleed, but if they were up for a journey they might emit the unmistakably musky scent of paradise.

Italians were responsible for some of the most notorious and meticulous relic thefts. In the early ninth century, Venetian merchants set a southeasterly course from their lagoon, sailing through the Adriatic and out across the open Mediterranean to the Nile delta and the proud city of Alexandria. They had come for the bones of Saint Mark. Under cover of darkness, the merchants opened Mark's tomb, taking care not to disturb it. At once, a rich and wonderful scent wafted through Alexandria, alerting its Christian citizens that something strange was afoot. Some rushed to their saint and pushed back the lid of his tomb. But everything was fine. Mark's bones were apparently still there. Unbeknown to the Alexandrians, however, Mark was actually on his way to Italy. The Venetians had left Saint Claudia's relics in place of Saint Mark's and then hidden the evangelist's bones in a barrel filled with cuts of pork. They had correctly assumed that the Muslim customs agents in Alexandria's harbor would not inspect such cargo too closely.

Meanwhile, the merchants of medieval Bari—a port city on the heel of the Italian peninsula—had their own plan. They needed no reminding that the Venetians were the superior shipbuilders and traders, but they hoped that their own city, which was much closer to the Mediterranean's major shipping lanes, could top Venice in the flow of pilgrims' dollars. The problem was that Bari had no Saint Mark. Maybe, they reasoned, Saint Nicholas would help?

The story of the theft of Saint Nick exists in several versions, but there are common threads: one is the saint's appearance in a vision. In these visions, Nicholas tells the merchants of Bari that he is ready to leave his tomb in Myra, the city in Asia Minor where he had worked as a bishop, to retire farther west. The merchants who were responsible for the saint's requested transport formed a civic organization, the Societas Sancti Nicolai, and once Nicholas's relics were successfully acquired and relocated, the long-hoped-for pilgrims began to arrive in Bari in droves.

In a fifteenth-century depiction of Nicholas's new shrine in Bari, Gentile da Fabriano presents an imagined lineup of pilgrims beneath the saint's elevated tomb, from which holy oil dripped. The crippled and sick hobble in at the center and on the right, hoping to catch a drop of Nicholas's oil, while a man who has already been healed by Santa's secretions walks away on the left, a now-useless pair of crutches slung over his shoulder (see plate 2).

The society's gamble paid off: Bari's merchants were rich. But the Venetians would not be so easily outflanked. The most spectacular relic heist was still to come.

Martyrs' relics healed, and they also protected. The broader civic importance of relics—which were credited with guarding cities against the three great horrors of war, plague, and famine—transcended even the longest list of individual healing miracles.

By this municipal math, Constantinople was extremely well protected. (Its strategic location on a small peninsula reinforced by massive land walls and a well-funded navy may have helped too.) Of all the major Christian centers in the late antique, medieval, and Byzantine worlds, Constantinople could claim to have the most martyrs' relics by a very sizable margin. A Russian pilgrim counted almost fifty relic shrines within Constantinople, its suburbs, and its nearby villages at the beginning of the thirteenth century. This only scratched the surface. One scholar estimates that at the height of the Byzantine Empire there had to have been at least thirty-six hundred relics from nearly five hundred saints and martyrs scattered throughout the city. The count includes relics of both early Christian martyrs and Jesus's apostles. The bones of Timothy and Andrew had been moved to the city in the mid-fourth century. Others soon followed.

Unsurprisingly, Constantinople also boasted the largest collection of relics from Jesus's passion. More had been sent there from the earliest days of the Christian relic cult than to anywhere else. The stock of the city of Rome, despite its historical importance, was a far distant second. Most of Constantinople's passion relics were gathered in one place, under the immediate protection of the Byzantine emperor. From the eighth century onward, they were housed in the emperor's private place of worship, the Chapel of Saint Mary of the Pharos (or "Lighthouse"), which was adjacent to the imperial family's residence and the throne room. The passion relics at the Lighthouse included all the expected ones—fragments of the cross and stones from the tomb—but also a seeming inventory of anything and everything that Jesus might have touched during his last days on earth: the cloths he used to dry his apostles' feet before the Last Supper, the links from the chains that bound him when he was scourged, the reed and the wine-soaked sponge that were used to slake his thirst on the cross. Keeping all these relics of Jesus's passion so close to the emperor publicly communicated a powerful notion of mutual protection. Just as the emperor guarded Christ's relics, so did Christ guard the empire.

Among the many passion relics that the Byzantine emperor protected was a notable latecomer. It did not arrive in Constantinople until the middle of the tenth century—and then only as part of a broader arrangement with the Muslim rulers of Edessa, that famous Syriac-speaking Christian city in northern Mesopotamia. Recognizing the relic's value to the emperor, these Muslims successfully bartered it for two hundred captives, twelve thousand pieces of silver, and a solemn vow that the Byzantine army would not lay siege to their city. The relic they handed over in return was the Image of Edessa. After it arrived in Constantinople, it became known as the Mandylion. It was yet another image of Jesus imprinted on cloth.

For centuries, the Image of Edessa was believed to have protected its city from one invader after another. But strangely, the earliest written account of the legend that would become attached to the image never mentions an image at all. We know the story from Eusebius, whose *Ecclesiastical History* tells the fabulous tale of King Abgar, the ruler of Edessa during the days of Jesus.

Eusebius explains that the story comes from Edessa's archives and was translated word for word from the original Syriac into Greek. King Abgar, he tells us, was desperate. Suffering from some incurable malady, Abgar had written a letter to Jesus, knowing that the Galilean was a wonder-worker who had the power to heal afflictions and even raise the dead. Might Jesus agree to travel to Edessa from "the region of Jerusalem" to heal a foreign king?

Eusebius quotes Abgar's letter in full and, more than that, transcribes a brief response said to have been written by none other than Jesus himself. According to Eusebius, Abgar's courier took the king's request to Jerusalem and then returned with Jesus's reply. In his letter to Abgar, Jesus is cordial but brief. He blesses Abgar for believing in him but declines the invitation to visit Edessa. Instead, Jesus promises that he will send one of his disciples to see about the king's illness. In an appendix to this exchange, Eusebius quotes an unnamed narrator who relates how the dutiful apostle Thomas sent Thaddeus (also known as Jude) to Edessa after Jesus's death and resurrection. When Thaddeus found the sick king, he laid hands on him in Jesus's name. Abgar was immediately cured, "without drugs and herbs, just as in the healings of Jesus."

A similar story appears near the end of the fourth century. This time it is recorded in the Latin itinerary of Egeria, who wrote about the Holy Sepulchre's cross-chomping pilgrim. Egeria knew all about the letters between Jesus and Abgar even before she arrived in Edessa during her peregrinations in and around the Holy Land. In her telling, there is still no mention of any miraculous image of Jesus on cloth. Instead, Jesus's *letter* is a powerful relic. Egeria cites the comments of the bishop of Edessa, who gave her a personal tour of his city. According to him, Jesus promised Abgar that Edessa would never be conquered. As proof, the bishop tells Egeria a story. Once, he says, when the Persian army was advancing on Edessa, someone stood atop the city gate and waved Jesus's letter to Abgar around in the air. Immediately, darkness overtook the land. Though the Persians laid siege to the city for months, the walls of Edessa never faltered.

As the legend about the Jesus-Abgar correspondence developed in various Syriac and Greek sources, the city's protective talisman slowly transformed from Jesus's letter into his image. Meanwhile, the courier who transported the two letters changed into a learned scribe, the keeper of Edessa's archives, and even an artist of some renown. Depending on the source, he is said to have returned to Edessa carrying a letter from Jesus, a transcription of Jesus's words, or a painting of the Lord done "in choice colors."

By the end of the sixth century, there was still an image of Jesus in the story, but by that point it was no longer a painting. Even the most skilled artist could never dream of capturing Jesus's divinity on canvas. Instead, what gets delivered to Abgar is an impression of Jesus's face on cloth. The miraculous image, not the letter or the visit of Thaddeus, is what heals Abgar and protects Edessa.

The Image of Edessa remained in the city for centuries before the Byzantine emperor acquired the relic from the Muslims there in 944 and had it processed around Constantinople's walls, infusing them with the same protective power from which Edessa had benefited for so long. Its new home also meant that a new account of the image's history had to be written. In the Byzantine version, the Image of Edessa (now called the Mandylion) is described as the cloth that dried Jesus's face in the Garden of Gethsemane when he was in such agony that sweat fell from it like drops of blood. In a combination of biblical, quasi-biblical, and apocryphal traditions, we learn that it was there in the garden that the sweat-and-blood-soaked towel was given to Thomas, along with instructions to pass it on to Thaddeus, who, in turn, later delivered it to Abgar. When the Byzantine emperor finally secured the Image of Edessa, he added it to his collection of passion relics, ensuring that the holy towel was properly "affixed to a board" and mounted in a golden frame.

Thanks to the Venetians, King Louis acquired the Byzantine emperor's private collection of passion relics, including the towel affixed to a board. The circumstances were complicated. In 1201, the master sailors and shipbuilders of Venice agreed to temporarily halt much of the shipping and trading that had made their city rich. The pope had persuaded them to put their skills toward the service of a more important, collaborative goal: the fourth Christian attempt at reclaiming the Holy Land from the Muslims.

The Venetians promised they would build and sail the ships that would transport some thirty-five thousand crusaders to Egypt for a land assault north on Jerusalem. They were supposed to be paid for their efforts, but only about a third of the anticipated army, toting less than half the fee the Venetians were due, showed up when the ships were ready to sail. The blind doge of Venice, Enrico Dandolo, was less than pleased. Eventually, the Venetians did deliver the army of the Fourth Crusade, but first they needed to settle accounts. Dandolo had a plan. As his fleet progressed through the Adriatic and came in sight of the Dalmatian coast, the city of Zara hove into view. It was the first Christian city sacked by the crusaders on their way to the Holy Land. Constantinople was next.

In 1203, as the Venetians and their army of crusaders overwintered in Zara, a visitor arrived: Alexius was the son of the recently deposed Byzantine emperor, and he had come to offer the Venetians a solution to their problem—and his. He promised the Venetians that he would fully cover the outstanding balance they were due, give them preferential trading privileges with Constantinople, supplement their holy war against the Muslims with Byzantine troops and naval vessels, and pay out hefty bonuses once all was said and done. In short, Alexius offered the moon. In return? He wanted the Venetians' help in regaining his throne.

By August of 1203, the Venetian-crusader army had diverted to Constantinople and successfully upheld its end of the bargain, reinstalling Alexius as emperor. But yet again, the Venetians were stiffed. Alexius could not deliver what he had promised, as he lacked the funds—and, with so many barbaric Latins now tromping about the city, the goodwill of his subjects. Within months, he was deposed and assassinated, but the unpaid and increasingly restless Venetians, along with all the other crusaders, were still in Constantinople. The following spring, they murdered and raped their way through the city, looting everything of value they could find, including the riches of Constantinople's many churches, which they divided among themselves.

Thirty years later, the now Latin empire of Constantinople was in dire straits. With insufficient financial and military backing from the various kingdoms of western Europe that had supported the Crusades in the first place—and with Greeks, Bulgars, and Seljuk Turks all seeking to take (or retake) Constantinople—the empire's ruler, Baldwin II, turned to Venice again. Venetian merchants loaned him plenty of money to pay his mercenaries and fund the city's defense, but this time they demanded collateral: the crown of thorns.

Unsurprisingly, Baldwin defaulted on the loan, but not before arranging to sell the crown to his cousin King Louis IX. When the two French Dominican friars sent by Louis arrived in Constantinople to claim the crown, they found that it was in the hands of a Venetian banker named Nicola Quirino. The friars dutifully accompanied Quirino to Venice, where the crown was deposited in Saint Mark's Basilica (next to the apostle's stolen relics) until full payment could be arranged.

In 1247, the year before the Sainte-Chapelle was completed, French officials drew up a bull listing all the relics that had been transferred to Paris. The text of the document makes it seem as if the relics had been ceremoniously gifted to a new caretaker rather than looted, held as collateral, pawned to a banker, and then sold to the highest bidder. With the relic finally acquired, it was Louis's turn to travel to the Holy Land. Leading a Crusade himself, he eventually reached the Latin stronghold of Acre, on the Mediterranean coast northwest of Jerusalem, but his attempt to win back the Holy Land was a farce. At one point the king was even captured and ransomed. On returning to France, Louis spent years as a pious ascetic to atone for his failure. This was an unprecedented transformation for a ruler of his line.

Louis tried to make one last attempt on the Holy Land in 1270, but he never got there. Instead, he died from dysentery along the way. Before his remains were returned to Paris, the flesh was boiled from the bones in a grand vat of wine. The relics of the king who would become Saint Louis eventually joined his most prized possessions in the Sainte-Chapelle. For the next five centuries, there they would rest: near the crown of thorns and, it seems, an image of Jesus on a towel affixed to a board.

Today, only the crown remains. At some point it was moved to Notre-Dame, where it and a tunic that had once belonged to Louis were rescued during the terrible fire that destroyed the church's iconic spire in 2019. Most of the other relics from the Sainte-Chapelle had been lost or destroyed centuries earlier, during the French Revolution. But there is seemingly one last reference to the holy towel in a late eighteenth-century relic catalog. It mentions a "sliding box containing a portrait." Maybe this was the image of Jesus that had once protected Edessa and Constantinople but then had its history rewritten and upstaged by Rome's veronica and Turin's shroud.

Maybe it was something else.

4   *The Feasts of the Dead*

As the Puerto Rican late afternoon faded into night on September 13, 1928, a ferocious hurricane roared ashore. Its torrential rains and devastating winds killed hundreds of people. Tens of thousands of homes were damaged or destroyed, and the year's sugarcane, coffee, and tobacco crops were all but wiped out. Until Hurricane Maria hit Puerto Rico in 2017, it was the single most powerful storm ever recorded to have made landfall on the island.

Those were the days before the US Weather Bureau (now the National Weather Service) and the World Meteorological Organization began to officially name tropical cyclones. With no central naming authority in place, hurricanes tended to get local monikers—usually geographic ones. In the United States, this hurricane, which first ravaged the Leeward Islands before plowing through Puerto Rico and then the Bahamas, was known as the Okeechobee hurricane, since its most severe effects on the American mainland impacted the area around Lake Okeechobee in southern Florida.

Puerto Ricans gave the storm a different name. Their tradition was to name hurricanes with reference not to where they did the most damage but to *when.* Storms were named according to the calendar—the Roman Catholic calendar of the martyrs.

September 13 was the feast of Saint Philip, a second-century Roman prefect from Alexandria who resigned his post after converting to Christianity and was subsequently martyred along with several members of his family, including his virgin daughter, Eugenia, who had already spent several ascetic years in an Egyptian desert monastery disguised as a man. Among Puerto Ricans, the Okeechobee hurricane was thus known as San Felipe Segundo, the second Saint Philip's day hurricane. The first Felipe had barreled through on the same date more than fifty years earlier, when Puerto Rico was still a Spanish colony.

Although it may seem doubly morbid to associate a beloved saint and martyr with two deadly storms, using saints' days as the cardinal points of the year, a way of marking seminal dates and the passing of time, was once quite common. This is especially true in the Caribbean, where nearly every other island is named for a martyr, often because it was that saint's day on the calendar when the land was "discovered" by Europeans. The Caribbean island known as Saint Lucia, for instance, is named for another islander: Saint Lucy of Syracuse. She was a lovely Sicilian woman who had her eyes scooped out and a sword plunged down her throat during Diocletian's reign. According to legend, some French sailors were shipwrecked there on Lucy's feast day: December 13.

Lucy was killed because she refused to renounce her Christian vow of virginity and marry a pagan—a story line that gets repeated in quite a few martyrdom narratives of virgin saints from late antiquity. When Saint Philip's virgin daughter fled to an Egyptian monastery disguised as a man, it was to escape marriage, not martyrdom. Similarly, Philip's story has much in common with that of Saint Eustace, the namesake of the Dutch Caribbean island of Sint-Eustatius, whose martyrdom is celebrated one week later, on September 20. Philip and Eustace were both high-ranking Roman officials who resigned their duties, converted to Christianity, and were subsequently killed along with their families. The popular medieval story about Eustace claims that he was a general in the Roman army who served under Emperor Trajan and was roasted alive with his wife and sons inside a bronze bull.

Being martyred inside a bull was a fitting coda for Eustace, since his life as a Christian began when he was converted by a deer. The saint-to-be had hunted the deer to the edge of a precipice, but before the chase could come to an end, Eustace was shocked to see a glowing crucifix shining like a beacon between its antlers (see fig. 16). Then the cornered beast started speaking to Eustace—in the voice of Jesus. The green stag-and-cross label on bottles of Jägermeister, a German herbal liqueur that would be called Hunt Master were its name translated into English, still pays homage to this forest scene and to Eustace, the patron saint of hunters.

Not surprisingly, many Caribbean islands owe their names to Christopher Columbus. The Italian-born explorer and angel of death for Indigenous Caribbeans named the Virgin Islands for Saint Ursula and the eleven thousand beheaded virgins of Cologne—a German city on the Rhine that became one of the preeminent destinations for medieval pilgrims because it housed both the relics of Ursula and her followers and those of the Magi, the "Three Kings" from Matthew's Gospel. During his second voyage to the Americas, Columbus sighted an island he called Saint Martin on November 11, that saint's feast day. On his third, Columbus claimed for his Spanish patrons an island he named for their nation's first martyr, Saint Vincent of Saragossa. Like Lawrence, Vincent was roasted on a gridiron. But Vincent survived his grilling and died only after his burns were opened on the floor of a prison cell littered with shards of broken pottery.

I once spotted an amateur painting of Vincent hanging near the altar of a tiny Anglican church in Port Elizabeth on the island of Bequia in Saint Vincent and the Grenadines (see fig. 17). The artist's de-

FIGURE 16. *Saint Eustace* by Albrecht Dürer, c. 1501. Metropolitan Museum of Art, New York.

FIGURE 17. *Saint Vincent of Saragossa*. Saint Mary's Anglican Church, Port Elizabeth, Saint Vincent and the Grenadines. Photograph by the author.

piction blends traditional iconography with a nod to the islands and their colonial past. As aquamarine waves roll in on the sunlit shore behind him, a dark-skinned and white-robed Vincent (representationally complete with a deacon's stole across his chest) stands on a pile of what look more like Royal Navy rum jars than like broken Roman wine vessels. In his outstretched hands, Vincent holds a palm frond. It is the unmistakable symbol of Christian martyrdom.

Both Martin and Vincent are well-known saints, still widely venerated among Christians, but some of Columbus's other baptismal names were decidedly more personal. His own link with the moniker of Saint Kitts—a diminutive of *Christopher*, the name of the martyred patron saint of travelers—needs no explanation. Meanwhile, Saint

Barts, now a ritzy yachting destination, honors its martyr in much the same way. The name refers not to the flayed apostle but to Chris's younger brother: Bartolomeo Colombo.

Today the economies of many Caribbean nations depend on the holiday travelers who visit for a week of rum and relaxation. Though Caribbean tourism would seem to have little in common with the Christian cult of the dead—saintly names of the islands aside—the two are not entirely unrelated. The major feasts of the saints were holidays too. They were red-letter days on the calendar and celebrated times of luxuriance and leisure that were set apart from the tedium of the rest of the year. No wonder their dates were remembered.

Holidays were baked into the Christian calendar early on. Sundays were set aside for rest, of course, but according to the *Apostolic Constitutions*—a set of rules that were attributed to the apostles and governed church organization and worship—so were scores of other days. One passage ascribed to Peter and Paul designates a remarkable number of days, at least 125 each year, as those when servants and slaves were to be free from labor. This fits with Paul's genteel approach to slavery in the New Testament. His response to the escape of a slave named Onesimus is to send him back toting a letter of measured rebuke addressed to his owner. Even though Paul urges the letter's recipient, the slave-owning Philemon, to welcome Onesimus back "no longer as a slave but as more than a slave, as a beloved brother," he never condemns the institution of slavery itself.

Centuries later, some American Christian commentators seized on the apostle's omission and used it to justify slavery as a hedge against anarchy. Preaching one Sunday evening in May 1850, the Reverend James Henley Thornwell, a Presbyterian minister in

Charleston, South Carolina, railed against what he called the "vituperation and abuse" that Northern abolitionists were hurling at Southern Christian slave owners. In a sermon titled "The Rights and the Duties of Masters," which was delivered at the dedication of a church erected in Charleston "for the benefit and instruction of the coloured population," Thornwell speaks of Christianity as a faith "proclaimed by the Apostles and Prophets, and sealed by the blood of a goodly company of Martyrs and Confessors." Citing Paul's letter to Philemon, Thornwell argues that even though the apostle may have regarded slaves as their masters' brothers, they owe their toil and labor to their masters and God. In turn, Thornwell continues, slave owners have a duty to treat their slaves kindly, so as to uphold "the civil interests of mankind" and, more important, forestall "the social anarchy of communism" that slavery's end would surely bring.

Thornwell takes an interpretative approach in his sermon, one that plays biblical passages off one another to find scriptural support for the Southern status quo, but earlier in the nineteenth century, after a successful slave revolt in Saint-Domingue, the French colony that would become Haiti, English Christian slave owners, fearing a similar uprising in one of their own colonies, took a more brute approach to troublesome biblical passages. They deleted them. Heavily excerpted Bibles, specially commissioned and printed "for the use of the Negro Slaves in the British West-India Islands," kept verses that stressed obedience and servitude but axed those that might have inspired slaves to question their condition. In the book of Exodus, the story about Moses receiving the Ten Commandments was retained, but there is no mention of how he parted the Red Sea and led the Israelites out of bondage in Egypt. Paul's famous line from the letter to the Galatians—the one about there being "neither slave nor free" in Christ—was cut too.

One wonders what those English Christian slave owners or Thorn-well and those who heard him preach that Sunday evening at Charles-ton's Second Presbyterian Church would have thought about the unbelievable number of rest days prescribed in the *Apostolic Constitutions*. Would it further "the civil interests of mankind" for slaves to be idle so often? In addition to every Sunday, the apostles' list of holidays includes every Saturday, all of Holy Week leading up to Easter, Ascension and Pentecost, Christmas and Epiphany, every feast of an apostle, and the day honoring Stephen as "the first martyr." No other martyr is named in the apostles' list, but there is a good reason for this. The *Apostolic Constitutions*, like a number of other early Christian treatises attributed to the apostles, is not actually apostolic. It was composed in Roman Syria in the late fourth century. Had its author mentioned any martyrs killed after the apostles and Stephen, he would have belied the supposedly apostolic provenance of the text he was writing.

Ancient readers were not stupid. While it may have been hard to know whether a text really had been authored by an apostle, any reference in an apostolic list to a later martyr like Lucy or Eustace would have been immediately spotted as an anachronism. In purporting to convey the apostles' instructions and studiously trying to make his text *seem* as apostolic as possible, the author of the *Apostolic Constitutions* knew that his work would be taken seriously. These were, after all, the decrees of the founding fathers. Still, even though the author of the *Apostolic Constitutions* could not list any of the post-apostolic martyrs by name, he does manage to glorify them in a general way at the end of his list of rest days. Speaking as Peter and Paul, he declares that Christians should rest "on the day of the first martyr Stephen" and the days honoring all "the other holy martyrs who preferred Christ to their own life."

This blanket reference to *other* holy martyrs did two things: it suggested that Peter and Paul had witnessed the spread of Christian martyrdom, and it left a yawning window open on the Christian calendar for the proliferation of many feasts of martyrs still to come.

Just how many additional martyrs, and therefore days of rest, the reference to "the other holy martyrs" may have meant in the late fourth century, when the *Apostolic Constitutions* was written, is uncertain. What is clear is that the number of rest days included on Christian calendars throughout the Roman Empire quickly multiplied once Christianity was legalized in the early fourth century and, within just a few decades of that, Christian bishops began to appreciate the economic value of martyrs' shrines and the annual celebrations that drew scores of pilgrims to them.

At their most basic, the earliest Christian martyrologies were just lists of names and dates, as we saw in chapter 2. But the *Apostolic Constitutions* does not go even that far. It refers to the feasts of Stephen, the apostles, and "the other holy martyrs" but fails to specify the dates on which any of these days of rest were to be observed. Though there was no universal Christian calendar in that early period, the Roman Empire's bureaucratic inclinations—including an interest in keeping calendars and measuring the ticktock of time—did hasten the development of a generally agreed-upon list of the major feasts of the saints. One of the more intriguing quirks of history is that the calendar of ancient Rome is still in use today, thanks entirely to the spread of Christianity.

The first Christian calendar known to us, the *Chronograph of 354* (or, as it sometimes called, the *Codex-Calendar of 354*), is, as its name suggests, a calendar book prepared for the year 354. The original is lost, but surviving later copies indicate that it was a deluxe compendium of material richly illustrated by a Roman calligrapher for a senator named Valentinus. Indeed, few others besides someone like

PLATES

PLATE 1. *Saint Veronica* by Hans Memling, c. 1475. National Gallery of Art, Washington, DC.

PLATE 2. *The Crippled and Sick Cured at the Tomb of Saint Nicholas* by Gentile da Fabriano, 1425. National Gallery of Art, Washington, DC.

PLATE 3. *The Wine of Saint Martin's Day* by Pieter Bruegel the Elder, c. 1565–68. Prado Museum, Madrid.

PLATE 4. Pontifical manuscript illumination depicting a bishop enclosing an anchoress, early fifteenth century. Parker Library, Corpus Christi College MS 79, f. 96r, University of Cambridge.

PLATE 5. *The Torment of Saint Anthony* by Michelangelo, 1487. Kimbell Art Museum, Fort Worth, Texas.

PLATE 6. *The Temptation of Saint Anthony* by Salvador Dalí, 1946. Royal Museums of Fine Arts, Brussels. © Salvador Dalí, Fundació Gala-Salvador Dalí / SOCAN. Art Resource, New York.

PLATE 7. *Saint Mary of Egypt Receiving the Holy Eucharist from Saint Zosimas* by Hieromonk Silouan Justiniano, 2016. Holy Ascension Orthodox Church, Mount Pleasant, South Carolina. Reproduced with permission of the iconographer.

PLATE 8. "The Hermits and the Pilgrims" from the *Ghent Altarpiece* by Jan van Eyck, 1432. Cathedral of Saint Bavo, Ghent. Scala / Art Resource, New York.

PLATE 9. The Cure of "Mad" Henry of Fordwich. Trinity Chapel, Canterbury Cathedral.

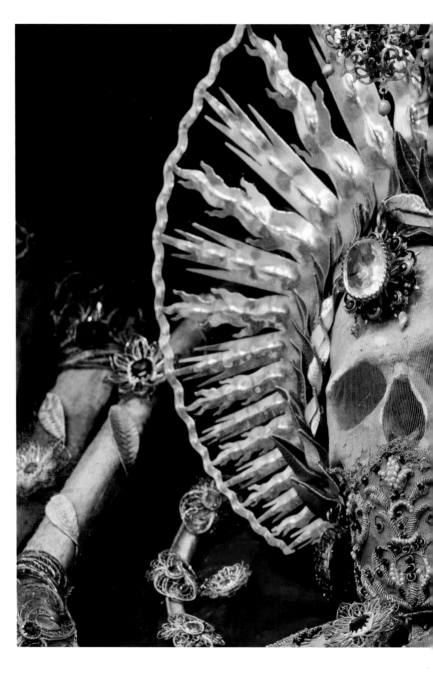

PLATE 10. Saint Leontius. Muri Abbey, Switzerland. Photograph by Paul Koudounaris.

PLATE 11. "The Procession of Flagellants" by the Limbourg Brothers, 1405–8/9. From *The Belles Heures* of Jean de France, duc de Berry, f. 74v. © The Cloisters Collection, Metropolitan Museum of Art, New York. Art Resource, New York.

PLATE 12. Central panel of *The Martyrdom of Saint Sebastian* by
Giovanni del Biondo, 1380. Opera del Duomo Museum, Florence.
Scala / Art Resource, New York. See fig. 26 for the full triptych.

PLATE 13. *Saint Sebastian Interceding for the Plague Stricken* by Josse Lieferinxe, 1497–99. Walters Art Museum, Baltimore.

PLATE 14. *Pietà* by Michelangelo, 1498–99. Saint Peter's Basilica, Vatican City.

PLATE 15. *The Body of the Dead Christ in the Tomb* by Hans Holbein the Younger, 1521. Kunstmuseum Basel. Erich Lessing / Art Resource, New York.

PLATE 16. *The Anastasis,* c. 1315–21. Church of the Holy Saviour in the Chora, Constantinople.

Valentinus could have afforded to pay for the time, materials, and expert workmanship needed to hand-produce such a singular book.

The *Chronograph*'s list of dates when the martyrs were buried, the *Depositio martyrum,* includes several expected luminaries (Stephen and Sebastian among them), and plenty of later Christian calendars followed its model of listing when and where the martyrs were buried, with some piling up multiple saints on any given day of the year. But in addition to its lists of burial dates, the *Chronograph* contains very different sorts of calendrical information, such as the dates of important pagan festivals, the dates when courts would be in session, the dates when markets would be open, and detailed notes on the astrological signs of the zodiac and their influence on world affairs.

If it seems strange that Valentinus would have been as interested in knowing which martyrs were buried in January as in understanding what an alignment of Mars and Jupiter might mean for the health of his vineyards in July, consider the context: Christianity was still a new cult for the elite families of fourth-century Rome, and it only made sense for a Roman senator living in that era to want to keep apprised of all the year's goings-on, Christian and pagan alike. In this regard, the *Chronograph* is, like all calendars, a mirror of the time and place in which it was produced: in this case, the Roman Empire's long transitional period when traditional pagan practices slowly declined while a newly robust and imperially sponsored form of Christianity was on the rise. Soon enough, Christian feasts would eclipse pagan ones, but the spread of Christianity hardly brought an end to the study of astrology. Knowing the movements of the heavens was fundamental to maintaining an accurate Christian calendar—even to understanding time itself.

Despite serving as annual reminders of the dates on which the martyrs met their ends, saints' feasts were far from somber affairs. These were occasions for Christians to celebrate their heroes. Festivities would usually begin with a nighttime vigil the evening before the saint's day was observed. Miracles were recorded at some. The evening's solemnity usually incorporated a reading of the martyr's *passio*—a brief account of the saint's suffering and death—which was often followed by a sermon preached in the saint's honor. Scores of these sermons survive, including several by John, a fourth-century preacher in Antioch whose oratorical skills were so admired that he was known as John Chrysostom—John "Golden Mouth."

The most well-known Christian martyrs were celebrated in major cities throughout the Roman world (Antioch, Rome, Alexandria, and Constantinople most prominent among them), but many saints' feasts were smaller and more local affairs. Wherever they were held, the presiding bishop had to walk a fine line between encouraging his flock to rejoice in the saints and discouraging them from taking their celebrations too far. A frequent target of the bishops' ire was the refreshment taken by some as part of their commemorative meals for the dead.

In Saint Augustine's *Confessions,* his famous autobiography of a raucous youth and eventual adulthood conversion to Christianity, the North African bishop recounts how his mother, Monica, in accord with the customs she knew from home, would often bring a picnic of homemade cakes and wine to celebrate with the martyrs atop their tombs. Saint Ambrose, Augustine's spiritual mentor and the bishop of Milan who discovered the relics of the long-dead saints Gervasius and Protasius, seems to have censured Monica rather sternly for her indulgence. Augustine hastens to defend her, saying that she "was not obsessed by excessive drinking," as Henry Chadwick puts it in his classic translation of the text. No, Augustine explains, that was not his mother's way of honoring the saints. In fact, he protests (a bit too much), Monica would never take more than "a sip" from a "tiny glass of wine diluted to suit her very sober palate." Her purpose in sharing her cakes and sips of wine with others who had gathered at the tombs was "devotion," Augustine insists, "not pleasure."

Obligatory defenses of one's own mother notwithstanding, Augustine, Ambrose, John Chrysostom, and other important Christian bishops throughout the Mediterranean world knew that they were fighting an uphill battle to control how the saints were celebrated. In his note on this episode, one that effectively calls Monica out as a tippler, Chadwick writes that Augustine "vainly tried to stop the inebriation at martyrs' shrines in Africa," knowing all too well that "drink was a major social problem."

Drunkenness at martyrs' feasts was not the only issue that concerned Augustine. In multiple sermons preached about the martyrs and their cults in the years before and after the close of the fourth century, Augustine refers to his own eating, drinking, singing, and dancing at martyrs' tombs. He admits that he thoroughly enjoyed the feasts of the saints in his youth, especially the close quarters and unconventional sorts of social mixing they occasioned. He even mentions "rubbing up beside women" in a juvenile bid to win their attention. On the other side of the Mediterranean, a fifth-century historian of the monks in Syria wrote of an ascetic who boasted of having maintained his virginity despite all the martyrs' festivals he had attended in his youth. Everyone wanted in on the fun: "Brethren," Augustine begins in a sermon preached at Carthage, the ancient coastal city near present-day Tunis, "see how it is that when a feast of the martyrs or some holy place is mentioned, to which crowds might flow to hold high festival. See how they stir each other up, and say, 'Let us go, let us go.' And each one asks the other, 'Where to?' They say, 'To that place, to that holy place.'"

Eventually, saints' feasts so saturated the calendar that on any given day of the year, as the historian Peter Burke once put it, some village somewhere was enjoying, recovering from, or eagerly anticipating such a celebration. Given the deeply agrarian nature of the medieval economy, the rhythms of the agricultural year often influenced how a saint's feast was kept. Hazelnuts are also called filberts because they ripen in late summer and were eaten around August 20, the feast of Saint Philibert. Sometimes the season's produce even shaped the saint's backstory. For sanitary purposes in an era before refrigeration, sausages were typically prepared during the colder times of the year. As the mincing and salting often coincided with the feast of Saint Anthony of Egypt on January 17, the famous monk soon became known as the patron saint of swine and swineherds. According to one medieval legend—no doubt invented to explain the odd porcine connection—Anthony is said to have kept a pet pig as a clock. It knew to nuzzle the monk at the hour of prayer.

One of the most widely venerated saints of the Middle Ages was another monk, the hermit Saint Martin. Despite his pleas to be left alone, Martin was popularly acclaimed the bishop of Tours, a Roman city in the Loire valley southwest of Paris. Martin missed the grand era of martyrs, coming of age only after Constantine had become the emperor of Rome, but he was one of the earliest saints to be venerated as enthusiastically as the martyrs. Not surprisingly, the story about Martin—this beloved monk and bishop who came to occupy a central place on the Christian calendar—is written in the style of a martyr's tale.

According to Martin's biographer, the orator Sulpicius Severus, the saint was a convert to Christianity who had served in Roman Gaul as a member of an elite cavalry unit. Martin must have left military service prior to the brief reign of Julian the Apostate in the early 360s, but Sulpicius frames Martin's departure from the army as a rejection of Julian, the last non-Christian Roman emperor, in favor of

Christ. The saint's bold refusal to serve the interests of a pagan king narratively links his story with those of earlier Christian soldier-martyrs, all of whom quit the Roman army after converting to Christianity. For abandoning his post, Martin was accused of cowardice and jailed. But to prove that it was fear of God, not fear of death, that led him to leave the military, Martin volunteered to serve unarmed on the front lines of the next battle. He never got the chance. Rome's Germanic adversary sued for peace, and Martin was released from prison and discharged from further military service. Centuries later, on November 11, 1918, the Allies signed an armistice with their own Germanic adversary. Remembrance Day, or Veterans Day as it is known in the United States, still coincides with the feast of Saint Martin of Tours—a patron saint of Christian soldiers.

If any story about Martin remains widely known today, it is that of Martin the cavalryman who cut his cloak in half to clothe a freezing beggar. (The Caribbean island now named for the saint is similarly divided, with only a soft border separating the French Saint-Martin from the Dutch Sint-Maarten.) The timing of Saint Martin's day in mid-November, as autumn starts its turn to winter, perhaps explains the further expansion of the cloak-cutting legend. It holds that Martin gave the other half of his cloak to a second threadbare beggar. Though ice already covered the ground, the clouds cleared at Martin's good deed, warming the cloakless soldier and melting the frost around him. "Saint Martin's summer" still refers to a brief period of unseasonably warm and windless days after the season's first frost. Per the adage in the *Old Farmer's Almanac*, "If All Saints' [on November 1] brings out winter, St. Martin's brings out Indian summer."

Saint Martin's Day was one of the primary divisions of the agricultural year. It was a time when contracts and leases began and ended. It was a harvest holiday when fieldwork was done and farmhands sought new jobs at hiring fairs, while any animals deemed unfit to overwinter were slaughtered. Well into the twentieth century, animals were still being sacrificed on the eve of Saint Martin's feast. In Ireland, the tradition was known as "spilling blood for Saint Martin." Geese and other fowl were the most typical victims, and goose remains a feature of the Saint Martin's Day menu in many parts of Europe. But just like the sausages associated with Saint Anthony, the goose on the Saint Martin's Day platter needed an explanation. Everyone already knew that Martin had to be cajoled from his hermitage to serve the public as bishop, so a further anecdote was added: Martin, it was said, had tried to avoid those pressing him into service by hiding in a goose pen. The birds' incessant honking gave him away.

Another joy of the late autumn harvest and the slaughter of meat for winter was that the summer's wine had come ready to drink. Martin was the bishop of a city in the heart of the Loire valley, a region still renowned for its excellent wines, so it is no surprise that he is the patron saint of vintners. Drunkards and innkeepers too.

In Pieter Bruegel the Elder's grand vision of early modern peasant life and the popular celebration of Martin's mid-November feast, a painting called *The Wine of Saint Martin's Day,* the saint himself is secondary (see plate 3). Mounted on a white horse, Martin rides past a crowd. Among the few who notice him are two invalids, who are themselves unnoticed by all except for Martin. Without breaking his horse's stride, the saint draws his sword across his cloak, cutting half for the footless man on crutches and half for the man whose legs are on the wrong way round. Everyone else in the painting—a roiling heap of men, women, and children—clambers over one another beneath, beside, and atop the massive cask that sits on a scaffold in the center of the scene. The nearly invisible stream of liquid spouting from it is woefully inadequate to fill all the vessels of those jostling for a sip of the season's new wine. Many hold up an empty something. The lucky have an earthenware bowl or maybe a broken pitcher. The rest make do with a shoe or a hat. The early arrivals who have had their fill are at the left of the painting: fighting, vomiting, passed out, or, in the case of two men steadying each other hand in hand, staggering home past a cross obscured by the trees in the distance. Steps away from all the chaos, a stout woman offers the eager child strapped to her chest a sip of new wine from a shallow bowl.

In the liturgical cycle of opposites, a feast this intense must always precede a fast. Nowadays, the pre-Christmas fast of Advent begins on the Sunday nearest to Saint Andrew's Day, which is on November 30. But Advent used to start earlier, spanning the forty days (minus Saturdays and Sundays) from the feast of Saint Martin all the way past Christmas to Epiphany. If Bruegel's painting is any indication of how Martin's feast was kept, it might have taken that long for everyone to recover.

The time of day is not something that we speculate much about anymore, given how all our devices keep us in sync to the second, but relatively accurate knowledge of the passing of time was no less important to Christians in the medieval period, perhaps especially beginning in the early sixth century with the *Rule of Saint Benedict,* a guide for monastic communities that came to regulate daily life throughout much of Europe. Benedict's *Rule* worked, and became so widespread, because it was flexible. Though it is often very specific— Benedict does not shy away from stipulating what monks should wear: a coarse cowl and a tunic; how much they should eat and drink: a pound of bread and half a pint of wine per monk per day; and even how they should sleep: in dormitory bunks with a single candle burning—the *Rule* always defers to local conditions and the wisdom of each community's abbot. That really is the hallmark of Benedict's *Rule:* a specific instruction followed by a qualification along the lines of "or as the abbot deems fit."

Despite regulating what would be a very difficult daily discipline for most of us, Benedict's *Rule* has both humor and kindness. It outlines a manageable form of monastic asceticism born of an acceptance of the human frailty that Bruegel rather less lovingly painted. The *Rule*, for instance, declares that monks should sleep "clothed and girded," so they can rise without delay on waking. Ordering men to sleep with their belts tightened may seem unduly rigid, but Benedict follows this rule with the suggestion that the brothers "gently encourage one another as they rise for the Work of God, because some may feel drowsy and listless." As for drink, Benedict writes that although he has "read that monks should not drink wine at all," he also realizes that the monks "of our day cannot be convinced of this." Therefore, he concedes, "let us at least agree to drink moderately, and not to the point of excess, for wine makes even wise men go astray."

Above all, Benedict structured the monk's day around two things: *ora et labora,* prayer and work. Taking his cue from Psalms, which speaks of the need to praise God seven times daily, Benedict established seven times for prayer during the day, plus another in the middle of the night. (This may explain the apocryphal story about Anthony and his need for a time-keeping pig.)

Following Roman tradition, Benedict's first hour, *prima hora,* was that of the sunrise. The exact time of sunrise varies widely throughout the year, of course—later in the winter and much earlier in the summer—but the first monastic hour, Prime, was supposed to be observed at about six o'clock. This was when the daily martyrology was read, that litany of saints whose testimony in blood was sufficient to get them fixed on the Christian calendar forever. Three other hours of prayer followed Prime at regular intervals: Terce, the third hour, at nine o'clock; Sext, the sixth, at midday; and Nones, the ninth, at three in the afternoon. The setting sun signaled the hour for Vespers (monastic evening prayer), and Vespers was followed by Compline once the fall of night was "complete." Several hours later, a bevy of robed and girded monks would rise from their beds to keep the night office of Vigils. With the first light of dawn, they would gather again to sing the hour of Lauds.

The monastic concern with order, with regulating life into hours for prayer, work, and sleep, was the day-to-day part of a much broader Christian preoccupation with time—one that extended far beyond the walls of the monastery. Observing sunrise and sunset, which respectively signaled the hours of Prime and Vespers, and determining the times for prayer in between took no special training, but keeping an accurate tally of days over the course of months and years was rather more complicated. Without intimate knowledge of the moon's phases and the sun's solstices and equinoxes, Christians had no way of knowing when to celebrate the annual memorial of the very first martyr's death: that of Christ himself.

On average, a lunar month lasts about 29½ days, but those who follow a lunar calendar usually split the difference with months of 29 or 30 days, each of which begins with the sighting of the crescent moon. By the midpoint of the month, on the fifteenth day, the moon will have waxed to full; the month ends when the moon has waned back down to new. Once the edge of the next month's crescent creeps out from shadow, the cycle begins again.

Just as the rising and setting of the sun marks out the course of a day, the waxing and waning of the moon is a ready-made month, a nighttime calendar hung in the sky for all to see. The regularity of its phases and the ease with which they can be observed explain the moon's appeal as a premodern means of measuring time, but lunar months do not multiply evenly into the solar year. Twelve lunar months have just 354 days, a little more than eleven short of the 365¼ in a full solar year. As a result, any unadjusted lunar calendar, such as the Islamic Hijri calendar, will not keep pace with the seasons. Likewise because of the discrepancy between lunar and solar years, a specific date on the Islamic calendar will fall in one season one year and quite another just a few years later. In 2020, for instance, the Muslim New Year, on 1 Muharram, fell in late August, but in 2030 it will be celebrated in early May.

By contrast, the Jewish calendar is lunisolar. It still records twelve lunar months over the course of a year, but in seven out of every nineteen solar years a thirteenth lunar month is added. Thanks to these so-called intercalary months, Rosh Hashanah, at the beginning of the Jewish civil year, on 1 Tishri, always falls in September or October, early autumn in the Northern Hemisphere. Two weeks later, the midmonth's full moon on 15 Tishri signals the start of Sukkot, the annual harvest festival. Without the regular addition of a thirteenth month to the Jewish calendar, a seasonally dependent holiday such as Sukkot would make no sense: in some years the harvest moon would come in autumn, but in others the "harvest" might coincide with the dead of winter or even the planting. The intercalations of the Jewish lunisolar calendar do make it more cumbersome than the purely lunar Islamic one, but these complexities pale in comparison to the royal mess that was the ancient Roman calendar.

Like most other ancient calendars, the earliest Roman one was lunar too. But, at least initially, the Romans used a ten-month calendar, which began with March. With the month named for Mars at the head of the year, those named for the Latin numbers *septem, octo, novem,* and *decem* were once the seventh, eighth, ninth, and tenth months of the year. In this earliest version of the Roman calendar, January and February did not exist. After the year ended in December, there was a long span of uncounted winter days until the new year began during the month of the vernal equinox. Though it may seem strange that the ancient Romans dismissed what were later called January and February as an indeterminate time of hibernation, this makes plenty of sense to me, as one who has endured many Canadian winters.

Soon enough, the Romans added January and February to the calendar. By the fifth century BC, they had scrapped their old lunar calendar in favor of a solar one. But not every vestige of the lunar calendar disappeared. The Romans still kept the length of their months at twenty-nine or thirty days. As a result, the new calendar was about eleven days short of a full solar year. To solve this problem, the Romans transformed every other February into an extra-long month by appending twenty-two or twenty-three days.

Another remnant of the old calendar was the continued use of three monthly date markers: the calends, the nones, and the ides. Because the calendar was not originally intended to be public, it fell to a Roman priest, a pontifex, to guard it and make it work. He was the one who had to formally announce the beginning of each month upon the sighting of the crescent moon. This is where we get our word *calendar*. It comes from the Latin verb *calare*, with reference to the priest who would "call out" the beginning of each month. Appropriately, the first day of every Roman month was known as the calends. The nones, on the other hand, corresponded to the appearance of the moon's waxing half disc, while the ides arrived with the full moon in the middle of each lunar month. The Romans did not bother to mark either the waning half disc or the new moon later in the month.

That the Romans continued to use three lunar markers each month even after having transitioned to a solar calendar which had nothing to do with the observed phases of the moon was only the start of the confusion. The calends was not a problem. It remained the first day of the month, even though it no longer referred to the "calling out" of the crescent moon. Because the ides used to fall on the fifteenth day of a lunar month, coinciding with that month's full moon, that date was kept too—sort of. In the transition to a solar calendar, the ides was fixed on the fifteenth day of a "long" month, with thirty days, but moved up to the thirteenth day of a "short" month, with only twenty-nine.

The nones, which means "nine" in Latin (think of the monastic name for the ninth hour of prayer), is the most baffling of the three lunar markers, since it does not correspond to the ninth day of the month. Instead, the nones was the ninth day prior to the ides by the Roman practice of inclusive counting: to arrive at the nones, one would have to tally backward nine days beginning with, and including, the ides. In a long month, this meant starting on the fifteenth and descending nine days to the seventh; in a short month, with the ides on the thirteenth, it put the nones on the fifth. This style of inclusive counting was in common use throughout the Roman Empire and explains why the authors of the New Testament refer to the Sunday of Jesus's resurrection as "the third day" after Friday.

The monthly date markers and the practice of inclusive counting take some getting used to, especially since the Roman system always counted backward. For a long month such as March, for example, when the ides was on the fifteenth, the Romans would express a date like the thirteenth by saying "Ante diem tertium idus Martias," or "The third day before the ides of March." Any date after the ides, the last marker in a month, was reckoned by noting how many days it was before the calends of the following month.

The year before Julius Caesar was assassinated, on the ides of March in 44 BC, his sorely needed revision of the Roman calendar went into effect. The Julian calendar's main innovation, made at the urging of Caesar's Egyptian astronomers, was to eliminate all those troublesome extra days that were appended to every other February. This was done by extending the twelve months of the year to their present lengths of thirty and thirty-one days—save poor February, mostly stuck at twenty-eight. With this change, January, Sextilis (August), and December became long months, of thirty-one days, but—adding confusion upon confusion—their ides were kept on the thirteenth. Meanwhile, March, May, and October remained long months (now with an extra day each), as did Quintilis, the fifth month counting from when the year began, in March, but its name was changed to *July* to honor Julius and his calendrical innovations. Finally, as Caesar's astronomers had calculated the length of the solar year at 365¼ days, they prescribed adding just one day to February every fourth year to account for the extra quarter day in the earth's annual trip around the sun.

The Julian reforms were brilliant, altogether a major improvement over previous Roman calendars, and they worked quite well, except for two small problems. Both were caused by the addition of the leap day. The first problem was remedied quickly once it was spotted. Ironically, the Romans had confounded themselves with their own system of inclusive counting, adding a leap day every third year instead of every fourth, as Caesar's astronomers had instructed. Somehow, this error went undetected for thirty-six years, until 9 BC, when Augustus Caesar's astronomers finally realized the mistake and temporarily halted the addition of leap days until the calendar could catch up. For his contribution to the proper keeping of time, Augustus was honored with the renaming of Sextilis. Now "August" followed "July."

The second issue with February's quadrennial leap day took longer to see and *much* longer to correct. Though the Egyptian astronomers' calculations were remarkably accurate, the length of one solar year is about eleven minutes shy of 365¼ days. As a result, each leap day tacked an extra forty-four minutes on to the calendar. At first they were scarcely noticeable. It took over a century for the calendar to be off by just a single day. But over many centuries even minutes can start to add up.

Christian calendar makers were aware of the miscalculation of the length of the year by the early Middle Ages, but the mistake went unremedied until the end of the sixteenth century. By that time, when Gregory XIII was pope, ten days too many had accrued on the calendar. To fix the problem, Gregory shortened 1582 by skipping ten days that October. In Catholic countries, this meant that October 15 immediately followed October 4 that year. From then on, the pope decreed, the addition of leap days would have to change. February would still get one in every year divisible by four, except in years that were also divisible by one hundred—unless that year was also divisible by four hundred. This explains why 2000 was a leap year, while 2100 will not be.

It took several centuries, but most of the world eventually adopted Pope Gregory's changes. Catholic countries were the first, followed by Protestant ones, while many Orthodox Christians still refuse to accept the pope's calendar. Because the Julian calendar is now not ten but thirteen days behind the Gregorian one, Orthodox Christmas—still December 25 according to the Julian calendar—currently falls on January 7. If the Orthodox "Old Calendarists" continue to use the Julian calendar through 2100, when the Gregorian calendar does not add a leap day, Orthodox Christmas in 2101 will slide a further day, to January 8.

For the earliest Christians, the date of Jesus's birth was much less important than that of his death. Pagan emperors celebrated birthdays; Christians celebrated the birth of their martyrs in heaven. In fact, only two of the four Gospels in the New Testament (those attributed to Matthew and Luke) even mention Jesus's birth. Matthew's infancy narrative opens with a long genealogy, a monotonous series of *begat*s ranging across forty-two generations from Abraham through David to Jesus, but his Gospel says nothing (at least not initially) about the year, the month, the day, or even the season when Jesus was born.

Luke is more specific. A good Roman citizen, Luke begins his account of the nativity by explaining that Jesus was born during the time of a census, or, as he puts it, during the time when "a decree went out from Caesar Augustus that all the world should be registered." We know that the ruler for whom August was named reigned from 27 BC to AD 14, which narrows the range of possible years when Jesus could have been born. But, like Matthew, Luke is silent about the month, the day, and the season of Jesus's birth.

Luke's next verse, in which he explains that the census "was taken while Quirinius was governor of Syria," winnows the range of possible years even further, but it also creates an intractable problem: Quirinius, a Roman aristocrat, did not become the governor of Syria until AD 6, several years after Jesus was supposedly born. Even more confusingly, both Luke and Matthew tell us that Jesus was born during the reign of Herod the Great. But Herod died in 4 BC. Clearly, something is wrong: there was no year when Herod was king and Quirinius was governor. Given that Luke was writing generations after Jesus's birth, his error can be forgiven. In fact, most biblical scholars believe that Jesus was likely born before Herod's death and before the governorship of Quirinius—sometime between 6 and 4 BC.

Despite the Gospels' silence about the month and day on which Jesus was born, Christians were already observing the nativity on December 25 in late antiquity, even though Christmas was far from being the major holiday that it later became. Theologically, it made sense that the Messiah, the one anointed the "light of the world," would be born in the world's darkest hour. December 25 is around the time of the winter solstice in the Northern Hemisphere, the point after which the days slowly grow longer again. The more established Roman holiday on December 25, the feast of Sol Invictus, the "Unconquered Sun," already celebrated the return of the light. Perhaps not surprisingly, one of the very earliest references to the celebration of these two feasts occurring on the same day can be found in the *Chronograph of*

354, that deluxe calendar book prepared for the Roman senator Valentinus. This is how the *Chronograph* abbreviates the date of Christmas:

> Hoc cons. dominus Iesus Christus natus est VIII kal. Ian. d. Ven. luna xv.

> When these ones [i.e., Gaius Caesar and Aemilius Paullus] were consuls, Lord Jesus Christ was born eight days before the calends of January, on the day of Venus, the fifteenth day of the moon.

The *Chronograph*'s reference to two consuls, the annually elected chief magistrates of Rome, is intriguing. Gaius Caesar was Augustus's grandson, while Aemilius Paullus was married to the emperor's granddaughter. As other records confirm, these two men served as consuls in the year that we would call A D 1, although the "A D" style of counting years had not yet been invented. The *Chronograph*'s date for the nativity, which translates to December 25 of A D 1, cannot have come from Luke. Instead, it seems that the *Chronograph* relied on a source that assumed Jesus was crucified in what we would call A D 31 and was thirty years old at the time. Whatever the source, the date in the *Chronograph* undeniably confirms that by at least the middle of the fourth century, if not earlier, Christians had accepted our "A D 1" as the year when Jesus was born.

The rest of the *Chronograph*'s abbreviated date for the nativity is easier to parse. We know that the fifteenth day of the moon ("luna xv") was a full moon in the middle of a lunar month; we also know that counting inclusively backward eight days from the calends of January gets us to December 25. Because the Romans named the days of the week after the planets, which, in turn, were named for the gods, the *Chronograph*'s reference here to the "day of Venus" ("d. Ven.") means that Jesus was born on a Friday. "Day of Venus" is more intelligible in Latinate languages like French, in which *Friday* is *ven-*

dredi, but the English word is related. *Friday* comes from the Old English *Frigedæg,* the day of Odin's wife Frigga, who, like Venus, was a love goddess.

Whether Jesus was born on a Friday when the moon was full is anyone's guess. It is more likely than not that this was just the *Chronograph*'s way of establishing a direct parallel between the day of Jesus's birth and that of his death—since, according to the Gospels, Jesus was crucified on a Friday when the moon was full. And this gets us to why the earliest Christians still had to rely on the Jewish lunar calendar.

The Gospels do not narrate the details of Jesus's death in the same way. There are many discrepancies in their stories. But they do agree that Jesus was killed on a Friday at the start of the Jewish Passover: the multiday festival after the spring equinox that commemorates the Israelites' exodus from slavery in Egypt. According to the Bible, the last of the ten plagues that God called down upon the Egyptians came with a requirement for the Jews: Moses had to instruct his people to mark their lintels and doorposts with lamb's blood so that the Angel of Death, who came to slay the firstborn of Egypt, would recognize the houses of Israelites and "pass over" them.

For Christians, Jesus himself was the sacrificial lamb, God's own firstborn slain when the moon was full so that death might pass over all people in spite of their sins. But when, exactly, were Christians to celebrate Easter—on Passover? Passover is observed beginning at sundown on the night of 14 Nisan, in advance of the next day's full moon, but Christians were divided on whether it was the full moon that was important or the Sunday following it, the day of the resurrection. Though a large majority quickly embraced the Sunday rather than the full moon, Eusebius explains in his *Ecclesiastical History* that there was still some debate about this question even into the fourth century. He says that those in "the Asian provinces" (modern-day Turkey) insisted that Christians had to align themselves with the Jewish calendar and celebrate Easter on 14 Nisan, the eve of Passover.

The emperor Constantine helped resolve the issue of Easter's date. The bishops at the Council of Nicaea, the church's first official convocation, in 325, decreed that it was the Sunday that mattered—but so too did the phase of the moon and the date of the equinox, which they fixed on March 21. According to the canons of the Council of Nicaea, Easter must always be celebrated on the first Sunday following the first full moon following the spring equinox on March 21.

Twelve and half centuries later, Pope Gregory's reform of the Julian calendar was spurred by a problem with the observed date of the equinox. Though the bishops had pegged it to March 21, they could not control the sun or the erroneous addition of leap days. By 1582, the equinox's supposed date was ten days ahead of what even the most novice astronomer could easily observe was the actual equinox. Put another way, the Gregorian reform of the Julian calendar had everything to do with correcting the date of Easter. It was a way of resyncing the observable equinox with its ecclesiastically decreed date of March 21.

Calculating Easter's correct date has always been taken seriously. In 525, the pope at the time directed Dionysius the Humble, a monk from the Black Sea coast of modern-day Romania, to compute it for the following year. Dionysius was well versed in the science of the *computus,* a term that comes from the Latin verb for "computation" or "reckoning." He followed the pope's instructions but did more than just calculate the next date of Easter. Like many before him who had intimate knowledge of the movements of the heavens, Dionysius was aware of the Metonic cycle. Its namesake, Meton of Athens, a Greek astronomer of the fifth century BC, had discovered that the phases of the moon recur on exactly the same days of the solar year every nineteen years. (This is why the Jewish calendar inserts a thirteenth lunar month in seven of every nineteen years.) With the Metonic cycle in mind, Dionysius decided that he would calculate the dates of Easter for the next five nineteen-year cycles beginning with 532. That way, no one would have to bother him about the calendar again. For the next century, anyone who wanted to know an upcoming Easter date could just look it up in the helpful table that Dionysius had prepared.

Dionysius's Easter table was not the first, but it turned out to be far and away the most influential. In fact, he relied on a set of tables prepared by astronomers in Alexandria. Theirs ended in 531, which explains why Dionysius began his in 532. But neither the Alexandrians nor anyone before them had referred to a year as *anno Domini*, "in the year of the Lord." In fact, their Easter tables referenced a very different AD: *anno Diocletiani*. In other words, the Alexandrian Easter tables counted the years from the beginning of the reign of the most notorious persecutor of Christians: the Roman emperor Diocletian. This was not done to honor him, of course, but rather the Christians he had martyred. It seems, however, that Dionysius was less keen to remember the name of a persecutor. So, in preparing his fresh set of Easter tables for the pope, Dionysius coined a new "AD" and with it an entirely new way of counting the years. He began with the nativity in AD 1: the first year of the Lord.

Dionysius's way of counting the years did not catch on quickly. The first Christian historian of any note to use the AD style was the English monk Bede, who availed himself of Dionysius's system to record the events in his *Ecclesiastical History of the English People,* which he finished by 731 and from which we know the story of Saint Alban's martyrdom. Bede's monastery in Northumbria, a Benedictine foundation dedicated to Saints Peter and Paul, may have been cold and muddy for much of the year, but this was no Dark Ages backwater where learning had no sway. Until Vikings destroyed it in the ninth century, Bede's monastery was a hub of Anglo-Saxon arts, science, and letters. Bede himself was a genius—a polymath who studied languages, history, astronomy, and calendars too. More than eight centuries before Pope Gregory corrected the Julian calendar, Bede had already seen that it was out of sync with the observable solstices and equinoxes.

Among Bede's many intellectual interests were the calculation and measurement of time. His most notable chronological work, composed around the year 723, is known today as *On the Reckoning of Time*. The science of the *computus,* the way of properly calculating the date of Easter, is a focus, but Bede's concerns went beyond the merely practical. *On the Reckoning of Time* is a wide-ranging study of ancient and medieval calendars. It addresses historical conceptions of the cosmos, how the moon moves through the zodiac, and how—in its revolutions around the earth—the moon affects the tides. Armed with all this astronomical knowledge, Bede used the lights of the sky to illumine the path of history.

History, as Alan Thacker once put it, had a *moral* purpose for Bede. In combining biblical history with the study of the cosmos, Bede unfolded time itself for his readers, explaining how the epochs of the past would eventually culminate in the conclusion of time. As Bede saw it, he and his Benedictine brothers in England were living in the sixth of seven ages. The five before had spanned from Adam to Noah, from Noah to Abraham, from Abraham to David, from David to the Babylonian exile, and from the exile to the birth of the Messiah. This sixth era, which had begun with Christ's nativity, would come to an end when he returned. The second coming would then inaugurate the seventh and last era of the world—one of judgment and a terrible war of Christ versus Antichrist.

For Bede, the luminaries of the sixth era were the martyrs. They were the ones through whom his era of history was best understood.

And in linking the reckoning of time with historical chronicles and the memorials of martyrs on their feast days, Bede produced the first truly historical martyrology. It was a register of every feast of every holy martyr he could find. In his work, Bede not only named the martyrs but also specified when and how they had been killed—and who had killed them.

Like the Alexandrian scholars who used Diocletian's name in numbering the years (and the bishops at the Council of Nicaea, who included Pontius Pilate in the Nicene Creed), Bede had no intention of erasing the names of Christian persecutors. His work, as Bede himself put it, endeavored to record "not only on what day, but also by what sort of combat or under what judge they [the martyrs] overcame the world." To complete his account of the sixth era's heroes, Bede drew upon a vast array of sources: calendars and martyrologies, passions of saints, histories and chronicles by Eusebius, and the roster of miracles in the *Dialogues* of Pope Gregory the Great—the same Gregory to whom Eulogius of Alexandria had written to ask about that mismeasured shipment of Roman lumber.

Despite all his research, the days that Bede collected into an annual cycle of sanctity covered less than half the year, with entries for only about a hundred saints—almost all of them martyrs. But Bede's calendar was soon expanded by others. The zenith of martyrological writing occurred in France, a century later, under the rule of the Carolingian kings. As stalwart proponents of history, literature, and culture, the heirs of Charlemagne expected their priests to know how to calculate the date of Easter without cheating by reference to tables. Several of these holy men continued the work that Bede had begun, including Florus, a deacon of Lyon, and Ado, the archbishop of Vienne.

Ado stuffed nearly a hundred martyrs per month into his calendar, listing multiple saints on every day of the year. His book was an advancement over Bede's, but it was also too long and cumbersome for daily use. In the 860s, a Parisian monk, Usuard of Saint-Germain-des-Prés, took it upon himself to abridge Ado's martyrology. Ultimately, Usuard's calendar was more polished and uniform than any before. Soon, every Benedictine monastery in the world had a copy of it, or some subsequent revision. Meanwhile, martyrs had become a central part of monks' daily prayers, with the saints' names and ordeals read out at sunrise during the hour of Prime.

Remarkably, the ancient Roman calendar still remains a part of the daily martyrology. When read at Prime, the martyrology begins with the announcement of the calends and the phase of the moon. But each day's saints are "anticipated," in the parlance of the church—which is to say that they are remembered on the day before their feast. In the case of Saint Martin, whose feast is November 11, his name is read aloud on the morning of November 10, with the next day's date given as "tertio idus novembris," three days, via the practice of inclusive counting, before the ides of the short month of November.

In addition to the names of the saints who are remembered each day, the martyrology usually includes information along the lines that Bede himself incorporated, such as where and how the martyrs died and who killed them. In the case of unmartyred saints, other details are given. This, for example, is the Roman Catholic martyrology for November 11:

> At Tours, in France, the birthday of blessed Martin, bishop and confessor, whose life was so renowned for miracles that he received the power to raise three persons from the dead.—At Cotyaeum, in Phrygia, during the persecution of Diocletian, the celebrated martyrdom of St. Mennas, Egyptian soldier, who cast off the military belt and obtained the grace of serving the king of heaven secretly in the desert. Afterwards coming out publicly, and freely declaring himself a Christian, he was first subjected to dire torments; and finally kneeling in prayer, and giving thanks to our Lord Jesus Christ, he was struck with

the sword. After his death, he was renowned for many miracles.—At Ravenna, the holy martyrs Valentine, Felician and Victorinus, who were crowned in the persecution of Diocletian.—In Mesopotamia, St. Athenodorus, martyr, who was subjected to fire and other torments under the same Diocletian and the governor Eleusius. He was at length sentenced to capital punishment, but the executioner having fallen down and no other person daring to strike him with the sword, he passed to his repose in the Lord whilst praying.—At Lyons, St. Veranus, bishop, whose life was illustrated by his faith and other virtues.—In the monastery of Crypta-Ferrata, near Frascati, the holy abbot, Bartholomew, companion of blessed Nilus, whose life he wrote.—In the province of Abruzzo, blessed Mennas, solitary, whose virtues and miracles are mentioned by Pope St. Gregory. And elsewhere in diverse places, many other holy martyrs, confessors, and holy virgins.

In the wake of the liturgical modernizations imposed during the Second Vatican Council in the 1960s, the martyrology is rarely read aloud at Prime anymore. No official English translation of the martyrology even exists. (The one for November 11 quoted above comes from before Vatican II.) Concerned with the annual commemoration of saints like Eustace—and any others who might have been converted by talking animals—the documents of the Second Vatican Council sought to ensure that public claims about the saints were "made to accord with the historical facts."

This was not the first time the calendar was purged of implausible legends.

In the late eighteenth century, the victorious revolutionaries in France swept all the saints from the calendar. Under the leadership of Fabre d'Églantine, the French Republican calendar completely erased the religious history of France. No longer would the stories of the saints, which d'Églantine deemed "a collection of lies," dominate the days. Gone were all the saints, and even Jesus too. Moreover, instead of seven-day weeks, each month of the year was reconfigured into three weeks of ten days each. These decades of days and the days within each were renamed in honor of the rural economy: agricultural tools, animals, trees, fruits, minerals, and the seasons replaced Lent, Christmas, Ascension, and Pentecost. This, according to the Republicans, was to prove that the true riches of France were the "useful products of the soil"—not, as d'Églantine acidly put it, "beatified skeletons pulled from the catacombs."

5 The Living Dead

The ritual began with the novice recluse prostrate on the floor of the church—the seeping coldness of stone hard against her face. She was sinful and unworthy, dead in the sight of others, but submissive as a saint. Her senses must have been heightened during this spectacle, during these last moments that she would share with the living. Circling her three times, the bishop sprinkled the recluse with holy water and then enveloped her in a cloud of incense, the rising smoke from his swinging thurible a visual and olfactory reminder that this woman was a burnt offering to God—still alive but already dead. Ritually speaking, this was her funeral. Soon she would be led to her tomb, a barnacle held fast to the northern wall of the church. After the bishop bolted it shut, it would never be opened again.

The recluse would stay enclosed in her cell for years, decades perhaps, until her natural death pulled her into the earth. From inside her tiny necropolis—population: one—she would still be able see the candlelit altar where she had pledged her life to Christ, but her view through the oblique slit in the church's wall, a splayed window called a squint, would be severely constricted: she could see nothing but the altar. This is what she would gaze upon for the rest of her life.

After the bishop blessed the recluse, two elders raised her from the ground, then each handed her a lit candle to hold. As the candles symbolized, the recluse herself was extinguished. Now her only light would come from the love of God and the love of neighbor. Everything in this ceremony was significant, every gesture meaningful, every prayer carefully chosen.

The liturgy's first reading, from the Old Testament's book of Isaiah, urged the recluse to enter her chamber and shut its door: "Hide yourselves," warns the prophet, "until the wrath is past. For the Lord comes out from his place to punish the inhabitants of the earth for their iniquity." The recluse's cell was to be a refuge from wrath and all the sins of the world. For all its chill darkness, it was a locked garden and "pleasant vineyard," as Isaiah puts it, into which only the Lord, its keeper, could enter. The cell was the recluse's refuge, but it was also her citadel. Inevitably, her prayers would draw the arrows of the adversary.

The ritual's second reading, from the Gospel of Luke, was more heartening. This passage tells the story of Jesus's arrival at "a certain village," presumably Bethany on the Mount of Olives, "where a woman named Martha welcomed him into her home." Luke is sparing with his narrative details, commenting only that Martha "was distracted by her many tasks," but we can assume some things about the hospitality she must have provided: a basin for washing, a comfortable place to sit, the restoration of food and drink. Meanwhile, as Martha saw to the needs of her guest, her sister, Mary, "sat at the Lord's feet and listened to what he was saying." Annoyed by her sister's neglect of the necessary work of welcome, Martha turns to Jesus to complain: "Lord, do you not care that my sister has left me to do all the work by myself?" Martha expects Jesus to see things from her perspective, but instead of rebuking Mary he chides Martha, his gentle tone evident in the repetition of her name: "Martha, Martha," we can hear him sigh, "you are worried and distracted by many things," when only one thing is needed. In setting aside all but the word of the Lord, "Mary has chosen the better part, which will not be taken away from her."

For the recluse who heard this passage, its meaning would have been clear: the "better part" ascribed to her was prayer, a single-minded focus on God, as the blinders imposed by her squint and her view of only the altar attest.

In the twelfth century, liturgical books called pontificals, which outline the rituals that only popes and bishops are allowed to perform, began to include an official enclosure liturgy like the one described above. Rites specific to the consecration of churches, monasteries, and the people (priests, abbots, monks, and nuns) who lived in them had long appeared in pontifical manuscripts, but now a new category was added to the list of persons: the anchorite (see plate 4).

Anchorites were not new, but a special ritual for enclosing them was. The term *anchorite* comes from the Greek verb *anachōrein*, which means "to retreat" or, more poetically, "to flee up-country" to the rural regions (*chōra*) beyond the reach of a city. In late antiquity, led by the example of Saint Anthony and the other desert fathers and mothers of third- and fourth-century Egypt, the hermit retreated to the literal desert, the arid and uncultivated lands at the fringes of civilization. For the medieval anchorites of western Europe, the desert was more of a metaphor, the *chōra* reenvisioned as any place isolated from the rest of the world.

Born of a long history of Christian asceticism, one that preceded even Anthony's flight to the desert, the medieval practice of enclosure was more immediately a development of a rigorous monastic reform movement that began in the late eleventh century. But the almost unimaginable physical and psychological difficulty of the enclosed life, truly a form of living entombment, meant that it was a rare subspecies of Christian asceticism, afforded to a select few—most of them women. For much of their history, anchoresses outnumbered anchorites on the order of two or even three to one, although the total number of recluses, both male and female, was never large. In England, there were only about a hundred inhabited reclusories in the twelfth century. Most of these cells were attached to churches or monasteries, but some were carved right into city walls. Over the next three centuries, the number of active British reclusories more than doubled until they were all abruptly emptied in the 1530s with the dissolution of the monasteries and the general suppression of Roman Catholicism during the English Reformation.

Few anchorholds (as recluses' cells are known) still survive. In the half millennium since the end of enclosure in England, most were demolished or otherwise overwritten by later construction. Among those that do remain is one attached to the northern wall of Saint Anne's Church in Lewes, near the seaside city of Brighton. There, as the British medievalist Mary Wellesley put it, "an anchoress was buried in the exact place she would have knelt at her squint in order to see the high altar." And it would have been to that place, to that grave of an anchorhold and its squint, that the anchoress of Lewes would have processed near the end of her enclosure ritual. As she walked from church to cell, those gathered round her would have sung, "In paradisum deducant te angeli" (May the angels lead you to paradise). The same antiphon was used in the funeral liturgy when conveying a body from church to grave.

The close association between a Christian initiation ritual and death did not begin with the medieval anchorites: it is much more ancient. In the first century A D, when Paul wrote to a growing community of Christ followers in the city of Rome, he told them that they had died and been buried with their Lord in baptism. All those who sought Christ were called to ritually imitate his death in baptism so that they might be reborn into life with him. Just as a medieval bishop circled a novice recluse three times, dousing her with incense and holy water in the name of the Father, the Son, and the Holy Spirit, many late antique baptisteries had three steps leading down to the rectangular pool where initiates were fully immersed in a watery grave in order to, as Paul explains, "put to death the deeds of the body," the stain of sin dissolving in the waters of baptism. The now baptized Christian who ascended the three steps on the pool's far side would have been clothed in a fresh white alb, at once a symbol of newfound purity and of the shroud of burial and anticipated resurrection with Christ.

Becoming an anchoress meant embracing a daily process of putting the body to death. The anchoress had permanently fled the land of the living and with it all the frittering mundanities of Martha's housekeeping and the related domestic anxieties of marriage and child rearing. Considered in the context of medieval society, which offered few options to even wealthy and well-educated women, life as an anchoress might (paradoxically) have been an escape, a way of grasping hold of some semblance of freedom, even if the anchoress remained governed by men: her bishop, her confessor, the author of her *Rule*.

The Greek word *anachōrein* suggests just such an escape from the strictures of civic life. Constantinople's famous Chora Church, built in the fields outside the city's original fourth-century walls, both literally and linguistically affirms the *chōra* as a place beyond the confines of the urban sphere, and the word *chōra* is itself loaded with theological and philosophical meaning, signifying that which is neither present nor absent, neither living nor dead—precisely the sort of liminal space that an anchoress inhabited and the sort of angelic existence sought by the desert fathers.

When Anthony withdrew into the desert, he briefly dwelled in some of the tombs he found in that wasteland. Athanasius, the fourth-century bishop of Alexandria who promoted Anthony's desert forays to readers throughout the Mediterranean world, quotes Paul to explains that Anthony sought to "die daily" as a martyr to the sins of his conscience.

Early in his own monastic career, Saint Simeon the Stylite, a fifth-century Syrian ascetic, attempted an especially perilous feat of enclosure. Unchallenged by five days alone at the bottom of a waterless cistern, he pursued increasingly drastic forms of deprivation in his isolated hut, slowly training his body through its confinement. "Always eager to grow richer in virtue," as Theodoret, the bishop of Cyrrhus, explains in his account of Simeon's life, the monk "wanted to endure forty days without eating like the divine men Moses and Elijah." But Simeon knew his strength could not rival that of the prophets.

To stop himself from breaking his fast before his forty days were up, Simeon asked a country priest who visited him from time to time to shut the door to his hut and seal it from the outside with clay. Aware of Simeon's plan, the priest demurred, wanting no part in the monk's potential suicide. "Well then, father," Simeon responded, "leave me ten loaves of bread and a pitcher of water. If I see that my body needs nourishment, I will partake of them." Forty days later, when the priest returned to remove the seal, he was astounded to find the loaves untouched, the pitcher still full. Simeon, however, was on the ground, "breathless, unable to speak or move." The priest soon revived him with a bit of the Eucharist, then fed him "a moderate amount of nourishment—wild lettuce, chicory, and the like—which he chewed into small pieces."

Theodoret does not tell us how Simeon spent the forty days he was enclosed in his hut, but from everything else the historian says about him we can infer that it must have been in near-constant prayer. An anchoress's days were an extension of this devotion, a life-long Lent within the walls of her enclosure, with years spent praying, reading, and contemplating death.

The basic physical demands of the body meant than an ethereal existence was impossible for an anchoress so long as she was alive, and although her daily fare was undoubtedly plain and meager, she could not be sealed up like Simeon with a lifetime supply of bread and sop. Her door had been bolted shut, but the cell of an anchoress had two small openings in addition to the squint through which she could see the high altar. A second interior window faced a servants' parlor. Through it the women who assisted the anchoress could pass food and drink and remove and return her chamber pot. According to Aelred of Rievaulx, a monk who wrote a guidebook for his sister—an anchoress in the twelfth century—a recluse should always rely on two servants: a younger woman capable of carrying things to and from the anchorhold, and an older woman whose wisdom and sensibility might be of spiritual benefit.

The cell's third window, by far the most dangerous of the lot, opened onto the exterior of the anchorhold. It was usually covered with a heavy curtain. The anchoress was not supposed to receive regular visitors, most especially male visitors besides her confessor, but it was to this exterior window that those seeking counsel (or something nefarious) might come.

An anchoress might have chosen a life of isolation, cut off from the warmth and touch of others, but her vocation still required the support of the church. Before she could enter her cell, it had to be built. The earliest anchoritic enclosures appear to have been simple lean-to structures of timber and thatch, but as the ascetic practice developed and spread, reclusories slowly became more permanent accretions of stone. Though there was no standard architectural plan for anchorholds, most were small and rustic, typically storeroom-size enclosures attached to a church's outer wall. Even so, building one cost money. For this, a patron would have to be found—often the local lord. His bequest, coupled with the community's alms, was usually sufficient to keep the recluse fed, clothed, and housed for the rest of her life.

This does not mean that anchoresses came from the poor. Wealth has long been associated with ascetic women. Julia Eustochium, a pious young woman who lived in the late fourth century, was a member of one of the wealthiest families in Rome. Her family controlled vast estates, with thousands of slaves and servants, that stretched from the city far into the countryside. In her ascetic endeavors, Eustochium had the support of her widowed mother. In fact, the two women joined Saint Jerome in Bethlehem for years. They worked to endow convents and monasteries while he lived and wrote in a cave believed to be where Jesus was born. In a notorious letter written to Eustochium when she was no more than sixteen, Jerome quotes from Luke's story of Martha and Mary to imagine Jesus doting on the girl as if she had been the one in that house on the Mount of Olives who hung on the Lord's every word: "My dove," Jerome's Jesus coos to Eustochium, "my undefiled."

Regardless of her means, however, a medieval anchoress was still dependent on men. In addition to a lordly patron, her choice to pursue the ascetic life would have required the approval of her bishop: it was he who would gauge whether she was suited for the hardships of a life enclosed, he who would examine whether her desire for such a life was to serve God or—just as masochistic as it sounds—merely to pursue the praise of others. The bishop reminded the anchoress of her lowliness during her enclosure ritual. It was not that her privileged consciousness qualified her to live a life apart; it was that she was unworthy to continue to dwell among others.

Despite such public abasement from the mouth of a bishop, an anchoress would often achieve a spiritual authority, thanks in part to her impressive asceticism and to her lifelong acquisition of wisdom. The first book in English known to have been written by a woman was authored by an anchoress: Saint Julian of Norwich, who died in the early fifteenth century. In fact, we know almost nothing about her—not even her real name. She is called Julian simply because her anchorhold was attached to a church in Norwich that was dedicated to a much earlier Saint Julian, the martyred bishop of Le Mans. Nevertheless, the female Julian's *Revelations of Divine Love* is still read and celebrated as a brilliant account of one woman's mystical union with God. Undoubtedly, Julian was exceptional, but she was also unexceptional. Not even she could escape the men who advised and controlled her, who decided what she could and could not publish and edited it as they saw fit.

Julian's *Revelations* aside, much of our evidence for the anchoritic vocation comes from texts like those liturgical rites at the back of medieval pontificals. More still comes from bequests, wills, and other sorts of wax-sealed documents that stipulate grants of money and land for a church to use in support of the needs of its local ascetic. But our best written sources about anchoresses are the guidebooks that were composed for them. There is *De institutione inclusarum* (*On the Formation of Anchoresses*), the one that the monk Aelred of Rievaulx wrote for his sister. Another is by Goscelin of Saint-Bertin, a Flemish monk living in England: his *Liber confortatorius* (*Book of Consolation*) is dedicated to his former student—and possible love interest—the anchoress Eve of Wilton. But the best known of them all is the thirteenth-century *Ancrene Wisse,* or *Guide for Anchoresses,* which was anonymously authored in Middle English rather than Latin.

We cannot say who wrote the *Ancrene Wisse,* but we do know that it was intended for three sisters living in the West Midlands near the Welsh border. Whoever wrote it was clearly a serious student of the Bible and the church fathers. He—assuredly, it was a *he*—frequently showcases his learning by citing long passages from scripture and the ascetic and theological treatises of the saints, including the original Latin prose of clerics like Saint Jerome and Saint Gregory the Great. He also cites the work of pagan philosophers, such as the first-century A D Roman Stoic and statesman Seneca the Younger. For the benefit of his female readers, who presumably did not understand

Latin, he provides an accompanying Middle English translation of his florid sources.

In a play on words that inverts the etymology of *anchorite* as a term for a monk who has fled to the desert, the author of the *Ancrene Wisse* likens an anchoress, an *ancre* in Middle English, to a ship's anchor—also an *ancre*. And in describing an anchorhold not as a place apart, not as a tomb on the outskirts of its city, but as the central, unmoving foundation of its church, its brace against storms and demons, the author of the *Ancrene Wisse* highlights the principal role of an anchoress for her local community. She was a saint, a set of living relics, whose intercession for those around her was invaluable. At the same time, the author warns the women to whom he writes against venturing too close to the thick of village life. The first and last parts of the *Ancrene Wisse* purposefully bookend its "inner" sections so as to explain the "outer" rules for an anchoress. Like the *Rule of Saint Benedict,* these outer rules regulate practical matters—such as what the anchoress should wear and how much she should sleep and eat—but they also specify that she should never teach children, never send or receive letters, never hold money in trust for others, and never engage in gossip. As one recent editor of the *Ancrene Wisse* put it, the very fact that the guidebook's author felt compelled to remind his readers that the anchorhold was not to serve as a schoolhouse, a post office, a bank, or a newspaper implies that some may have functioned in just those sorts of municipal ways. But such public-facing activities, the outer rules of the *Ancrene Wisse* explain, draw the anchoress out from her anchorhold and distract her from the much more important inner rules guiding her spiritual life.

Prayer was the work of an anchoress. That is why her bodily needs were seen to by others. A fifth-century Syriac text known as the *Book of Steps* offers a parallel example of similarly distinct groups: those whose work it is to pray and those who are responsible for serving those who pray. The work's anonymous author describes a Christian community somewhere in northern Mesopotamia, near what is now the Iraqi city of Mosul, that was divided between what he calls "the Perfect" and "the Upright." Like medieval anchoresses, the Perfect were devoted to prayer; it was their helpers, the Upright, who were supposed to aid them in their devotion by providing them with sufficient food, clothing, and shelter. In defense of this two-tiered hierarchy, one that unambiguously promotes the ascetic life as superior, the author of the *Book of Steps* points to the Gospel of Luke. Because she imitated Christ, taking "up his cross in lowliness and holiness," he says, "Mary's portion came to be larger than Martha's." Martha was an upright woman, no doubt about that, but it was Mary who "died to the world and its business and spiritually lived in our Lord."

Likewise, the inner rules of the *Ancrene Wisse* explain the extent to which the anchoress and all five of her senses were to be dead to the world while her spirit lived on in the Lord. But the windows of an anchorhold posed a problem: they opened the living world into that of the dead—and into the anchoress's very body itself. For this reason, the *Ancrene Wisse* says, an anchorhold's windows are to be as small as possible. They must shut the anchoress off from the world. Deprived of external stimuli, she would thus be forced to develop a sixth sense: her spiritual sight. Still, as little as the anchoress might have been able to see through her windows, the sounds and smells of the world would continue to penetrate her enclosure.

The persistence of these nonvisual intrusions is a central concern of Robyn Cadwallader's beautiful historical novel *The Anchoress*. Much of it is set in the anchorhold of a twelfth-century Midlands church into which the seventeen-year-old Sarah has been nailed. Sarah wants to flee her body (and her past), but the more she tries the more acutely she becomes aware of how everything outside her cell still presses in: the smells of rain and cooking fires; the sounds of birds in the eaves; the thud of church doors closing, "wood on wood."

Sarah also hears Agnes. Agnes used to live in Sarah's anchorhold, but her bones are buried there now, right beneath Sarah's feet.

There was another reason that an anchorhold's windows were supposed to be small. As the enclosure liturgy's first reading from the book of Isaiah reminded the anchoress, the outside world is filled with deceit, "false tales and idle talk," as Goscelin of Saint-Bertin explains to Eve in the *Book of Consolation*. The *Ancrene Wisse* also warns against this sort of gossip. Still, the most serious problem was not the spoken words of others: it was the others themselves. In Cadwallader's novel, the bishop who advises young Sarah warns her that a lifetime of enclosure is the only way that her virginity might remain intact. The nonfictional monk Aelred of Rievaulx told his sister the same thing. If, he said, the portals of her cell were stretched wide enough for someone to enter, it would turn into a brothel.

Rievaulx Abbey now lies in ruins on the banks of the river Rye. When Aelred was its abbot, he wrote lovingly of monasticism as a practice of friendship: friendship with his fellow monks and friendship with God. Yet in writing to women, especially his sister, Aelred remembered the lustful "cloud of desire" that had occluded his youth. He knew the ancient history of Christian monasticism as well as anyone in twelfth-century England, and the stories about female ascetics from late antiquity, coupled with the memories of his own lust-filled youth, seem to have colored his assessment of the danger his sister was in as an anchoress.

One of those stories tells of the young Maria and her old uncle, a monk named Abraham. Maria was orphaned as a child and Uncle Abraham was her only surviving relative, so even though he lived as a hermit, she was taken to stay with him, which she did for twenty years. Abraham kept to his prayers and other ascetic devotions in the protected inner chamber of their two-room house, occasionally instructing his niece in the monastic disciplines through a small window, while Maria lived alone in the exposed outer room. It would prove to be a tragic domestic arrangement.

As the story goes, another monk, who visited Abraham on occasion, came to desire the beautiful Maria. Out of Abraham's earshot, he would speak to her sweetly, coaxing her to open her door. Eventually, she did. It is not clear from the tale whether Maria was seduced from the safety of her cell and freely opened herself to the monk or was lured out and raped, but this distinction seems not to have mattered to the narrator—if it occurred to him at all. It seems not to have mattered to Maria either. Whatever happened, she knew that she had been corrupted, and she knew that she could not speak with her holy uncle again, much less continue to live with him. As penance for her sin, Maria left her uncle's house and—perplexingly—took up life as a prostitute. As for Abraham, so absorbed was he in his prayers that it was some time before he even noticed that his niece was gone.

Two years later, tipped off by a friend, Abraham finally found Maria, plying her trade at an inn. He arrived in disguise, dressed as an old soldier in need of some company. Thinking the man just another customer, Maria winsomely drew near. But as soon as she was close to her holy uncle, she became agitated by what the narrator refers to as Abraham's "familiar scent of asceticism." After the monk revealed his identity, uncle and niece were reconciled and returned home to resume the ascetic life together—this time with Abraham in the outer and Maria in the protected inner room.

The lesson supposed to be gleaned from this tale may not be obvious to us, but it would have been to Christian monks. Maria's story communicates two things: the dangers that lurk outside the cell for less-than-vigilant hermits, and the foolish lustfulness of women. According to Galen, a Greek physician of the second century A D whose ideas about medicine and the functioning of the human body remained widespread and influential well into the Renaissance, women are wantonly sexual creatures. They are also failed men: as Galen theorized, female reproductive organs are simply undescended male ones turned outside in—a developmental imperfection caused by a lack of body heat.

As Abraham's soldierly costume is supposed to signal, the wandering ascetic who seduced the unwary Maria was in disguise too. The narrator calls him a monk "in name only." He is why the enclosure liturgy's reading from the book of Isaiah warns the recluse to enter her chamber and shut its door. If Satan's minions could not penetrate the cell of an anchoress, they would try to draw her out instead. Exposed, she stood no chance.

In the early days of the coronavirus pandemic in 2020, one commentator explained the necessity of "enclosure as a way to starve the searching virus of bodies to inhabit." The virus visualized as a watching army of drones waiting for their moment to strike is an apt parallel to the swirl of demons above the hermit's cell, conceived by the desert fathers as a place of shelter from their attacks.

In one story from the *Sayings of the Desert Fathers,* as a famous collection of ascetic vignettes is known, we learn about an Ethiopian monk, Moses the Black, and his struggle against sexual desire. (How to combat sexual urges is a recurring theme in these stories.) Moses's need to free himself was so overpowering that he sought counsel from the wise Abba Isidore, begging the old man for a word. Isidore was blunt: he told Moses to return to his cell. When Moses insisted that he simply could not, Isidore took him outside and pointed to the west. Moses looked in the direction of the setting sun and "saw hordes of demons flying about and making a noise before launching an attack. Then Abba Isidore said to him, 'Look towards the east.' He turned and saw an innumerable multitude of holy angels shining with glory. Abba Isidore said, 'See, these are sent by the Lord to the saints to bring them help, while those in the west fight against them.

Those who are with us are more in number than they are.' Then Abba Moses gave thanks to God, plucked up courage and returned to his cell."

Isidore's advice was sound. Later in the collection of sayings, Moses offers the same instruction to another monk, thereby distilling the wisdom of the desert down to a single sentence: "Go," Moses commands. "Sit in your cell, and your cell will teach you everything."

The *Ancrene Wisse* often alludes to the *Sayings of the Desert Fathers* and the encouraging examples of monks like Moses and Anthony even as it acknowledges that remaining hidden in one's cell is no guarantee of protection. When Anthony fled to live in the tombs and, like Simeon the Stylite a century later, asked an acquaintance to shut his door and occasionally bring him some bread, the demons "could not endure it." They were terrified that Anthony would "fill the desert with discipline."

One night, as Anthony was praying in his tomb, so many demons attacked him that he was knocked unconscious and left for dead. Fortunately, his bread deliveryman was slated to come the next morning. On his arrival, he found Anthony and carried him to a nearby church, where the villagers kept watch over the comatose monk "as round a corpse." Late that night, when all but the bread man were asleep, Anthony finally came to. He gestured for his friend to move closer. Then he whisper-shouted a simple command: "Take me back!"

Anthony's encounters with demons, more than one episode of which his biographer describes, are an important theme in Christian art. The most famous depictions of the monk's battles, alternately known as *The Torment* or *The Temptation of Saint Anthony*, include those by artists as different as Michelangelo and Salvador Dalí.

Michelangelo's version of Anthony's torment, which is modeled on an engraving by another artist, is especially noteworthy, as it is the earliest surviving work by the master—completed when Michelangelo was just twelve or thirteen. It depicts Anthony suspended in midair as eight fantastical beasts rip at his robes in a frenzy (see plate 5). One winged demon with goat horns yanks on Anthony's halo. Another, some sort of spiny seahorse, swings at him with a flaming club. So much for Abba Isidore's promised angelic counterforce.

Dalí's interpretation, by contrast, shows a naked Anthony on the ground, reeling backward on one knee (see plate 6). In his hand, Anthony brandishes a cross against an approaching parade of elephants led by a horse. The animals teeter on impossibly spindly and rickety legs that somehow support an obelisk, a grand villa, and a giant of a woman who cups her fulsome breasts in her hands as her luxuriant hair flows loose around her. Though we cannot see his face, Dalí's Anthony seems no less tormented than Michelangelo's—in this case by all these surrealist demons, these symbols of the temptations that afflict the monk, these icons of sex, money, power, and knowledge.

If Michelangelo's Anthony endures a threat of literal beady-eyed beasts while Dalí's are more figurative, it was not modernism that led Dalí to reimagine the attacks on the monk as more psychological than physical. The idea that the truest demons are temptations can be traced back to the time of Anthony himself.

In the late fourth century, when Evagrius of Pontus—a brilliant diagnostician of monastic psychology—was still a young man, he abruptly left a successful career in Constantinople for a monastery in Jerusalem. News of his affair with the wife of a powerful court official was about to become public. Eventually, Evagrius made his way from Jerusalem to the ultimate monastic proving ground: the deserts of Egypt.

As Evagrius understood it, the demons that attack monks are best conceptualized as a set of eight *logismoi*, or categories of "evil thoughts." Thoughts do not come zipping down with teeth from out of the desert sky, but that is precisely what makes them even more dangerous: where can one hide from a demon that wells from within?

According to Evagrius, the first of the eight evil thoughts is gluttony. By *gluttony*, he meant not the desire for a table laden with cakes and dainties but simply the urge to fill the belly to fullness—even if only with stale bread and beans. As Jerome puts it in his letter to the young Eustochium, "First the belly is stuffed; then the other members are roused." Evagrius grasped that the first need of the body is food. If the monk can master the desire for food, then he can slay the next seven demons, one after the next. These include lust, greed, sadness, acedia, anger, vainglory, and pride—the self-love that keeps a Christian from loving God and neighbor. The demon of acedia, alternately interpreted as "depression" or "boredom," is the most menacing of all. It attacks with the heat of the midday sun, urging the monk to flee the absurd rigors of the ascetic life and return home. Acedia pulls the monk back to the world by reminding him of all the pleasurable things he has forsaken. This is the demon that can end the monk's struggles for good.

The anchorites of Egypt had fled the world, but the demon of acedia made it difficult for them to stay fled. A medieval anchoress had no such choice, physically barred as she was from leaving her anchorhold, but that did not mean she was free from demonic combat. She still had to fight what attacked her, especially the demon that smuggled listlessness into her cell.

Aelred of Rievaulx describes the mental turmoil caused by idleness as another evil thought. It breeds "disgust for the cell" in the heart of an anchoress. Aelred's inventory of the diabolic—naming the demons and explaining how they attack—was no mere academic exercise: it had immediate practical consequences for his readers. If the anchoress was to defeat her enemy, she had to know her enemy. For this reason, the largest of the eight sections in the *Ancrene Wisse* focuses on battle strategy, offering point-by-point instructions on how to expel each evil thought—each of the eight *logismoi,* which, by the thirteenth century, had become the seven deadly sins.

The ascetic retreat to the desert to do battle with demons was done in imitation of Christ. According to the Gospels, Jesus withdrew into the Judean wilderness for forty days after his baptism. There, in the tree-less and rocky scrub between Jerusalem and the Dead Sea, he was "tempted by the devil" three times. When "the tempter" goaded Jesus to sate his hunger and prove his powers by turning stones into bread, he was unmoved. As Matthew's Gospel puts it with characteristic under-statement, Jesus fasted for forty days, "and afterwards he was hungry."

"Forty days" has long been understood as biblical shorthand for an indeterminate time of testing. There were forty days and forty nights of rain during the great flood in Genesis, it took forty days for the prophet Elijah to reach Mount Sinai, and on three separate occa-sions, Moses retreated to the summit of the same mountain—the mountain of God, also known as Mount Horeb—for forty days. After one such visit he returned with the Ten Commandments. "Forty days" remains entrenched in our lexicon as the length of the Lenten fast and our term for a time of protective isolation. In Italian, *quaran-tena* refers to the forty days that port cities kept foreign ships waiting in the harbor to help stem the spread of the plague. One hopes they were well provisioned.

As the New Testament describes it, Jesus's forty-day retreat into the Judean wilderness was a time of preparation. He was readying himself for the labor of his public ministry, which began only after he returned from the desert. In Luke's telling, Jesus's visit to the house of Martha and Mary came later, well after his time in the wilderness, but as Nikos Kazantzakis reframes the encounter in his controversial

1955 novel *The Last Temptation of Christ,* Jesus emerged from the desert only to stumble upon the open door of their house. Inside, Kazantzakis writes, it "smelled of cypress wood and quince." Martha set a stool before the hearth, then gathered kindling to light a fire. She had no idea who Jesus was or from where he had come, but she offered the stranger "bread, honey and a brass pot of wine."

In Martin Scorsese's cinematic adaptation of Kazantzakis's novel, Martha and Mary's house is perched at the edge of the wilderness, the last stop before the land of the living gives way to the desert of demons. After an exhausted and sunburned Jesus—played by a young Willem Dafoe—has rested and eaten, he thanks Martha and Mary for their hospitality. Then he speaks with them kindly. He says nothing about Mary having chosen the better part. In this telling of the story, it is Martha who admonishes Jesus. She tells him that God wants a man like him not out fasting in the desert but married, making a home and raising children. This last temptation of imagined domestic tranquility is what pulled the desert fathers back to civilization too.

Though it may seem innocuous, few interpretations of Jesus's life have spurred as much outrage as the idea that he might have been married. In 2012, before it was discredited as a forgery, an ancient scrap of papyrus inscribed with a few lines of Coptic set off a furor when reports emerged that it quoted Jesus as saying, "My wife . . ." Conveniently, the rest was cut off.

For many unmarried celibates in late antiquity, the Judean Desert was a permanent abode. Wandering from their monasteries into the *paneremos* of the open desert was a Lenten retreat, one that evoked both Jesus's forty days and the forty years of the Israelites. Today, walking into the Judean wilderness, almost all of it in Israeli-occupied Palestinian territory, is inadvisable without a backpack full of water. Many of the region's Christian monasteries are now in ruins, as are the elaborate catchment systems that once channeled rainwater from rare desert downpours into underground cisterns before it was lost to wadis, the usually dry river valleys that scar the wilderness there and whose name comes from Arabic.

Some of the Judean Desert's monasteries, however, are still inhabited. Clinging to a cliff high above the Kidron Valley east of Bethlehem is the Greek Orthodox Monastery of Mar Saba, which was founded in the late fifth century (see fig. 18). Saint Saba's body is still there, dressed in priestly finery and displayed in a glass case. Stacked neatly nearby are hundreds of skulls, remains of some of the monastery's other inhabitants over the past fifteen hundred years. As one of the very oldest Christian monasteries in the world, Mar Saba has a well-earned reputation as a rigorous place. Years ago, when I lived in Jerusalem, I received permission to visit the monastery for a few days and, when I was not in its church or its library, got to know an American monk: a former hippie from San Francisco. One night, as we stood together sipping our tea, leaning out over a railing to gaze into the valley below, he told me about some of the demons he had seen in the desert. Then he gestured down to the wadi and said that one day it would run red with the blood of heretics. I left for Jerusalem the next morning, ahead of schedule.

During several other visits to the Judean wilderness, always with a backpack full of water, I walked among the ruins of its abandoned monasteries with the late Israeli archaeologist Yizhar Hirschfeld. His book *The Judean Desert Monasteries in the Byzantine Period* remains the authority on its subject. Yizhar showed me how to make my way on foot from Jerusalem to Qumran, where the Dead Sea Scrolls were discovered. That stretch of the desert is mountainous, and the final escarpment that descends to the valley floor hundreds of feet below sea level is vertiginously steep, but there are ways through. Parts of ancient footpaths connecting the monasteries are still visible too, including some routes described in detail by Cyril of Scythopolis, a sixth-century historian of monastic life in Palestine. Cyril wrote admiringly of the monks who wandered in the desert, foraging like John the Baptist on roots and grasses to sustain their travels. I usually brought hummus and hard-boiled eggs.

For other late antique writers, wandering in the wilderness was a way of repenting for sins. The seventh-century *Life of Saint Mary of Egypt* tells of a woman who is commemorated annually in Orthodox and Byzantine-rite Catholic churches during the fifth week of Lent. Mary of Egypt was known throughout medieval Europe via the Latin translation of her story in Jacopo de Voragine's *Golden Legend,* and her self-abasement is still upheld as the quintessential example of the Lenten practice of penitence. According to her tale, Mary spent forty-seven years alone in the Judean wilderness, decades of exposure that left her so emaciated, bent, and sun blackened that she was scarcely recognizable as human. Icons of Mary usually depict her white haired and barefoot, ribs exposed beneath a sagging tunic. But it was not always thus with Mary.

In her youth, in the bustling port of Alexandria, Mary worked as a prostitute—except that, by her own admission, her appetite for sex was so unrelenting that she never charged for her services: doing so would just slow the flow of customers. Instead, Mary made her living by spinning flax and begging.

One day, Mary got word that a ship filled with Christian pilgrims was about to set sail for Palestine. She decided to join and paid for her own passage the only way she knew how. Eventually, she arrived in Jerusalem and tried to enter the Holy Sepulchre to venerate the holy cross along with the tide of other pilgrims, some of whom had been her clients. They went into the shrine, but Mary found her way blocked. An unseen force was preventing her from entering. On seeing an icon of the Virgin outside the church, Mary immediately realized that it was her dissolute life that was keeping her from the holy shrine of Christ. Sobbing before the icon of the Virgin, the mother of God, who is described as "immaculate in body and soul," Mary of Egypt prayed that the door to the Holy Sepulchre would be opened to

FIGURE 18. Mar Saba Monastery, Judean Desert.

her. If it was, she promised, she would renounce her past and go wherever the Virgin told her to go. As Mary's plaintive tears fell to the ground, the force blocking the door dissipated and was replaced with an enveloping warmth. Mary adored the cross inside the church, then returned outside to the image of the Virgin. The icon spoke to her. It told her to head east to the Jordan River, which flows south from the Sea of Galilee and empties into the Dead Sea near Qumran.

It was the third hour, nine o'clock in the morning, when Mary left Jerusalem and began walking toward the wilderness. By sunset, she was there.

This part of the story is supposedly of Mary's own telling, but it is embedded within a larger narration by Zosimas, a priest from one of the monasteries in the Judean Desert. According to him, it was a tradition of his monastery for the brothers to wander alone in the wilderness during Lent, toting with them whatever provisions they liked. Zosimas mentions his own supply of figs, lentils, and dates.

One year during his Lenten wanderings, Zosimas approached the banks of the Jordan. There he encountered a white-haired phantom, which scurried across a wadi and up the slope of its farther side. After a brief chase, the monk caught up to his quarry and saw that his phantom was actually a naked old woman. He averted his eyes and tossed her his cloak. Then Mary began to tell him her story.

For years, she explained, she had struggled against a blazing fire, an incandescent desire for meat, sex, and wine. Through great asceticism and unceasing prayer that flooded the desert with her tears, Mary slowly extinguished her desires. Moved by this story of ascetic repentance, Zosimas returned to the Jordan the following Lent to bring Mary the Eucharist (see plate 7). When he found her, she was on the river's far side. Before he could think up a plan to reach her, Mary made the sign of the cross and strode atop the water.

The next Lent, Zosimas returned to the desert again. This time he found Mary dead. He also found a note, apparently written by Mary herself, inscribed in the ground by her head: "Father Zosimas," it said, "bury the body of the humble Mary in this place. Return dust to dust and pray always to the Lord for me." Lacking a shovel, the priest struggled to dig her a grave. Then a lion arrived and began licking the dead woman's feet. Sensing that the beast was mourning Mary's death, Zosimas warily enlisted its help. After the digging was done—by paw and by hand—the two went their separate ways: the lion to the inner desert, gentle as a lamb; the monk back to his monastery, where he told his brothers the story.

Tales of so-called holy harlots like Mary of Egypt are a beloved subgenre of Christian hagiography. In yet another, one written and narrated by a man named Jacob the Deacon—women's stories are always retold by men—we learn about Saint Pelagia, an actress and courtesan from Antioch. Attesting to its great popularity, the *Life of Pelagia* is preserved in scores of manuscripts in multiple languages: Greek, Latin, Syriac, Arabic, and Old Slavonic just some among them.

After a kindly bishop converted Pelagia to Christianity, she traded in her pearls and perfume for the white alb of baptism. Then the devil appeared, shrieking at her, furious to have lost his lady to Christ. Like Mary of Egypt, Pelagia soon found her way to Jerusalem. But instead of wandering into the wilderness, she began a new life as a hermit, enclosed in a cell on the Mount of Olives near the village of Bethany. Her reputation for holiness spread quickly among the monks of Jerusalem and the city's nearby desert. But they knew nothing of her past. In fact, they knew nothing of *her* at all. The severity of Pelagia's asceticism had withered her once remarkable beauty away, erasing every trace of femininity. Insofar as the monks were concerned, Pelagia was a man: a beardless eunuch named Pelagi*us*. Her true identity and her past were revealed only in death, when the body of the actress and that of the eunuch became one, stripped naked to be anointed with myrrh.

These stories about Mary of Egypt and Pelagia of Antioch communicate a discomfiting truth about saints in the Christian tradition:

women cannot be holy as women. By nature, all women are Eve, the cause of the Fall. For a woman to become holy, she must transcend her sex—through either a martyrdom that kills it or an asceticism that shrouds it.

Take the remarks of Gregory of Nyssa as an example. Even as the fourth-century saint and bishop celebrated the life of his sister, the holy ascetic Macrina, he balked at calling her a woman. In a letter to the monk Olympius, Gregory chummily reminds his friend how they had bumped into each other in Antioch when Gregory was on his way to Jerusalem. Gregory recalls that their conversation was wide ranging, befitting his interlocutor's expansive intelligence, and that it touched upon the life of a holy woman—his sister Macrina. But Gregory quickly corrects himself: "If, that is, she should be called a woman," he writes, "for I do not know if it is fitting to call her by her sex, she who has so risen above her nature."

Women are bodily creatures. It is only men like Gregory and his learned friend who naturally manifest the higher virtues of mind and spirit. The rare woman—the Macrina, the Mary, the Pelagia—who can shed her body and surpass men with her wisdom occupies a tertiary category of existence: no longer a woman, but not a man either.

The Virgin who showed Mary of Egypt the way from Jerusalem to the Jordan was the icon for all women to emulate. Most late antique and medieval interpreters understood the Virgin's body itself as an enclosure, a locked garden that was never corrupted or penetrated. Even so, the Bible says relatively little about Mary's relationship with Joseph or the conception and birth of Jesus—despite the cultural ubiquity of the Christmas story, which might lead one to think otherwise. Of the four Gospels in the New Testament, only those attributed to Matthew and Luke even mention the nativity, and they do not tell the same story. For those inclined to defend Mary's perpetual virginity, Matthew's Gospel is the problem.

Luke explains that the angel Gabriel went to Nazareth and visited "a virgin engaged to a man whose name was Joseph." The angel in Luke tells Mary not to fear, then says that she will become pregnant by the Holy Spirit even though she is a virgin. Later, Luke tells us that Joseph and Mary traveled to Bethlehem to enroll in the census. There, Mary gave birth to Jesus and—as everyone knows—laid him "in a manger, because there was no place for them in the inn." Throughout the rest of his Gospel, Luke refers to Mary and Joseph as Jesus's parents, but he never comments on any specifics of their marital relationship.

Matthew, by contrast, clearly suggests that although Mary was a virgin when Jesus was conceived, she did not remain that way after he was born. Two passages in the opening chapter of his Gospel are key. First, Matthew says that when "Mary had been engaged to Joseph, *but before they lived together,* she was found to be with child from the Holy Spirit." The operative verb here in Greek, *sunethein,* means "to live together," but it can be used euphemistically in the same way that we might say two people "slept" together. Even if *suneithein* is taken plainly, the way Matthew structures his sentence presumes that Mary and Joseph followed through on their engagement and "lived together" at some point, but that Mary had become pregnant through the Holy Spirit before then.

If this passage does not fully communicate Matthew's meaning, consider a second just a few verses later. This next one is more specific, and it differs from Luke's account in several important ways. Unlike Luke, Matthew says nothing about the angel Gabriel visiting Mary; instead, he tells us that an angel appeared to *Joseph* in a dream. The angel did not come bearing news of Mary's pregnancy—Joseph already knew that the woman to whom he was engaged had somehow become pregnant but "being a righteous man and unwilling to expose her to public disgrace, planned to dismiss her quietly." The purpose of the angel's appearance in Matthew's narrative is to dispel Joseph's fear over taking Mary as his wife, "for the child conceived in her," the angel explains to Joseph, "is from the Holy Spirit." Matthew concludes by noting that the now angelically reassured Joseph did take Mary "as his wife, *but had no marital relations with her until she had borne a son.*" Combined, these two passages point to a single and unambiguous conclusion: for Matthew, Mary's conception of Jesus was divine, but her later relationship with her husband was thoroughly human. Of course, this is not the end of the story.

Another ancient gospel, one not included in the New Testament, tells a radically different tale about Mary. This second-century Greek text, known as the *Protoevangelium of James,* deeply influenced the development of Marian theology in the Christian tradition and the practice of early and medieval Christian asceticism. In blending elements of the nativity stories from Matthew and Luke with its own novel account of Jesus's birth, the *Protoevangelium* agrees with these Gospels that Mary was a virgin when she conceived Jesus by the Holy Spirit, but then it goes on to insist that the physical nature of Mary's virginity remained intact during and after Jesus's birth. As its name suggests, this "Pre-Gospel" of James is intended as a prequel to the good news: it narrates the events leading up to and including Jesus's birth but then, after a brief denouement, quickly comes to an end. Said another way, the *Protoevangelium* tells not Jesus's story but Mary's.

According to the *Protoevangelium,* Mary's birth and upbringing were special. An angel had appeared to Mary's aging mother, Anna, and told her that she would conceive a child. In thanksgiving, Anna promised the child as a gift to the Lord. True to her word, Anna and her husband, Joachim, brought their daughter to the Temple when she was just three years old. Mary lived there peacefully until she reached the age of twelve. But then the priests and elders grew concerned. Mary was on the verge of becoming a woman, and her first menstruation would "defile the sanctuary of the Lord."

To find a new home for her outside the Temple, the priests summoned every widower in Judea to come to Jerusalem and wait for a sign. A dove landed on Joseph's head, indicating his divine selection as the one to take the "virgin of the Lord." But his union with Mary is not anything like the one that Matthew described. Initially, Joseph resists his selection, explaining to all who will listen that it is improper for him—an old man with grown sons—to take a twelve-year-old girl into his care. Here, as elsewhere in the tale, the author of the *Protoevangelium* is quick to contrast Joseph's age with Mary's youth. The reason is obvious: Joseph will never be Mary's husband. He is her guardian.

Four years later, when Mary is sixteen, Joseph is called away for some time to oversee a building project in another city. When he returns, Mary is six months pregnant. As Joseph wails in shame, wracked with anxiety over how the priests will deal with the corruption of this young Temple virgin who had been entrusted to him, Mary insists that she has never known a man. Soon, her word is confirmed. The high priest forces Mary and Joseph to drink "the water of the ordeal," which is supposed to strike down those who partake of it unworthily. But nothing happens. With the stain of Mary's impurity erased and her miraculous pregnancy confirmed, the *Protoevangelium* takes its cue from Luke's Gospel and explains that Caesar Augustus called for all in Judea to return to their homes to be enrolled in the census. Again, Joseph is anxious: he can enroll himself and sons, but what is he to say about this pregnant girl who is neither his wife nor his daughter?

As Mary is unable to walk the distance to Bethlehem, Joseph saddles an ass for her. One son leads the animal while Joseph follows on foot. When they are still at the outskirts of Bethlehem, in the *chōra* beyond the city, Mary calls for Joseph to take her down, explaining that her child presses forth from within. Joseph spots a cave in the desert in which to hide Mary from view, then hurries toward Bethlehem in search of a midwife. By chance, he encounters one coming down from the hills. Hastily, he explains that he was selected to care for a virgin, that the virgin then conceived a child through the Holy Spirit, and that they must now return to the cave in the desert where she is about to give birth.

Meanwhile, a luminous cloud hovers above the cave where Mary waits for the midwife. But before the midwife can enter to help, Jesus is born in a blinding flash of light. Then the awed midwife visits Mary and her newborn son in the cave. Eventually, she leaves to return to Bethlehem, but before she has gone very far she encounters a woman named Salome. Explaining herself, the midwife tells Salome that she has just witnessed a miracle: a virgin gave birth in a cave. Scoffing at the preposterous story, Salome tells the midwife that she will never believe such a thing until she can manually inspect the supposed virgin's condition herself. So, like doubting Thomas extending his fingers into the gash on Jesus's side, Salome enters the cave and reaches for Mary. At once, her hand withers as if blackened by fire. Salome's faithlessness is quickly forgiven when an angel appears and tells her to hold her hand out for the infant to heal.

Soon we are back in more familiar territory. Now borrowing from Matthew, the author of the *Protoevangelium* tells of the star that leads the Magi to Jesus with their gifts of gold, frankincense, and myrrh. After the wise men depart for home, Mary wraps her baby in swaddling clothes and, fearing the wrath of King Herod, hides him in an ox stall.

Parts of the *Protoevangelium* remain quietly hidden in the Christmas story as we know it today. Luke mentions shepherds and the manger, of course, but neither he nor Matthew ever says anything about an ox or an ass. Yet there they are, curiously watching over Jesus in every nativity scene from your grandmother's crèche to Duccio's *Maestà* (see fig. 19).

Some of the most enduring depictions of the incidents in Mary's life as they are narrated in the *Protoevangelium* are also among the best remaining examples of high Byzantine art. At the Chora Church

FIGURE 19. Center panel of "The Nativity with the Prophets Isaiah and Ezekiel" from the *Maestà* by Duccio di Buoninsegna, 1308–11. National Gallery of Art, Washington, DC.

in Constantinople, otherwise known as the Church of the Holy Savior in the Fields—the unsown, virgin fields beyond the city walls—there are Greek inscriptions in the mosaics that play with the word *chōra* to name Jesus and Mary. Jesus is the *Chōra tōn Zōntōn*, or "Land of the Living." Meanwhile, Mary and her holy womb are honored as the *Chōra tou Achōrētou*—the "Enclosure of the Unenclosable."

6 *The Miracles of the Dead*

The tale is set across the Narrow Sea, at a tavern in Flanders, where the riotous cursing of three drunk young gamblers and their shouts for more wine join with the rattle of dice, the songs of "syngeres with harpes," the quick steps of dancing girls, and the lows of those hawking fruit. Then, deep over the tavern's cacophony, a funeral bell tolls.

Sobered by its sound, one of the gamblers sends his young servant out to see whose corpse it is "that passeth heer." But the boy already knows. Last night, he tells the gambler, "an old felawe of youres" was taken by Death, he who "hath a thousand slayn" during "this pestilence." Fortified by a desire for vengeance and the "wyn of Spaigne," the gamblers spring to their feet "al dronken" in rage, and together they swear "many a grisly ooth" to bring death upon Death.

Not "fully half a mile" from the tavern in their quest for Death, the gamblers cross paths with a hooded old wanderer, a man pale and withered of face who knows more than it seems. If the gamblers wish "to fynde Deeth," the man says as a simple matter of fact, they need only "turne up this croked way." They will find him waiting for them in a grove beneath an oak tree. Yet instead of Death beneath the oak, the gamblers find "eighte busshels" of lustrous gold coins. Abandoning their search for Death in favor of the unexpected riches, "the worste of hem" turns to the other two. Jolly though their find may be, they must wait, he says, to carry it off "by nyghte," lest the villagers see and have them hanged as thieves.

The gamblers draw lots as they wait for darkness to overtake the grove. The marked one, and with it the errand to fetch "breed and wyn" from town, falls to the youngest of the three; the others stay behind, promising to watch the "tresor wel." Once the youngest is gone, "the worste" hatches his plan: Surely, he asks the other, gold is better divided two ways than three? Later, when the youngest returns with the evening's bread and wine, the others welcome him back rowdily, as if in "pleye." Then, as he sets his burden down, they pull their daggers and "ryve hym thurgh the sydes."

With the youngest dead, the worst relaxes his guard: "Now let us sitte and drynke, and make us merie, and afterward we wol his body berie." But a few toasts into their merrymaking, the two murderers realize with horror that they were not the only ones who had coveted coins "faire and brighte." During his trip to town, the youngest had stopped at an apothecary's shop. Explaining himself to the proprietor, he feigned need of a "confiture" to kill his rats and, for added effect, the pesky polecat that kept devouring his chickens. On the next street over, the youngest borrowed "large botelles thre." One he "kepte clene for his drynke." Into the others? "His poyson poured he."

This sordid tale of the three gamblers who did find Death beneath an oak is a late medieval exemplum about greed. It takes as its theme a four-word passage from the Vulgate, the common Latin version of the Bible: "Radix malorum est cupiditas"—loosely translated, "The love of money is the root of all evil."

Medieval preachers often relied on exempla like this to make moral lessons more vivid in their sermons. It was, after all, one thing to condemn unbridled greed and then quote the Bible for support, but quite another to explain the Bible's message through a tale that memorably exemplifies the consequences of cupidity.

The irony of this particular exemplum about greed is that its narrator enriched himself through its telling. For this is "The Pardoner's Tale," one of at least two dozen stories composed by Geoffrey Chaucer for his late fourteenth-century collection *The Canterbury Tales*. Chaucer's tales, which are framed as entries in a storytelling contest that helps to pass the time during a sixty-mile pilgrimage from London to Canterbury, are told by a motley (and mostly corrupt) group of fictional travelers. Among them are a monk, a knight, a ploughman, a friar, a wife, and three nuns. As the title of the tale about the three gamblers suggests, its teller is a pardoner—which is to say, someone who sells papal indulgences, or pardons of punishment for temporal sins. In his case, these transactions are by way of fund-raising for a London hospital founded by the Spanish sisters of Our Lady of Roncesvalles.

The pardoner's labors on behalf of a Catholic hospital may sound charitable, but he has no more scruples than the gamblers in his tale. In the prologue to his story, he admits to his traveling companions that he has no desire to follow in the footsteps of the apostles. He wants to live pleasantly, full of purse and belly, and that means acquiring "moneie, wolle, chese, and whete." He boasts that he would pocket the last coin of "the povereste wydwe in a village" even if he knew it meant that her children would "sterve for famyne."

The pardoner dresses the part of a pious pilgrim—a badge certifying his visit to see Rome's Veronica is sewn on his hat—but everything about him is false. When he preaches in a village church, his theme is always the same: "Radix malorum est cupiditas." He begins by telling the villagers who he is and where he is from. Then, to silence potential objections to his demands for money, he brandishes his official-looking papal seals and letters of authorization. To warm up the crowd and impress them all the more with his learning, he peppers his sermon with some well-placed phrases in Latin. Once his preaching has neared its crescendo, he pulls out the grand finale: a traveling bag stuffed with rags and bones. Among the tools the pardoner carries to pry coins from the credulous is a tattered bit of sail from Saint Peter's fishing boat and the shoulder bone of a "hooly Jewes sheep." His mutton broth is curative, the pardoner explains. Just dip the bone in a well, and its water will heal any animal that drinks from it.

Despite detailing his deceptions to those traveling with him, the pardoner still has the gall to warn his fellow pilgrims against "the synne of avarice." Not to worry, though: his "hooly pardoun" can heal their sin, but only so long as they "offre nobles or sterlynges, or elles silver broches, spoones, [or] rynges." The host of the traveling party, the one who organized the storytelling contest, curses the pardoner for his greed and accuses him of being so foul a liar that he would surely offer his own shit-stained underpants for others to kiss and then swear their lips had touched "a relyk of a seint."

Chaucer invented the pilgrims in his *Canterbury Tales,* but Canterbury itself—and the renowned shrine of its martyred archbishop, Saint Thomas Becket—is anything but fictional. Just before vespers on December 29, 1170, a cold Christmastide Tuesday, four knights acting at the behest of King Henry II split open the archbishop's skull and scattered his brains across the floor of his own cathedral.

Within little more than two years of his death, Thomas Becket had already been papally and popularly proclaimed a saint. One monk who knew him had nearly finished the first narrative collection of the saint's posthumous miracles; a second, and ultimately longer, collection by another Canterbury monk was also under way. The martyr's blood, mopped from the stones of the cathedral, was preserved as a wonder-working elixir, heavily diluted and distributed to pilgrims in healing phials. Doses of this "Canterbury water" are cited as the cause of dozens of miracles in the monks' collections.

In the summer of 1220, fifty years after Becket's death, a new shrine was erected for his relics at the eastern end of Canterbury Cathedral, which began attracting as many as two hundred thousand pilgrims per year. The Kentish Downs, near the White Cliffs of Dover, thus became one of the most important pilgrimage sites in the medieval world, surpassed by only Rome, the Holy Land, and Santiago de Compostela—the shrine of Saint James in Spain.

Despite Becket's wide reputation as a healer, the number of new miracles attributed to him waned over the course of the thirteenth century. By the end of the fourteenth, when Chaucer was writing, new ones were rare. In part, it seems that monastic registrars simply lost interest in recording the story of yet another woman who had regained her sight, yet another ship the saint had saved from a storm. Or maybe, some wondered, did a saint just have a limited ration of miracles to give?

The nature of divine intervention in the world was in question too. In the middle of the fourteenth century, the Black Death wiped out up to half the population of Europe, slaughtering an estimated twenty-five million men, women, and children at the peak of its virulence, between 1347 and 1351. The incomprehensible magnitude of loss that the living were left to confront profoundly affected every element of medieval society, from its economic and civic organization to its art, religion, and literature. When the gambler's servant mentions the thousands taken by Death during "this pestilence," he means the plague. Although cults of new, so-called plague saints arose in response to what had happened, by then the formerly luminous era of medieval pilgrimage had entered its twilight.

Peregrinus, the Latin word for "pilgrim," has never had an exclusively religious connotation. The term is more general, used to refer to any sort of nomad or stranger—hence the name of the peregrine falcon, the most widespread raptor on earth, with a range that covers much of every continent except Antarctica. Unlike the speedy falcon, most medieval travelers kept relatively close to home. Still, there were many thousands of long haulers who wandered very far afield, enduring journeys of months—sometimes years.

In addition to visiting Rome, Santiago de Compostela, and the Shrine of the Three Kings in Cologne, Chaucer's Wife of Bath made the trip to the Holy Land three times. Impressive as this is, the earliest nonfictional itinerary of a Christian pilgrim to the Holy Land is that of an anonymous voyager from Bordeaux who logged his travels between 333 and 334. The Bordeaux pilgrim's terse journal entries, which chart his day-to-day progress across an extensive network of Roman roads, are an exercise in good record keeping, an odometer of milestones walked between each turn and stop.

By the era of Thomas Becket, such pilgrimage routes were well worn. The twelfth-century *Peregrinatio Compostellana,* possibly the world's first tourist guidebook, is a medieval *Lonely Planet* that advised travelers on local food and customs, safe river crossings, alternate routes, and ancient relics. Written for French visitors to the shrine of Saint James, the *Peregrinatio* focuses primarily on northern Spain, leading pilgrims westward over five hundred miles of daily stages from Roncesvalles, on the southern slopes of the Pyrenees, to the eventual terminus of the way at Santiago de Compostela, near the Atlantic coast. The guidebook's haughty author (likely a French monk from Poitou) singles out the Basque for especially rough treatment, comparing their language to barking dogs and their custom of eating from a communal dish to gorging pigs at a trough. As for swarthy Navarrese men, they were fond of cunnilingus, which they performed on both "women and mules." Cultural prejudices aside, the *Peregrinatio* is a wealth of knowledge that warns its readers where they might encounter every conceivable sort of danger—from horseflies and quicksand to bad wine and ruthless toll collectors.

Pilgrims were supposed to be exempt from tolls, and some were shielded from extortion and harassment by letters of safe passage, but the very existence of these letters only underscores the dangers and other difficulties of long-distance travel. Even in the best of circumstances, a pilgrimage was hard. Overland progress was slow, and delays due to illness, injury, and inclement weather were all but inevitable. Many took the risk anyway. Some were compelled to travel as penance for sin. For others, a saint's shrine was a last resort, the only hope of relief from some persistent or incapacitating malady that local doctors could not cure. As saints preferred to work their wonders at their shrines, praying at home was not as effective. So for those most in need of a miracle, the journey was all the slower still.

Not everyone went on pilgrimage hoping for a cure. Some made the voyage to fulfill a vow or to thank a saint in person for a miracle that had already been granted. This reciprocal relationship is evidenced by the ex-votos (literally, "from the vow") that pilgrims left for saints at their shrines. Coins were common offerings. They were often intentionally bent in half, to signal their unusability as currency. Other pilgrims left wax molds of healed body parts: eyes, hands, feet. Miniature wax ships commissioned by anxious seafarers were especially ubiquitous memorials of gratitude. Simple wax candles were popular too. Pilgrims to Canterbury often called out to be "measured for Saint Thomas." A measuring thread was stretched from toe to crown, cut to size, and then twisted into a wick for the candle that would be offered to the saint.

Measuring was a practice with an ancient precedent. The anonymous sixth-century pilgrim from Piacenza (the one who mentioned the fizzing ampullae of oil at the Holy Sepulchre) explained how some pilgrims made their own "measures" at various sites in

Jerusalem. Thin strips of cloth, tailor-cut by pilgrims themselves, marked the distance between the imprints of Jesus's hands on the column where he was scourged. Others measured the gap between his footprints on the stone where he stood before Pilate. The Piacenza pilgrim noted that travelers wore these measures of their Lord's suffering around their necks, like scarves, to heal "all manner of ailments."

With so many wondrous things to see and to do, some pilgrims undertook their journeys voluntarily, as either expressions of piety or, quite simply, little adventures. The flourishing of prescribed routes to prescribed destinations following the prescribed advice of guidebooks like the *Peregrinatio Compostellana* transformed pilgrimage into a package tour. Pilgrims had high expectations for the experience, and each shrine had to deliver on its promise. Pilgrimage also meant participation. Who would travel all the way to the Holy Land just to gaze upon some empty desert vista? When the Piacenza pilgrim writes of those taking measures at the sites where Jesus was tortured, he adds that he saw "the sponge and the reed" that were used to hoist a mouthful of sour wine up to Jesus on the cross. Then he humbly brags that he drank from the same sponge himself.

Eventually, pilgrimage became so ensconced in the medieval economy and so choreographed to provide memorable moments for the tourist that it dictated how some churches were built. Trinity Chapel, into which Becket's relics were ceremoniously translated on July 7, 1220, was erected, as Robert Bartlett explains, in an "attempt to allow a smooth flow of pilgrims" through Canterbury Cathedral, by way of "an ambulatory around the east end." At Canterbury and other "so-called pilgrimage churches," Bartlett continues, visitors were herded through designated entrances and exits so they could venerate the saint without traipsing through the choir and disrupting the monks, who "maintained their perpetual round of prayer and chant."

Outside the shrine, or in the shops of the surrounding town, a pilgrim could buy a new walking staff for the journey home or maybe replace a worn scrip, as the traveler's shoulder bag was called. Of course, no pilgrimage was complete without a souvenir to remember the trip. By the twelfth century, this typically meant a pressed-metal badge bearing an image of the saint or shrine. Two small panels from Jan van Eyck's celebrated *Ghent Altarpiece* imagine hermits and pilgrims on the road (see plate 8). In the panel on the right, Saint Christopher—the giant of a man draped in red and the patron saint of Christian travelers—strides ahead. Behind him walks a pilgrim with two badges pinned to his hat. One is clearly a scallop shell, certifying a visit to the shrine of Saint James.

As pilgrims traveled to shrines to experience the holy and offer personal tokens of their gratitude, they occasionally left behind traces more permanent than the wax from their candles. The most indelible tactile memory I have of the Holy Sepulchre is of some of these traces. Covering the walls of the staircase that descends to the chapel built where Constantine's mother found the holy cross are thousands of other crosses, each inscribed on stone by a pilgrim. Their beveled edges, long since smoothed by centuries of fingers, repeat that most fundamental of human messages again and again: *I was here.*

The same message—if in different form—appears somewhere in Cana, the Galilean village where, according to John's Gospel, Jesus once attended a wedding. Though the Piacenza pilgrim admits his unworthiness to perform the act, he informs his readers that he carved his parents' names on what he was told was the same couch upon which Jesus was reclining at the wedding when he turned water into wine. The miracle, John says, was "the first of his signs."

A miracle is a cause of wonder, an event inexplicable through appeal to the natural order of things, and the first of Jesus's signs at the beginning of his public ministry in the Galilee was a portent of what was to come. The Gospels describe Jesus as an especially able manipulator of water. He could turn it into wine, he could walk across it, he could calm it in a storm, and he could order his disciples to cast their nets into it and haul up a catch so teeming with fish that it nearly swamped their boat.

Jesus could also use water in the form of his own spit to make broken men whole. John tells the story of Jesus encountering a man who was born blind. Jesus "spat on the ground and made mud with the saliva." Then, John says, Jesus "spread the mud on the man's eyes, saying to him, 'Go, wash in the pool of Siloam.' Then he went and washed and came back able to see." Mark relates a similar story about a man who was deaf and mute. Jesus took the man aside, "in private, away from the crowd, and put his fingers into his ears." Again, Jesus spat. This time he touched the man's tongue "and said to him, 'Ephphatha,'" Aramaic for "Be opened." At once, the man's "ears were opened, his tongue was released, and he spoke plainly."

The occasional quotation of an Aramaic word or phrase in Mark's Gospel, which, like the rest of the New Testament, is written in Greek, is usually tied to a momentous event. The deaf man was healed with spit and *ephphatha*. Mark refers to the spot where Jesus was crucified as *Golgotha,* which he glosses as "the place of the skull." And Jesus's lamentation from the cross "Eloi, Eloi, lema sabachthani" Mark renders as "My God, my God, why have you forsaken me?" In another healing story in Mark, Jesus again speaks to someone privately in Aramaic. In this case, it is a young girl who is believed to have just died. After dismissing the crowd around the girl's parents, Jesus leads them back into their house. Then he takes their daughter by the hand and says to her, "Talitha cum," which Mark helpfully translates for his non-Aramaic-speaking audience as "Little girl, stand up!"

John's Gospel takes things further. There we read that Lazarus, the brother of Martha and Mary, not only was dead when Jesus brought him back to life but "had been in the tomb four days." As if to emphasize the point, Martha audibly comments on the stench of her brother's putrefying corpse when Jesus tells his followers to "take away the stone" from the entrance to his tomb. Again, Jesus's command is direct, though this time recorded in Greek: "Lazarus, come out!" he shouts into the depths of the cave.

According to the Gospels, Jesus's ability to control both natural phenomena and death extended to the realm of the demons. Mark, Matthew, and Luke—whose works are collectively known as the synoptic Gospels, for their tendency, unlike John's, to narrate the events of Jesus's ministry in a similar order and in similar ways—all tell a story about a boy prone to seizures. Mark and Luke explain his foaming mouth and gnashing teeth as the results of his being seized by a spirit. Matthew calls it a demon. In Matthew's version, the boy's father tells Jesus that his son "often falls into the fire and often into the water." In Mark's account, the father says that when the spirit seizes his son, "it dashes him down." From Luke we learn that the boy shrieks and then the spirit "mauls him." Narrative details aside, the story is the same. And by all accounts, the boy's father was desperate. He had brought his son to Jesus's disciples, hoping they would be able to cure him, but they were not up to the task. Of course, Jesus has no trouble rebuking the spirit and casts it out of the boy at once, but he is exasperated with his followers and berates them as a "faithless generation." In a different episode, in John's Gospel, he scolds Martha again too. Before Jesus calls Lazarus out from his tomb, he has to remind Martha to be faithful: "Did I not tell you," he says, "that if you believed, you would see the glory of God?"

In yet another healing story told by the three writers of the synoptic Gospels, Jesus remarks approvingly on the faith of several villagers. They had brought him a paralytic, confident that Jesus would make him walk again. As Mark and Luke tell it, the villagers were so eager that instead of shoving their way through the crowd around Jesus, they tore off part of the roof of the house where he was speaking so they could lower the man down to him on a mat. As the man descends from the rafters, Jesus, in an unexpected twist, does not heal him. Instead, he says, "Your sins are forgiven."

Then the scribes who have gathered to listen to Jesus preach begin to whisper. Jesus knows why. They murmur of blasphemy, knowing that only God can forgive sins. "Which is easier," Jesus demands of them, "to say, 'Your sins are forgiven,' or to say, 'Stand up and walk'?" He does not wait for a response but rather seems to answer them: "So that you may know that the Son of Man has authority on earth to forgive sins . . ." Then he addresses the paralytic: "Stand up, take your mat and go to your home." When the paralyzed man does as he is told and simply stands up and leaves, all there to witness the miracle are stunned.

The story of the paralytic's healing was a reprimand of the scribes and Pharisees, those scrupulous observers of the Jewish law who were so assured of their own sanctity. In asking whether it is easier to forgive sins or command a paralytic to walk, Jesus tried to trap them in the same sort of rhetorical *either/or* that they so often used to test him. What cannot be overlooked here, though, is the clear connection that Jesus draws between moral virtue and physical health. The same link is made in the story of the man born blind. But there it is Jesus's disciples who ask whether it was the man's sins or those of his parents that had caused him to be unable to see. Neither, Jesus says. The man "was born blind so that God's works might be revealed in him." And "*we,*" Jesus says to his disciples, "must work the works of him who sent me while it is day; night is coming when no one can work."

The long night "when no one can work" never seems to have come. Not even after Jesus, "the light of the world," was gone. According to the Acts of the Apostles, his followers (despite the hiccup with the epileptic boy) remained capable of performing "signs and wonders" in his name. For ancient Christians, the saints and martyrs inherited the mantle of the apostles. They were the next intercessors between humans and God. They were the new lights who illumined the way to the Light.

Among the most renowned of these living lights was a man we have already met, Saint Simeon the Stylite: the monk who sealed himself in his hut for forty days in imitation of Jesus's time in the desert. But Simeon was much better known for a considerably longer and more public ascetic pursuit. According to his biographers, Simeon's ascetic magnum opus was a decades-long performance. Venturing out into the Syrian wilderness northeast of Antioch, he climbed atop an open-air pillar and proceeded to stand there in prayer—for the next thirty-seven years. While still alive and standing upright on his pillar, Simeon himself became a pilgrimage shrine whose wonders were known throughout the world (see fig. 20). As the bishop and church historian Theodoret of Cyrrhus explains in his account of Simeon's life, travelers flocked to the monk as if his column were the axis of a compass. Britons and Persians, Ethiopians and Scythians—all of them hastened to Simeon, hoping "to receive from him what they could not receive from nature."

Theodoret knew that many would doubt the stories of Simeon's miracles. But the skeptics, he says, are those not yet initiated "into divine things." Those who have already embraced the gospel know that Simeon was no charlatan. His miracles carried on the work of the Lord in imitation of the one "who told the paralytic to carry his mat." Transfigured in Christ, Simeon was a "dazzling lamp," Theodoret says, who "sent out rays in all directions," lighting the way to the

FIGURE 20. Clay token depicting "Mar Simeon" (Saint Simeon the Stylite) standing on his column and flanked by angels and pilgrims, c. 600. Courtesy of the Royal Ontario Museum, Toronto.

desert for those who had not yet heard the name of Jesus to come and receive "the benefit of divine baptism."

The most influential analyst of miracles in the ancient Christian world lived far from the Syrian wilderness, across the Mediterranean on the shores of Roman Africa. Before he was initiated "into divine things," Saint Augustine of Hippo was one of those skeptics to whom Theodoret refers. Augustine came to Christianity slowly—his interest was purely intellectual at first—but a miracle accelerated his embrace of the faith. He was there in Milan, in June 386, when Saint Ambrose discovered the relics of Saint Gervasius and Saint Protasius, and he wrote about the blind man who regained his sight when the martyrs' bones were processed to the city's new basilica. The following Easter, Augustine was baptized. He mentions the blind man in the *Confessions,* his memoir of conversion, but it was not until forty years after the fact, in the final book of his magisterial defense of Christianity, *The City of God,* that Augustine would use the events in Milan to more fully explain how miracles (and relics) bring people to Christ.

Milan, Augustine reminds his readers at the end of *The City of God,* is a large city. And the miracle of the blind man who regained his sight was witnessed by an immense crowd, one that included even the emperor and his entourage. But, Augustine continues, slowly making his point, if it is the case that miracles like the one in Milan exist to confirm the grandest miracle of all—the bodily resurrection of Christ—then even those quiet wonders that happen in out-of-the-way places far from imperial cities deserve to be publicized for all to hear. Following his own advice, Augustine then tells story after story of lesser-known miracles closer to his home, in Hippo and Carthage and all the littler villages that once dotted the coast of Africa Proconsularis. He writes of a doctor relieved of his gout, a comedian cured of paralysis, a farmer saved from a demon. (The farmer's trick was to hang a bag of Jerusalem dirt in the middle of his room.)

Then there is the story of the tailor who lost his coat. A poor man, he ventured to the shrine of the Twenty Martyrs in Hippo to pray that he might somehow get a replacement. Overhearing the tailor's plea, several youths at the shrine ridiculed him, mocking this ignorant old man as if he had asked the martyrs for money. He retreated in silence to the shore of the sea. There he came across a huge fish, just washed up and gasping for air. Augustine tells us that the old tailor, with the "good-natured" help of the youths, then lugged this miraculous catch straight to a cook, to whom he sold the fish for enough money to buy wool to make a new coat. But the story does not end there. The cook, Augustine explains, was himself a pious Christian, and when he sliced open the fish to clean it, he found a gold ring hiding in its gullet. Hurrying to the tailor with the ring, the virtuous cook exclaimed, "See how the Twenty Martyrs have clothed you!"

One of the central miracle stories in Augustine's collection is that of Innocentia, a noblewoman from Carthage. She was diagnosed with breast cancer, Augustine tells us, and given two options for treatment. Neither was palatable. A mastectomy beneath the knife of a fifth-century surgeon would mean trauma and danger that need no elaboration; alternatively, and as her physician advised, she could accept her inevitable death and thereby allow him to follow that old maxim of Hippocrates, "First, do no harm." But around the time of Easter, when the catechumens were being baptized, Innocentia had a dream. In it, she was instructed to ask the first woman who emerged from the waters of baptism to make the sign of the cross over her tumorous breast. This she did, and was immediately cured. Again, though, this is not the end of the story. After examining her, Innocentia's flummoxed physician agreed that her cancer had—somehow—disappeared, and he eagerly inquired after what herb or drug she had used to treat it. When Innocentia recounted her dream, the physician snorted in contempt, having expected that she was about to divulge some wondrous medical discovery. Innocentia wryly rejoined that her physician was right to scoff: Christ curing her cancer was nothing wondrous—not when compared to his raising someone who had been *dead* for four days.

When Augustine heard that Innocentia was healed by the sign of the cross, he went to see her himself. He was indignant that so great a miracle, to say nothing of one that had happened to a woman so well respected around town, had not been better publicized. Not even the women with whom Innocentia was most closely acquainted knew how she had been cured. "And," Augustine concludes, "as I had only briefly heard the story, I made her tell how the whole thing happened, from beginning to end, while the other women listened in great astonishment, and glorified God."

For Augustine, the value of a miracle went beyond its benefit to any single individual. Fundamentally, he understood miracle stories as an evangelical tool: a way of broadcasting how Christ, through his saints, continued to intercede in the world. Such is the conclusion of Saint Gregory the Great, who draws upon Augustine's writings about miracles in his *Dialogues,* which he completed in the late sixth century. Far from blithely accepting miracle stories at face value, Gregory encourages a skeptical and rational debate about divine intervention in everyday life. Ultimately, he concludes that miracles do happen. As Theodoret says about Simeon, Gregory says of the saints: they continue the work of the apostles. "We have new miracles," Gregory explains, "in imitation of the old."

In the old miracles—the biblical stories about Jesus and his apostles—wonders unfold with alacrity. With just a word or some spit, ears open, eyes see, and the dead stand. But in the healing stories told by Christians of the postapostolic era, miracles happen often considerably more slowly.

Theodoret is an example of one of these more gradually unfolding miracles. In the *Religious History,* his account of the lives of thirty Syrian monks (including Simeon the Stylite), he explains how his own life was entwined with wonder-working ascetics even before he was born. Years earlier, he says, his mother suffered from an eye problem that no doctor could heal. When she heard that a holy man called Peter the Hermit had cured another woman with a similar complaint just by making the sign of the cross, she "rushed to the man of God." At the time, Theodoret's mother was in the bloom of her youth, a twenty-three-year-old beauty partial to gold jewelry, rich makeup, and woven silk dresses. Peter the Hermit dutifully healed her eye through divine grace and the sign of the cross, but he scolded her for ruining "the image of God" by adorning herself as she had. Again, there is an unmistakable connection here between sin and disease: *vanity* had caused the eye complaint. On returning home, Theodoret's duly chastened mother "washed off her makeup" and from then on spurned fine clothes and jewelry. "In quest of healing for the body," Theodoret says, "she obtained in addition the health of the soul."

With his mother's trust in holy men established, Theodoret later explains that another of these living saints blessed his mother's womb, which had been "prevented by nature from bearing fruit." This time the story is about Macedonius, a monk who roamed the Syrian mountains subsisting on nothing but ground barley soaked in water. Theodoret's father had gone round to many other ascetics, begging each in turn "to ask for children for him from God." Eventually, Macedonius agreed. But—and here we arrive at the slowly unfolding nature of miracles to which late antique Christians had become accustomed—it was another *four years* before Theodoret's mother noticed a "burden in her womb." Macedonius was credited nonetheless.

Many centuries later, such was still the case: if a saint's help had been enlisted, then any cure, no matter how incomplete or long in coming, was ascribed to divine intervention. This connection between a cure and its later certification as a miracle may be key to understanding the monastic records of those medieval pilgrims who ritually engaged saints at their shrines. As Ronald Finucane puts it in his celebrated study of miracles and pilgrims in the medieval world, "Since about nine-tenths of the registered miracles were cures, by asking what the pilgrims meant by 'cure' we are also asking what the majority of them meant by 'miracle'."

Finucane's analysis of miracle registries—the collections of miracle stories written and compiled by monks—suggests that cures were often partial and not always immediate. Many of those who attest to having been cured of blindness, for instance, may not have been congenitally or permanently blind, nor did they necessarily understand blindness and sight as mutually exclusive, forming a binary of darkness and light. Finucane points to seasonal ophthalmia as one explanation. An eye inflammation that afflicted many in the medieval world, it is caused not by any direct injury or illness but rather by poor nutrition—namely, a deficiency of vitamin A. Predictably, eye complaints would spike in the lean winter months but often resolve on their own in the spring and summer (coincidentally, the height of pilgrimage season), which brought renewed access to fresh fruits and vegetables. Similarly, the foaming mouths, gnashing teeth, and spasmodic thrashings so characteristic of biblical demoniacs—and the possessed pilgrims who were chained overnight and left to incubate beside a saint's tomb—could, Finucane suggests, simply have been symptoms of convulsive ergotism, the result of ingesting the ergot fungus that infected the ears of rye and other cereal grains that formed such a central part of the medieval diet. Even the dead may not have been dead, Finucane says, as death was often determined by such vague indicators as body temperature and skin color.

Influential as Finucane's wonderfully readable study has been, it is not without its critics. Raymond Van Dam, in his analysis of saints and miracles in late antique Gaul, and Simon Yarrow, in his investigation into the miracle stories of twelfth-century England, both caution against trying to understand healing miracles in reductionist ways. Appealing to the natural remission of disease or even psychosomatic explanations of healing may make it easier for modern skeptics to apprehend what those in the Middle Ages understood as a miracle, but this also obscures the crucially important cultural value of miracles in the medieval world.

Fundamentally, miracle stories presume that God orchestrates the cosmos. Think of Peter the Hermit's admonition of Theodoret's mother for vanity: her eye complaint was a punishment for sin. Fortunately, at least in the written account of what happened, Theodoret's mother interpreted it that way too. She used Peter's correction as a spur to renounce her makeup and jewels and embrace a life of devotion instead. In this understanding of disease, especially when one's illness is so immediately obvious to others, a broken body is a public indication of a broken soul. A newly healed body, on the other hand, is an advertisement of divine forgiveness.

There was clearly a tension in the medieval world between natural and supernatural explanations of disease. Saints and holy men were the recourse when there was no other recourse—when the local doctor trained in the arts of Hippocrates proved to be ineffective and the social ritual of pilgrimage had become the only alternative. In fact, the communal attestation of a miracle is a central part of many stories in monastic registries. Those pilgrims who traveled to a saint's shrine in thanksgiving for a wonder already granted often brought along witnesses who were willing to corroborate a miraculous cure. Interrogating them and including their testimony demonstrated that the one recording the story had taken seriously his obligation to investigate and verify.

What we might call the responsible monk's "duty to doubt" is obliquely revealed in the sorts of miracles that got recorded. As quantitative analyses of the monks' registries have shown, medieval peasant women almost always told stories about their bodies: a healed eye, a cured breast, a miraculous pregnancy. By contrast, only a fraction of the miracle stories told by religious men—educated priests, monks, and bishops—have anything to do with bodily healing. Priests told about their dreams, about their visions, about uncanny and inexplicable experiences. In part, this distinction reflects how gender and social and educational circumstances shape people's experience of the world. But it is just as much a commentary on the biases of those re-cording the stories. A monastic registrar was simply much less likely to believe in the miraculous vision of an old washerwoman than that of a fellow monk from a neighboring monastery.

Caesarius of Heisterbach, a thirteenth-century monk from a Cister-cian abbey south of Cologne, compiled a grand collection of nearly 750 miracle stories, the *Dialogus miraculorum,* based on oral accounts told to him mostly by abbots, monks, priests, and nuns. They make for engaging bedtime reading. Preachers deployed Caesarius's brief tales as exempla, which circulated in the many copies that were made of his popular book.

As the title of Caesarius's compilation suggests, he presents his miracle stories as part of a dialogue. This frame, a discussion about miracles between an elder monk and a younger novice, gives Cae-sarius leeway to offer his own commentary on the tales—which, of course, makes it even easier for his readers to understand and use the stories and commentaries as moral lessons in their own sermons, for instance.

Quite unlike Chaucer's pardoner, Caesarius is acutely concerned with the truth of the miracle stories he relates, almost all of which are secondhand reports by his various informants. He identifies many of them by name, to absolve himself of responsibility should any of their tales turn out to be false. "The Lord be my witness," Caesarius declares, "I have not contrived one single chapter in this dialogue." And if, he continues, any of the events narrated here "did not happen as I described them," then blame should fall on "those who related them to me."

Because Caesarius relies on priests and monks for most of his col-lection's content, it is no surprise that relatively few of his miracle stories involve bodily healing. We read, for instance, about Conrad, the provost of Xanten, on the banks of the Rhine. One day, Conrad bent to wash his hands in the river. Unfortunately, his gold ring, lubricated by the cold water, slipped from his finger and sank to the bottom of the stream. A year later, Conrad encountered some fishermen near the spot where he had lost his ring. He inquired whether they had caught anything. Yes, they said, one good-size pike. But they refused to sell it to Conrad, explaining that the fish was already promised to the provost of Xanten. Informed that they were speaking with the provost of Xanten, they handed Conrad the catch. Later, when Conrad's cook disemboweled the fish . . . well, just guess how this story ends. Clearly, Caesarius's novice is right when he exclaims—as Theodoret and Augustine and Gregory all had before him—that "ancient miracles are renewed again in our time."

Other than the obvious similarities between some of these "renewed" miracles and those recorded in ancient times, neither Caesarius nor the elder monk in his dialogues offers the young novice any systematic method for identifying what should, or should not, count as a miracle. But the elder monk does define the miraculous in general terms, when he tells the novice that a miracle can be anything "at which we marvel" that appears to run counter to the natural course of the world. Understood this way, with the focus on the observer's reaction, a miracle is less an event than the awe and wonder caused by an event. In some of Caesarius's miracle stories, the impetus of an observer's wonder is investigated and found to have a perfectly rational explanation. Intriguingly, this does not mean that it no longer counts as a miracle. Again, sometimes the miracle is not the event but the wonder that the event generates.

For instance, Caesarius tells the story of Abbot Daniel of Schönau, who was preparing to say Mass at a small chapel near the Church of the Holy Apostles in Cologne. The summoning bell had been rung, the faithful were filing in, and Daniel was already "clothed with priestly robes" when, to his horror, he noticed a chunk of raw flesh clinging to the side of the chalice. Caesarius says that Daniel debated whether to continue with the liturgy, knowing full well that he would "scandalize the people if he were to take off his robes" and end the Mass before it had even begun. Opting to press ahead—apparently after having decided that the flesh on the chalice must belong to Christ—Daniel steeled himself once the water and wine had been sanctified. Then he lifted the cup and "consumed the whole together." After Mass ended, Daniel returned the chalice to the recluse in whose cell it was stored for safekeeping. Before he turned to go, he asked if she knew who had used it last. "Dom Bertolph," she replied at once, a gluttonous priest known as "the bacon guzzler." With the ignominious cause of the flesh on the chalice revealed, Caesarius says, Abbot Daniel "confessed to us, if not to me at that time, that never had he had so much comfort in any Mass either before or afterwards as he had in that one."

Other miracle stories that Caesarius tells remind the reader of the bookish monastic culture from which his collection arose. One day—Caesarius begins again—a cleric "with quite a good knowledge of letters" underwent a bloodletting, a treatment frequently administered by medieval doctors to rebalance the body's humors. With the lancet in his vein and his blood draining away, the cleric's knowledge of Latin seems to have drained away too. He was unsure how to process the bizarre experience. He described his loss of Latin "with sorrow" to many but also called it his "wonderful deprivation." One fellow suggested a remedy: maybe the cleric should be bled again at the same hour on the same day of the following year—perhaps that would bring back his knowledge of letters? Caesarius never implies that this fellow might have been an accomplice, a collaborator helping his friend secure a sabbatical, but a year later, after another round of bloodletting, the cleric's knowledge of Latin did return.

Several of Caesarius's miracle stories concern animals, such as the one about the children who were playing priest in a stream when they baptized a stray dog. The poor mutt was "unable to bear the power of that great name," and "at once went mad before their eyes." But God, Caesarius assures his readers, did not punish the little children. He knew that their misuse of the sacrament was done "in folly," not "wickedness."

Another of Caesarius's animal stories anthropomorphizes birds to make a moral point—like a monkish version of one of Aesop's fables. Caesarius tells us that he was "credibly informed" about a pair of storks whose nest was near the home "of a certain knight." Apparently something of a bird watcher, the knight noticed that whenever the male stork flew away, the female "committed adultery" and then washed herself in a ditch. Whether out of prudishness or piety, the knight had soon seen enough and "ordered the ditch to be blocked up." The next time the scenario of the adulterous stork unfolded, the female was unable to wash away the remnants of her illicit liaison. When the male returned and discovered his mate's misdeed, he tried to harpoon her with his beak. But "not being strong enough" to kill her himself, he flew off and returned with several companions, who helped him finish the job.

Thankfully, the subsequent dialogue about the storks between the monk and the novice offers some insight into just what lesson a medieval preacher was supposed to be conveying to his congregation when he used this exemplum in a sermon. "I suppose," deadpans the novice, "that the jealousy contains some sacred meaning?" "Your supposition is right," the monk affirms. In the scriptures, the monk continues, God often "compares himself to birds," and "his spouse is the faithful soul." Adultery is "every mortal sin" that pulls the faithful soul away from God and delivers it into the devil's clutches. But baptism, the monk concludes, is "repentance," and the water of the sacrament "washes away guilt" so thoroughly that even God will refrain from taking revenge. It seems we are to conclude that the female stork could have continued her dalliances indefinitely had the knight not blocked up her only ritual means of seeking forgiveness.

Yet another story about animals in Caesarius's collection involves two other species of birds: a kite and a sparrow. The sparrow was kept as a pet by a woman "who was a great lover of the blessed Thomas of Canterbury" and suffered from an illness that left her "tortured with pain." During the worst of her spasms, she would often cry out, "Holy Thomas, help me!" One day, when the sparrow was out of its cage and standing on a window ledge, a kite swooped down and seized the little bird in its talons. The sparrow, which had learned how to mimic his matron's voice, squawked, "Holy Thomas, help me!" as the raptor flew off with him in his clutches. The kite released the sparrow at once but still "paid the penalty for its pillage" and fell from the sky, "dead to the ground."

In the dialogue about this story, the novice begins with the question that any sympathetic reader might ask: why would holy Thomas respond to the singular call of the sparrow but not the repeated cries of the woman? The woman, the elder monk explains, had faith that she would be resurrected to live another life, but animals have no such heaven to enjoy. In any case, the monk continues, holy Thomas *had* heard the woman's cries just as well as those of the bird, and the sparrow's miraculous escape was a sign of this, but the woman would need to learn virtue through suffering.

By many accounts, Thomas Becket was himself insufferable. Born on the feast day of Saint Thomas the Apostle, Becket was the son of Norman immigrants who arrived in London in the wake of William the Conqueror. Thomas was a dozen years older than the future king Henry II, but the two became friends and hunted and played chess together as young men. Soon after Henry was crowned, he appointed

Becket his lord chancellor. Though Becket had been abroad to study Latin and canon law and had even worked in the employ of Theobald of Bec (the archbishop of Canterbury), there was little indication that he had any interest in the religious life—much less that he would go on to become an ascetic, a martyr, and a saint. But when Theobald died in the early 1160s, Henry seized on the opening to put his man in control of church as well as state.

Henry was keen to expand the scope of English law to encompass the church, which had a parallel—but notoriously toothless—system of justice. Even a priest who committed a serious crime was rarely punished with anything more than defrocking. But a change seems to have come over Becket once he was installed as archbishop. Resigning as Henry's chancellor, he took it upon himself to defend the church's autonomy, including its reviled legal system. Far from helping Henry consolidate power, Becket actively worked against the king. In October 1164, not three years into his tenure as archbishop, Becket was formally held in contempt of royal authority. He fled to France before he could be forcibly removed from his post.

Six years later, in the summer of 1170, Becket returned from his self-imposed exile after Pope Alexander III personally negotiated a truce between the former friends the king and the archbishop. It did not hold for long. Ahead of his arrival back in Canterbury, Becket dispatched several letters excommunicating the bishops who, in his estimation, had usurped his authority while he was gone by presiding over the coronation of Henry's young sons. This was an intentional provocation directed less at the bishops than at the king.

By Christmas of that year, when Henry was away from England at his castle in Normandy, he had reached the end of his patience with Becket's incessant interfering: "Will no one rid me of this meddlesome priest?!" he is famously said to have shouted. This was not an explicit order to assassinate Becket, but four Norman knights who heard the king's cry interpreted it as a command that something be done. On December 29, just days after Henry's outburst, Reginald FitzUrse, William de Tracy, Richard le Bret, and Hugh de Moreville landed on England's shores and confronted Becket inside Canterbury Cathedral, apparently with the intent to arrest him and return him to Normandy. Things did not go as planned. Becket resisted their attempt and ended up with a sword through his skull.

The beginnings of a cult dedicated to Saint Thomas the Martyr were in place overnight—literally. The very evening Becket was murdered, a townsman acquired a cloth soaked with the bishop's blood. He took his relic home, rinsed it out as best he could, and then gave the washing water to his wife to drink. At once she was cured of paralysis. The following April, pilgrims were granted access to Becket's first shrine. Its protective outer casing had large enough holes carved in it that the faithful could reach in and touch or kiss Becket's sarcophagus.

King Henry condemned Becket's murder and denied that he had ordered it, but the pope still compelled him to make amends. Among other reparations, Henry submitted to processing barefoot into Canterbury Cathedral, where he publicly confessed his sins and then received three blows with a rod from each of the church's monks. Meanwhile, the four knights who were responsible for Becket's death were sent to the Holy Land for fourteen years of penitential service. None ever returned.

Soon after Becket's death, two Canterbury monks began writing down the orally circulating stories about the miracles that the saint had wrought. These two collections, as the great Oxford medievalist R. W. Southern once put it, are the defining literary genre of monastic culture in high medieval England. Yet as Rachel Koopmans more recently, and more aptly, characterized them in her definitive study, the miracle tales about Becket curated by monks are better compared to an entomologist's collection of butterflies. An orally circulating story is alive in the world, flitting about breathless from person to person, changing slightly with every retelling; the literary version, by contrast, is a dried husk of what was once living—a dusty specimen pinned down with others like it to a moldering page.

The first of the two major collections to emerge from Canterbury was the one written by Benedict of Peterborough, which he began in 1171. A whole cluster of Benedict's stories tell of many people who were healed by drinking "Canterbury water" infused with Becket's blood. Some of these healings Benedict saw himself. Others he heard about from trustworthy men—which is to say, other monks and priests just like himself. Benedict's third category of miracle stories, Koopmans explains, are those he heard from people who had been healed and then traveled to Canterbury with witnesses to relate their experiences themselves. Benedict was least comfortable reporting these.

William of Canterbury started his collection of Becket miracles the year after Benedict, in 1172, and kept adding story after story until the end of the decade. By the time he was through, William had accumulated the largest collection of miracle stories in England. Unlike Benedict's collection, William's is flamboyantly written and filled with specific medical terminology—presumably because he had some medical training. But like Benedict and most other monastic registrars, William doubted what he was told by those who came to him to have their stories recorded. Ronald Finucane puts it bluntly: William assumed all that "beggars were liars" but "the nobility always told the truth."

Still, William of Canterbury was no Caesarius of Heisterbach. William's stories are not just those from the mouths of priests and monks. They deal with odd discoveries like hidden rings but also the many sorts of everyday accidents and illnesses that so frequently befell those in twelfth-century England. William may have doubted and interrogated those who brought him their stories, but it was in a bid to ensure authenticity. And this did not stop him, Koopmans says, from delighting "in the sensational stories they had to tell." William eagerly records how Becket intervened to bring about all kinds of miracles, and he regales his readers with, as Koopmans explains, "a woman who was given a ring by Becket in a vision, a man who put Becket relics near a lavatory, a woman tempted to have sex with a handsome knight, a boy kicked in the head by a horse, a boy gored by a bull, a boy run over by an iron cart, a young man struck by lightning, a jester slipping on a wet floor, a man hung on the gallows, a woman just missed by a falling tree, and many other stories about visions, drownings, sea rescues, and accidents."

Dramatic and intriguing as the monks' collections may be, the analogy that Koopmans draws between Canterbury's monastic registrars and later butterfly collectors is even more apt when we understand that these stories, at least in their written form, rarely escaped back into the world. They formed an archive, a historical record, that the monks gathered and transcribed for posterity. Once netted and pinned to the page, few seem to have left it. They were not read aloud to visiting pilgrims nor ever translated from Latin into the Middle English or Anglo-Norman French vernaculars that the local laypeople would have understood. Occasionally, an educated author who was writing yet another account of Saint Thomas's life—dozens circulated within decades of Becket's death—might have consulted the monks' miracle stories and made use of a few of them, but unlike the stories that Augustine had promoted throughout Roman Africa or even those that preachers had mined from Caesarius, the ones recorded by Benedict and William remained locked in the registry.

Beginning in the early thirteenth century, Becket's miracles were advertised to travelers to Canterbury not through written accounts but through stories told in glass. That said, the "miracle windows" of Canterbury's Trinity Chapel do repeat a handful of the stories recorded by monks, such William's tale about Adam the Forester. Adam was a guardian of animals in the king's wood who was shot through the neck by a poacher. A draught of Canterbury water healed his arrow wound.

Another window relates one of the miracles from Benedict's collection with brilliant economy and clarity. In two adjacent roundels we can "read" the story of Mad Henry from the village of Fordwich, just an hour's walk from Canterbury (see plate 9). In the roundel on the left, Mad Henry comes to Becket's tomb in a state of uncontrollable frenzy. This is exactly what the Latin inscription at the top of the roundel says: "amens accedit," "he arrives out of his mind." With his hands tied behind his back and a caretaker on each side who raises a club to strike him, Mad Henry stumbles over his billowing cloak. The chaos of the scene is further conveyed by the monk at the right, who reaches out to steady a lectern to keep the manuscript resting on it from toppling to the ground. Meanwhile, the cloak of one of Henry's caretakers seems to have snagged on a candlestick atop the protective casing of Becket's tomb—identifiable by the two large holes carved in its side for the benefit of pilgrims' reaching hands.

According to Benedict's story, Henry's hands were bound to Becket's tomb in the hope that the saint would come to him overnight in a dream and cure him of his mania. As the second roundel confirms, this is what happened: "orat, sanusq[ue] recedit," reads the inscription, "he prays, and departs sane." In the image, we see Henry kneeling calmly at Becket's tomb, his cloak draped properly back over his shoulders, as the two caretakers and the monk from the day before marvel at his transformation with outstretched hands. At the very bottom of this roundel are the things Henry no longer needs, his ex-votos that will stay behind at the shrine as gifts to holy Thomas of Canterbury: two wooden clubs and an untied length of rope.

7   The War for the Dead

The devotees of Saint Leontius filled the first book of his miracles within twenty years. They credited him, a Roman soldier who was roasted alive on a gridiron and then beheaded, with hundreds of healings. These ranged from the mundane to the astonishing. Some said Leontius once brought a stillborn baby back to life. Befitting his status as a martyr and miracle worker, Leontius's relics are kept in a glass-fronted casket on an elevated marble platform surrounded by cherubs. His skull, which sits upright on an embroidered cushion, is the centerpiece of a truly baroque display (see plate 10). Rays of hammered gold ripple from his laurel-wreath crown; oversize earrings dangle where there are no ears; an amber-colored gem rests on his forehead, poised as a third eye above two empty sockets. Symmetrically arranged around his skull on a backdrop of red velvet are a dozen intact long bones, a few vertebrae, parts of a pelvis, and two ribs. Each is individually wrapped in a fine silk gauze from which filigreed flowers bloom.

Leontius was one of several early Christian martyrs of that name, at least two of whom served in the Roman military. His bones might be ancient, but their fastidious adornment is not: his cult did not arise until the middle of the seventeenth century. That is when a captain in the Pontifical Swiss Guard brought Leontius's bones from

Rome to a Benedictine abbey near Zürich. His relics and the ledgers listing his miracles are still there.

Like hundreds of other "catacomb saints" who were dispatched from Rome to the Germanic lands north of the Alps as a skeletal army of the Roman Catholic Church, Leontius was disinterred by the *cavatori,* the official excavators of the catacombs who worked for the Vatican's Sacred Congregation of Rites and Ceremonies. The congregation was responsible for authenticating the bones of the martyrs it uncovered but was a relatively recent establishment at the time of Leontius's translation: it was founded in 1588, just ten years after a providential discovery.

On the last day of May 1578, the shovel of a vineyard worker inadvertently pierced the ceiling of a subterranean gallery on the Via Salaria, opening the catacomb of Saint Priscilla and revealing a vast treasury of forgotten bones. Hundreds of thousands of Christians and Jews were buried in Rome's suburban catacombs in late antiquity. The city's dozens of tomb complexes form a second metropolis beneath the soil, a sprawling and disconnected labyrinth cut into the soft volcanic tuff, with aisle after branching aisle lined on either side with the floor-to-ceiling bunk beds of the dead. But who among them were martyrs?

The *cavatori* required few signs to guide them. A carved palm frond or just the letter *M* might suffice. The catacombs' ancient art was helpful too, although one faded fresco's rather obvious depiction of a baptism was reinterpreted as the boiling of a martyr in oil. Sometimes, bones themselves were enough, as the relics of those christened Saint Anonymous and Saint Incognitus suggest.

While the vineyard worker's accidental find did spur antiquarian and archaeological interest in early Christian Rome, the catacombs had never really been forgotten. In the early 1550s, a quarter century before their supposed rediscovery, Philip Neri, a Florentine priest and later a saint himself, was already regularly leading groups of friends and pilgrims on walking tours of some of Rome's most iconic churches that usually included a visit to one of the city's catacombs. He was also famous for his ascetic sleeplessness and overnight vigils in the tombs. Believing he was in the company of martyrs there, not just run-of-the-mill dead, Neri was like an early modern Saint Jerome, who, in recounting his Sundays as a schoolboy in Rome, fondly recalled exploring "the tombs of the apostles and martyrs" and "the crypts which had been excavated in the depths of the earth."

Nonetheless, prior to the vineyard worker's breakthrough north of town, there was little interest in organized devotion to the catacomb saints. But the Protestant Reformation had changed a lot, including the Catholic Church's relationship to its martyrs. With Neri and his followers at the vanguard, Counter-Reformation Catholics began systematically excavating, studying, and even exporting Rome's immense underground warehouse of relics. Many bones, like those belonging to Leontius, were sent north to embattled Catholic communities that lost their saints during the upheaval and destruction of the sixteenth and seventeenth centuries. The bones of those presumed to be early Christian martyrs were now unwitting conscripts in a religious war.

Philip Neri was still a child on October 31, 1517—All Saints' Eve by the reckoning of the Catholic calendar—when an Augustinian friar who had been baptized on the feast day of Saint Martin of Tours posted a series of propositions on the entrance to the Castle Church in Wittenberg, a university town southwest of Berlin on the Elbe River. Martin Luther's nailing of his *Ninety-Five Theses* to the door of the church, and the accompanying *bang! bang! bang!* of his hammer strikes resounding from its stone walls, might appear revolutionary, but that would be a retrospective misunderstanding of the scene. Assuming

Luther really did nail his theses to the door, no one there to witness him would have given him a second glance. It was just the precocious Fr. Martin, a young theology professor still shy of his thirtieth birthday, tacking up a flyer in Latin about an upcoming academic debate—hardly revolutionary. Yet Luther's theses did spark a revolution.

Luther's main dispute was with the power of indulgences and the often unscrupulous pardoners, like our friend from the *Canterbury Tales*, who sold them. Indulgences were, in effect, get-out-of-jail-free cards. By the ponderous logic of the Roman Catholic Church, God's mercy means that most sinners will be spared from eternal damnation, but God's justice demands that the souls of the uncondemned dead must be fully cleansed of their sins before they can be admitted to heaven. The cleansing, which takes place in the neither-heaven-nor-hell washing room of purgatory, is neither brief nor pleasant. Depending on the extent and severity of sins committed in life, the slow ascent from purgatory to heaven can be a seemingly interminable slog of a climb. And it is a *climb*. Dante famously envisions purgatory as a seven-terraced mountain, mirroring the seven deadly sins of pride, envy, wrath, sloth, greed, gluttony, and lust. The earthly paradise lost by Adam and Eve is perched high atop the mountain's summit.

Fortunately for all these mountaineering Christians, there is a gondola ride to the top. Offering donations to the poor, saying a litany of certain prayers, and going on pilgrimage to saints' shrines are among the good deeds one can do in life to remit some, if not all, of one's later obligations in purgatory. In Luther's time, yet another way of satisfying the debt owed for sin was to buy an indulgence, an official pardon of temporal punishment. Indulgences could be purchased for oneself or on behalf of another—including those who had already died and presumably still had much languishing in purgatory left to do. The indulgences that so infuriated Luther were being sold door to door by a German Dominican in the villages near

Wittenberg. Sanctioned by the pope, they were intended to raise money for the construction and decoration of a marvelous new church in Rome: Saint Peter's Basilica.

From a vantage point of more than five centuries later, Luther's anger over the sale of indulgences may seem both entirely reasonable and easily addressed. So could the great rift in the church have been avoided had the pope simply stopped the sale of indulgences? In a word: no.

Luther was hardly the only reform-minded theologian of his day, and the concerns of others were manifold. These included the frustrations of such intellectual heavyweights as Luther's colleague at Wittenberg Philipp Melanchthon and their contemporary in Zürich Huldrych Zwingli. As many historians of early modern Christianity have said, the Reformation would have happened even if Luther had died in the cradle.

Luther's own disputes with the Roman Catholic Church went beyond those he listed on the door in Wittenberg. But even with those issues set aside, the logical implications of the *Ninety-Five Theses* alone were enough to cause a serious problem. The very existence of indulgences, to say nothing of the tawdriness of their commercialization and sale, presupposed that the pope had some knowledge of and even control over what happened to the souls in purgatory. Luther flatly rejected this. How, he asked, could the pope possibly know who God had pardoned and just what each person needed to do to obtain such a pardon? As Luther saw it, the whole life of a Christian had to be one of repentance for sin. It was a persistent and daily form of inner contrition. No act—neither the sacrament of confession administered by the clergy nor any meritorious deed—could substitute for faith.

But if the individual Christian was justified before God through faith alone, not any sacramental form of absolution or a pilgrimage to a martyr's shrine, then where did that leave the cult of the saints? For Luther, saints' shrines were no more remarkable than any other place. As for voyages to visit them, Luther saw such pilgrimages as both useless diversions from daily responsibilities and extended opportunities to commit more sins along the way (*see* Chaucer, Geoffrey). He was willing to concede that the story of a martyr's witness unto death could be pedagogically useful as a lived example of Christian holiness, but no other element of a saint's cult—not relics, not shrines, not pilgrimages, not feast days—should be of any concern to the true Christian.

Clearly, the challenges that Luther and others in his circle raised were far from peripheral. Their attacks cut to the heart of the institutional hierarchy and the centuries-old sacramental and devotional practices of the Roman Catholic Church. They could not be ignored. Perhaps the Reformation could have been suppressed for a time had they all been obedient monks whose quills and inkpots were taken away, but thanks to the advent of Johannes Gutenberg's system of movable type set on a simple wooden press, even the most isolated Reformer could disseminate his ideas (often in the local vernacular rather than Latin) with unprecedented range and speed. There was no need to write a whole book or even bother with having anything bound. Brief pamphlets were better anyway: they were quick, cheap, and easy to print, and they were foldable—which made them concealable.

Recent advances in etching and engraving techniques meant that even an ordinary sixteenth-century pamphlet could be embellished with detailed illustrations. The emotional allure of the visual image was doubly powerful for the Reformers. Illustrations moved people in ways that words alone could not, and printed images could reach both the educated elite and more rustic audiences alike. A woodcut

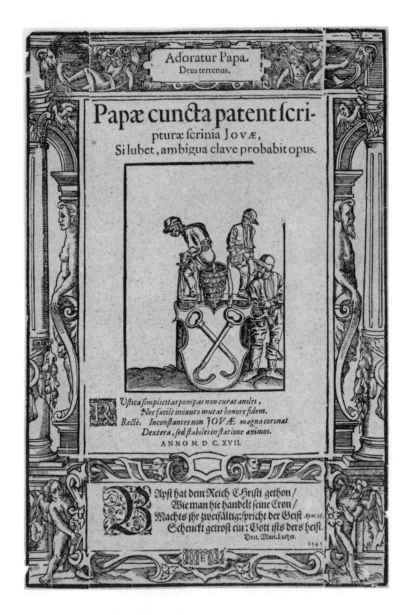

FIGURE 21. "Adoratur Papa Deus terrenus" (The Pope is worshiped as an earthly God) from the workshop of Lucas Cranach the Elder for Martin Luther's *Depiction of the Papacy*, 1545. British Museum, London.

from the workshop of Lucas Cranach the Elder that was made for the 1545 edition of Luther's *Depiction of the Papacy* shows the pope being "worshiped as an earthly God" (see fig. 21). Part of a series of nine broadsides, each of which circulated individually, it shows three German peasants, one in the act of defecating into an upturned papal tiara and the others waiting their turn. One need not be literate to grasp the gist of the message.

The Roman Catholic Church had to respond to Luther, but a ship as old and big as it was even then could not change course quickly. Catholics had just as much access as Protestants to new print technologies, but their response to the Reformers' critiques was slow, stiff, and imperious. Over the course of twenty-five meetings between 1545 and 1563, dozens of eminent priests and bishops met in the northern Italian city of Trento, or Tridentium, as it is known in Latin. After so many sessions spanning nearly twenty years, the written declarations of the Council of Trent can be summarized as a digging in of the heels. Against the Protestants' accusation that the church had strayed from the pure faith of scripture and the heroic witness of the earliest Christians, Roman Catholics defended themselves with a two-word thesis: "Semper eadem," "Always the same." Against the Reformers' insistence on the primacy of scripture alone, Catholics stressed the importance of scripture *and* tradition—the theological, liturgical, and interpretative traditions of the Roman Catholic Church. In short, the Catholic response to the Protestant Reformers was a historical one: from the structure and theology of the Mass through the organization of the ecclesiastical hierarchy to all the practices surrounding the cult of the saints and every other devotional custom of sixteenth-century Catholicism, the church claimed a continuity of many centuries. "Semper eadem."

At the twenty-fifth and final Tridentine session, in 1563, the Roman Catholic Church reaffirmed the importance of indulgences and relics—and pilgrimages to the shrines of the saints, where relics could be venerated and indulgences granted—but also tacitly acknowledged that the profusion of saints over the years, along with their often localized cults, had gotten a bit out of hand. The solution was to further centralize and systematize. Going forward, the admission of miracles and relics would require episcopal recognition and approval. A new saint's cult could no longer emerge organically, as it may have in the past, but would have to be authorized and directed by bishops. This bureaucratic resolve to institutionalize the saints helps account for the sharp downturn in the elevation of new ones throughout most of the sixteenth century.

In the meantime, the renewed organizational and institutional focus of the Roman Catholic Church meant that a lot of work had to be done. The calendar of the saints, for one, was in immediate need of updating and editing. Saints of purely local interest and those whose cults and shrines could not boast much of a history were quietly pushed aside in favor of those with longer pedigrees and wider appeal. But revising the *Roman Martyrology* to transform a collection of disparate local calendars into one that was more universal was not going to be easy. Nor could it be done in isolation: turning one crank moved multiple gears. Any change to the calendar necessitated a change to the breviary, the set of prayers and commemorations prescribed for each day. Further complicating matters was the church's insistence on history and tradition. If any part of the calendar or breviary was changed, then some historical justification for the decision was required. This was also true even if a current practice was simply confirmed and continued.

The massive calendrical, liturgical, and historical task of reorganizing the saints fell to Philip Neri's star student in Rome, Cesare Baronio. Neri's circle included several priest-scholars who, like him, were deeply devoted to the ancient martyrs of the church—to their stories, to their torments, to their bones. Under Neri's tutelage, Baronio matured into the most important intellectual of the Catholic Counter-Reformation. Late in his life, in recognition of his many scholarly achievements, Baronio was named a cardinal and appointed head of the esteemed Vatican Library.

In addition to revising the calendar and breviary throughout the 1580s and 1590s, a significant contribution in its own right, over much of the same period Baronio serially published a monumental, twelve-volume history of the church, the *Ecclesiastical Annals.* It is a century-by-century Catholic response to a similar historical undertaking (the *Magdeburg Centuries*) that had been completed a few decades earlier by a circle of Lutheran scholars. In that era, everyone was interested in church history.

Although Baronio is rightly credited with the *Ecclesiastical Annals* and his revisions of the *Roman Martyrology,* there is no way he could have completed either project alone. One of his most important research assistants, Antonio Gallonio, was another follower of Neri's. Gallonio remains a minor figure, overshadowed by Cardinal Baronio and Saint Philip Neri, the charismatic leader of their community, but his own publications on early Christian martyrs are more viscerally arresting than Baronio's. Gallonio recognized the power of images. His works include a collection of narratives about the virgin martyrs of Rome and, as we already know, an engrossing treatise on the instruments of torture used to kill the earliest martyrs. First published in Italian in 1591, his *Trattato degli instrumenti di martirio* is an especially novel contribution to the long history of Christian martyrdom.

As Neri's follower and Baronio's research assistant, Gallonio was steeped in history. He understood that research into the earliest Christian martyrs could be used to justify contemporary Catholic devotion to them. But, as he is said to have realized while reading aloud to Neri as his mentor lay on his deathbed, the ancient tales are frequently short on detail. A beheading is easy enough to envision, but what about more elaborate methods of execution? How can a reader visualize a martyr's suffering if the written account does not precisely describe the means of martyrdom?

Enter the *Trattato*: Gallonio's *Treatise on the Instruments of Martyrdom* is a near-thorough index of early Christian martyrdom arranged not by saint and date but by tool and machine. Fittingly, it begins with a survey of the various crosses and stakes on which Christian martyrs were hung. Eleven other chapters follow. They cover every imaginable tool of torture that Gallonio could find in his sources: cutting, chopping, and sawing devices; different sorts of pulleys, racks, and wheels; squashing presses and weights; handheld devices used to burn, whip, and rend the flesh of Christians. Gallonio's descriptions of these grisly implements draw from a wide array of literary sources. If a reference to an instrument of martyrdom was insufficiently clear in the Christian martyrological sources, which was often the case, Gallonio would look to the writings of non-Christian Roman historians and orators, such as Livy and Tacitus, for more detailed explanations of the ancient form of punishment.

But what makes Gallonio's book so incredibly useful is its inclusion of dozens of detailed engravings. Perhaps surprisingly, there is almost no blood or gore in these images and no gratuitous eagerness on the faces of the executioners. One might even describe the faces as staid—those of both the executioners and the martyrs themselves. While there are some illustrations of dismembered martyrs and painfully suspended saints, most of the images depict a horror that has not yet happened: a blow about to fall, a pulley about to turn. Appropriately for a book focused specifically on the instruments of martyrdom rather than on the individual saints and martyrs themselves, all the engravings in the *Trattato* depict the torture of nameless and unidentifiable Christians, most of whom sport only a loincloth.

Gallonio's meticulousness in his historical study of Roman instruments of martyrdom was a means to an end. His book is neither an archive of the macabre nor an annotated collection of violence for early modern voyeurs. Instead, Gallonio wanted his pious Catholic readers to *use* his detailed descriptions of Roman mechanisms of death, along with the images he commissioned to illuminate them, to visualize the torture of the saints and thus to sympathize with them. His book, in other words, is a devotional aid—a way of suffering along with the martyrs in prayer. This is why he includes scores of marginal references to Baronio's newly revised *Roman Martyrology*. A reader following the calendar of the saints could now cross-refer from the generic index of martyrological instruments in one book to the literary account of a specific saint's death in the other.

As Antonio Bosio (yet another follower of Philip Neri's) well understood, many of the earliest martyrs, most just as nameless and unidentifiable as Gallonio had made them, were still underfoot. Bosio's entire life's work, published posthumously in 1632 as *Roma sotterranea,* is a four-volume archaeological exploration of subterranean Rome: a four-volume study of the city's catacombs (see fig. 22). Bosio covers everything in his book, from early Christian burial practices to the art of the catacombs, complete with detailed maps, diagrams, and renderings. Although he is often touted as a pioneer of the new science of archaeology (one nineteenth-century admirer dubbed him "the Christopher Columbus of the catacombs"), Bosio's excavational interests were anything but academic and neutral.

Like Neri, Baronio, and Gallonio before him, Bosio used his historical scholarship to serve sectarian ends. As he saw it, the art on the catacombs' walls and the martyrs within them are time capsules that reveal how Christians of the most heroic age venerated their holy dead. Bosio is the one who interpreted that fresco depicting a baptism as showing a martyr being boiled in oil. The explanation for his misunderstanding is simple: his reading of martyrs' stories guided

FIGURE 22. Title page of *Roma sotterranea* by Antonio Bosio, 1632.

(and predetermined) his excavations. As Simon Ditchfield once put it, the ancient texts confirmed for Bosio in advance what his trowel would find. Right there, just below the surface of Rome, was proof against Protestant cries to the contrary of the centuries-old roots of early modern Catholic devotional practices. Right there, so Bosio believed, was material evidence for history and tradition—for the Catholic Counter-Reformation's rallying cry of "Semper eadem": Always the same.

The historically focused response of the Counter-Reformation was primarily a reaction to Luther and other Reformers in continental Europe, but the battle also had a western front.

In England, the year before Luther nailed his *Ninety-Five Theses* to the door, Thomas More published his *Utopia*. This imaginative and aspirational work, reflecting an idealist concern with the corrupting influence of wealth, describes a fictional society in which property is held in common. *Utopia* is also a satire that targets Catholic priests. But More was most certainly no Protestant. He had sharp words for lazy monks and rolled his eyes at those who would walk miles just to venerate a bone, but he also wore a coarse hair shirt against his skin in the fashion of the penitents and once contemplated taking up the monastic life. Before Luther, More could be both a devout Catholic and a stern critic of the church. After Luther, tolerance of criticism was rather less forthcoming.

Beginning in 1529, as King Henry VIII's newly appointed lord chancellor, More quickly earned a reputation as a vigorous anti-Lutheran enforcer. He imprisoned Protestant printers and burned the stock held by their booksellers. Though More denied it, some accused him of burning more than just books. When English Protestants looked back on his life, they saw him as a cause of martyrdom, whereas for English Catholics, More himself was the martyr.

In cooperating and then conflicting with Henry VIII, More acted out a one-man show that illustrates how martyrs and martyrdom dominated the religious anxieties of an uncertain and contradictory age. (Even today, as in his own time, More's memory is contested: he is celebrated by communists for his radical critique of privately held wealth and honored as the namesake of a far-right Catholic legal society that aided the effort to overturn Donald Trump's defeat in the 2020 US presidential election.) There had been disagreements over the status of martyrs before, but not until the Reformation were questions about who was and who was not a martyr so perilous. When Henry's House of Tudor lurched from Catholicism to Protestantism and then back and forth again, these were not spasmodic conversions of merely English annoyance. They had profound effects throughout the European continent—including hastening a hagiographic renaissance, as both Protestants and Catholics were eager to claim the history and literature of martyrdom as theirs and theirs alone. At the center of this convoluted story is Henry VIII, his many wives, and his multiple heirs.

Henry's first marriage was already difficult even before it happened. His wife-to-be, the Spanish princess Catherine of Aragon, had been wed before. In theory, this should not have been a problem—the Roman Catholic Church allows widows to remarry—but Catherine's first husband was Henry's older brother, Arthur. That Arthur had died of an illness just months into the marriage (and, as Catherine modestly insisted, before it was consummated) was beside the point. It was still a violation of ecclesiastical law for Henry to marry his own brother's widow. Henry's father, King Henry VII, knew this but urged the union anyway. The strategic alliance between England and Spain was too important to sacrifice on the altar of technicalities. So a papal dispensation for Henry's marriage was sought and eventually granted, and in 1516 a girl was born to Catherine. The girl, named Mary, would later rule England as a Catholic, but she was not the male heir that Henry (now King Henry VIII) so desperately wanted.

Years passed. By the time that Mary was a teenager, the line of succession remained unclear. Henry had long ago tired of Catherine, who was his senior and in the dimming twilight of childbearing age. Prospects for a male heir were slim. While carrying on an affair with Anne Boleyn, one of Catherine's attendants, Henry sought an annulment on the grounds that he and Catherine never should have been allowed to wed in the first place. Shameless as this argument may sound, Henry had not sought his brother's wife—he was a boy of just eleven when his father brokered the union. And ecclesiastically speaking, Henry was right: he and Catherine should not have been allowed to marry. But ecclesiastical laws aside and with a grant of annulment clearly not forthcoming from Rome, Henry and Anne Boleyn went ahead and married anyway—in secret. Their clandestine wedding in January 1533 marked the beginning of an extremely tumultuous year in the history of English Christianity.

In March, Henry's new archbishop of Canterbury, Thomas Cranmer, agreed with the king and declared Henry's marriage to Catherine invalid, thereby overruling his overrulers in Rome. The pope was furious. In June, Henry had Thomas More charged with treason and imprisoned in the Tower of London. More, always the principled Catholic, had quietly resigned as Henry's lord chancellor over the king's open defiance of the pope, but it was his conspicuous absence at Anne Boleyn's coronation that month that led to his arrest. A private resignation was one thing, a public rebuke another. In July, with it being obvious that neither King Henry nor Archbishop Cranmer was going to stand down, the pope excommunicated them both. In September, the first and only child of the new royal couple was born: Elizabeth. Unlike her elder sister, Elizabeth would rule England as a Protestant.

Throughout the next year, 1534, Catholicism's eclipse in England picked up speed. Parliament issued the Act of Supremacy, putting into civil law what Henry had already established among his bishops:

he was the supreme head of the Church of England, not the pope. The following year, More, still doggedly insisting on principle despite being offered every opportunity to save his skin, was beheaded.

In 1536, the Dissolution of the Monasteries began. Scores of bucolic monastic estates were wrested from the jurisdiction of the papal tiara and put under the control of the crown. As Catholic monks and anchorites fled for the safety of the Continent, the once grand monasteries of the English countryside were, as the novelist Evelyn Waugh put it in the preface to *Brideshead Revisited,* "doomed to spoliation and decay." Thomas Becket, found guilty of treason in absentia more than 350 years after his death, had his shrine plundered, its riches and ex-votos all carted away.

That same year, just the third since his second marriage, Henry soured on Anne Boleyn and had her beheaded. Among her faults? She had failed to produce a male heir. Henry wasted little time in remarrying. The day after Anne was executed, he was betrothed again—this time to one of Anne's attendants, a woman named Jane Seymour. Jane gave Henry the male heir he had long desired but died of labor-related complications soon after the birth of that son, Edward. It was said that Henry was devastated by her death. Perhaps. But his grief did not temper his zeal for more wives. In quick succession, Henry married another Anne and two more Catherines: first Anne of Cleves, a Protestant; then Catherine Howard, a Catholic; and finally Catherine Parr, another Protestant.

When Henry died in 1547, his young son by Jane Seymour was crowned King Edward VI. Edward, or the regents who ruled in the boy's stead, further hurried England's embrace of Protestantism. It was during Edward's reign that Archbishop Cranmer developed the *Book of Common Prayer,* thereby codifying the structure of daily and Sunday worship in the Church of England and setting it liturgically apart from the Roman Catholic Church. But in 1553, Edward died from tuberculosis at only fifteen, putting Cranmer and the church he supported in danger. Henry's eldest child, Mary, was now queen, and she immediately saw to it that her father's first marriage, to Catherine of Aragon (her Catholic mother), was deemed valid after all. This made Mary—not Edward, not Elizabeth, not any other child Henry may have fathered—the only legitimate heir to the throne.

Mary also sought formal reconciliation with Rome, overturned her late brother's anti-Catholic religious laws, and married a Catholic, the Spanish prince Philip. Throughout England, all the hidden accoutrements of Catholic devotion were brought down from rafters and dug up from under floorboards. Though Mary pledged that she would not forcibly impose Catholicism upon her subjects who rejected it, she did have a score to settle with Henry's enablers who had made her mother an outcast and yanked England away from the Roman Catholic Church.

In 1554, Thomas Cranmer—now the excommunicated and deposed archbishop of Canterbury—was arrested and imprisoned, along with several other prominent Protestant clerics, including the bishop of London.

In 1555, the burnings began.

When "Bloody" Mary started burning Protestants at the stake, John Foxe was living in self-imposed exile on the European continent. He was not nearly so well known as Archbishop Cranmer—not yet, anyway—but he was an outspoken Protestant, and those were perilous days. Foxe had already been expelled from Oxford, where Cranmer would burn, over his Protestant sympathies. Perhaps he surmised that he would have to write the story of Cranmer's martyrdom—or, if he failed to flee England, that someone else would have to write his.

If there are three literary pillars of the English Reformation, the first is the Bible, the second is Cranmer's *Book of Common Prayer,* and the third is Foxe's account of Mary's persecutions. The last may have been the most influential. By the close of the sixteenth century, even the poorest parish church in England owned a copy of the Bible, the *Book of Common Prayer,* and the work popularly known as *Foxe's Book of Martyrs.* This textual trinity of scriptures, prayers, and martyrs made one thing clear: to be English was most assuredly not to be Catholic.

The usefulness of Foxe's book as part of a broader anti-Catholic propaganda campaign was not lost on the Elizabethan government, which came to power after Mary's death. In 1569, just six years after the first English edition of Foxe's book appeared, Elizabeth's Privy Council realized that it was in their political interest to finance the publication of a second edition. Mary's reign, including her reimposition of Catholicism on England, was still in very recent memory, and for the sake of national unity Elizabeth needed all her subjects to support her religious reforms. Once the second edition of Foxe's book was published, in 1570, a synod of the Church of England decreed that every church should have a copy—despite the book's length and expense. Deluxe volumes were kept attached to chains inside English cathedrals; those held in private hands were recorded as prized possessions in rural wills and passed down from one generation to the next; captains in the Royal Navy were said to bring abridgments of Foxe's book aboard and read selections to their sailors to urge them on against their Catholic adversary, the Spanish Armada.

This commercial and political success was wholly unexpected. Foxe's interest in martyrs was not opportunistic, and his book was not some hastily thrown-together attempt at a best seller. He was a cautious scholar who had long been collecting primary source material for an ecclesiastical history of Christianity in England, one that would highlight his country's martyrs. Well versed in the languages, history, and theology of early and medieval Christianity, Foxe possessed all the intellectual sophistication needed to complete such a project. But he was not interested in writing a traditional church history; he wanted to tell the story of what he considered the *true* church in England. His history would celebrate the fiery witness of the Marian martyrs but also link them to proto-Protestant Reformers such as the fourteenth-century English priest and dissident John Wycliffe. More than a century before Luther was born, Wycliffe was already attacking the wealth and corruption of the Catholic ecclesiastical hierarchy and insisting that the Bible must be accessible in vernacular languages, such as English, and not only the Latin of priests and the educated.

While some Protestants on the Continent harnessed the power of the printing press to operate in the manner of journalists—distributing pamphlets, letters, woodcut images, and other ephemera to publicize and win support for their martyred brethren—others understood that the Reformers would have to respond as historians to the singularly most barbed of Catholic counterattacks. If the defensive parry of the Counter-Reformation was that the Catholic Church was "always the same," then its offensive punch against Protestants was a simple historical question: "Where was your church before Luther?"

Religiously speaking, being new was not a good thing. If Protestants were going to claim the Bible as their own, the age of the apostles and the persecuted church of the martyrs as the noblest Christian era, and themselves as its rightful heirs, then they could not simply write off the twelve hundred years between Constantine and Luther as an unfortunate diversion from the true path. It was possible to argue that the cult of the saints—with all its relics and shrines, pilgrimages, calendars, and feasts—was a regrettable *detour* from a more Bible-based faith and that the visible, Roman Catholic, church was a false one, but at the same time it was necessary to show how the teachings of the invisible and true church of the Reformers had, in fact, been quietly handed down and kept alive from antiquity to the sixteenth century. In other words, it was essential that Protestants tell a linear tale of historical progress. A long genealogy of martyrs from antiquity to the present was one way to do that, but the new age of martyrs was unfolding at the time. The fires, both literal and metaphorical, were still burning. Before Foxe could situate Mary's martyrs within any grander historical narrative, he had to make their stories known.

His first attempt, published in Basel in 1559, was a flop. Foxe wrote it in Latin, which makes sense, given that that language was still the shared tongue of European scholarship. If he wanted a broad continental readership of learned Protestants to understand what was happening in England, then he had to write his history in a universal tongue. But if his goal was to engage readers back home in England, then an altogether different approach was needed. Fortunately for Foxe, Mary was dead by the time his Latin account of her persecutions made it to print. The burnings, it seemed, were over. Elizabeth was queen, and the pendulum had swung back in the Protestants' favor once more. This meant that Foxe could return home to tell his tales in English to an eager audience.

The first English edition of Foxe's book was rushed into print in 1563. Its title doesn't exactly roll off the tongue. He called it *Actes and Monuments of these latter and perillous dayes, touching matters of the Church, wherein ar comprehended and described the great persecutions & horrible troubles, that have bene wrought and practised by the Romishe prelates, speciallye in this Realme of England and Scotlande, from the yeare of our Lorde, a thousande, unto the tyme nowe present.*

Such long and descriptive titles were common in the sixteenth century. Readers of the era relied on them to encapsulate a book's contents in much the same way that readers today might peruse a summary to see what's in store. A short title would not have suited

Foxe's book anyway: everything about the *Actes and Monuments* is long. The English edition represents such a massive expansion of the earlier Latin version that it is difficult to think of the two as even related. At more than eighteen hundred pages in folio, the *Actes and Monuments* is longer than any book that had ever been printed in England before then—including the Bible.

Unlike printing those one-page propaganda pamphlets, transforming Foxe's handwritten draft into a typeset product was not going to be quick, cheap, or easy. Producing it would have been a serious undertaking for any printer at the time, and those in England—as Elizabeth Evenden and Thomas Freeman explain in their fascinating study of the making of Foxe's book—had extra disadvantages. They not only lagged behind their continental colleagues in technical skills but also lacked a reliable domestic source of quality paper. Good paper had to be imported, at significant expense.

While even a small printshop, in England or elsewhere, could churn out books much more efficiently and cost effectively than a monastery full of scribes, the advent of print did not mean that a publisher's labor was automated. Indeed, the human costs per printed page were still considerable. And labor, like paper, had to be paid for in advance, before a single copy of a book could be sold. A printshop owner, as Evenden and Freeman explain, had to employ trained compositors, who set the metal type needed to print each page. The first edition of the *Actes and Monuments* is eighteen hundred pages long and (more to the point) has two million words—roughly twenty times as many as the book you are reading now. Every letter of every word, every space, every punctuation mark, had to be arranged by hand. And that was just the beginning.

For each page, the type had to be set and locked into place by a compositor, and then a requisite two men would secure it to the press, ink it, and put it to paper. But before the page commenced its full print run, a sample copy had to be delivered to a corrector, who would proofread it for errors. Inevitably, there were errors. Minor mistakes were accepted as just the price of doing business, but what about more serious ones—such as a missing line? Those overseeing the production had to decide whether the faults marked by the corrector were significant enough to stop pressing that page. If so, its type would have to be returned to the compositor, disassembled, fixed, and then reassembled, all while the pressmen waited, twiddling their thumbs. Downtime had its costs too.

Assuredly, a copy of Foxe's *Actes and Monuments* was going to be expensive. By some estimates, it would cost a skilled laborer as much as a month's wages. But if that was case, then even if English Protestants were interested in reading what Foxe had to say, how many of them could afford to buy it? That question seems to have been less on Foxe's mind than on that of his London-based printer and publisher, John Day. The spectacular success of the *Actes and Monuments* is a story as much about the book's contents and support from the Elizabethan government as about the collaboration between an inspired writer and his shrewd publisher. It was Day, not Foxe, who took the financial risk, and no book like this had ever been printed before. For that matter, what even *was* this book—how could something so unprecedented be marketed? Foxe and Day seem to have had different visions.

As Foxe saw it, his *Actes and Monuments* was a Protestant ecclesiastical history. For his second English edition, published in 1570, he greatly expanded its historical reach, going back beyond the first edition's arbitrary starting point of "the yeare of our Lorde, a thousande" to begin instead with the earliest church. All along, Foxe thought of himself as a scholar and writer in the mold of Eusebius. There is merit to this. Like Eusebius, he used his martyrs to tell a bigger story, relied on a veritable stable of primary sources, and was as much a compiler and editor of other people's work as a historical narrator in his own right. In the second English edition of his book, which he dedicated to Queen Elizabeth, he makes the comparison explicit, fashioning her as Constantine while describing himself as (who else?) her Eusebius.

Most of Foxe's readers saw things differently. They regarded his book less as a Protestant ecclesiastical history and more as a Protestant martyrology. Foxe had used Eusebius to write his book but, like Eusebius before him, had relied on a huge array of very different sorts of sources. In Foxe's case, this meant pamphlets, letters, trial reports, local archives, and the oral testimonies of eyewitnesses to Mary's executions. It was not the ancient past but current events—the deaths of Bloody Mary's martyrs—that captivated Foxe's readers. Some were so interested in what he had to say about martyred Protestants that they showed up at Day's printshop to give their own perspective on a burning or a trial that Foxe had narrated. They had often seen the events themselves or maybe talked to those who had, so they came to London with colorful details or corrections to offer. Foxe, for his part, eagerly welcomed such crowdsourcing, which he incorporated in the book's revised, second edition, begun scarcely before the ink had dried on the first.

Still, if Foxe wanted to be thought of as a historian rather than a martyrologist, he was swimming against the tide of popular opinion. The format of his second edition did not help matters. Instead of eighteen hundred pages in one folio volume, like the first, it is twenty-three hundred pages in two. Volume 2 specifically focuses on martyrs, as its title page indicates: "Ecclesiastical History conteyning the Actes and Monuments of Martyrs."

Before the first edition of Foxe's book was published, it was anticipated as something of a Protestant *Golden Legend,* that wildly popular medieval compilation of saints' lives. In the preface to that edition, Foxe complains that his work needs to be understood as more than just a "Booke of Martyrs," as people were already calling it. Although it seems bizarre that Foxe was worried—and even writing—about how his work was being received before a single copy of it had even been printed, stirring public interest in the forthcoming book was crucial if it was ever going to earn his publisher a return on investment.

Intriguingly, Day's interventions in the production of Foxe's book went beyond shaping the English public's perception of what was to come. As the printer and publisher, the one overseeing and paying those who were setting and pressing and correcting the type, Day had control over how Foxe's manuscript was packaged for print. Two of his interventions were crucial to the book's success: it was Day who included a calendar of martyrs, and it was Day who decided that the book should be illustrated.

The addition of a calendar was a curious choice, which Foxe likely would have rejected had he known of it in advance. Foxe's martyrs, like those of most other Protestant martyrologists who understood the historical stakes, were arranged chronologically, century by century. Again, the Reformers needed to chart the linear progression of the hidden church through the ages from the days well before Luther. But Day's calendar of martyrs, an annual cycle of red-letter days, was clearly reminiscent of Catholic liturgical calendars. Why would Day want to include what was sure to be seen as a Protestant calendar of saints? It seems his motivation was financial. If Foxe's book looked liturgical (like Cranmer's *Book of Common Prayer*), then it could be used as a sort of Protestant *Golden Legend*. Every church in every English village would want a copy, to replace its "popish predecessor," as Evenden and Freeman put it in their study of the book's production.

Foxe's calendar, ultimately too Catholic for the tastes of most Protestants, was withdrawn for the second edition, but aggrieved English Catholics seized on it as an opening to respond to the book.

In 1565, Thomas Harding maligned the work for its "dongehill" of "stinking martyrs." The next year, Nicholas Harpsfield, who wrote a life of Thomas More and a treatise on what he called the "pretended divorce" between Henry and Catherine of Aragon, pointed to Foxe's calendar as an example of the absurdity of Protestants thinking they had any martyrs at all. How, he wondered, could this lot of poor, ignorant traitors burned by Queen Mary ever hope to rival the illustrious saints and theologians of the Roman Catholic Church? At the beginning of the seventeenth century, an English Jesuit, Robert Persons, echoed Harpsfield's critique, even though the calendar appears in no edition of Foxe's book after the first. Persons wanted his readers to be aware of how Foxe had exchanged the towering martyrs, virgins, and saints of the Catholic calendar for "a multitude of artificers, labourers, shermen, weavers, cowherds, coblers, taylors, smithes, and spinsters."

The indignation of Catholics over Day's ill-advised calendar was nothing compared to their anger over the images of Protestant martyrs in the *Actes and Monuments*. Far from removing the images from the second edition, Foxe and Day doubled down on them, even adding what may have been the world's first pull-out poster. This oversize page in the 1570 edition, which predated Gallonio's *Treatise on the Instruments of Martyrdom* by twenty years, depicts three dozen small scenes of early Christian martyrs—all shown enduring various forms of torture during what Foxe calls "the first ten Persecutions of the Primative Church under the Heathen Tyrants of Rome" (see fig. 23). That the page could be removed from the book and hung up on a wall seems to have been the point.

Many of Foxe's martyrs were commoners. But belying the class-based criticism of Harpsfield and Persons, who pointed to the Marian

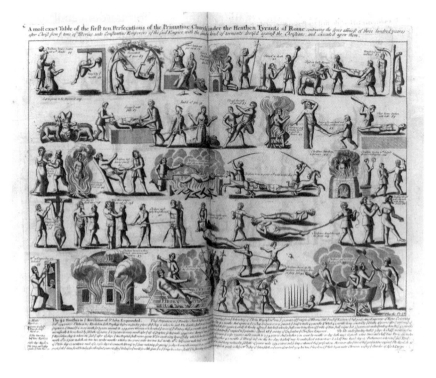

FIGURE 23. "A most exact Table of the first ten Persecutions of the Primative Church under the Heathen Tyrants of Rome" from a 1684 edition of John Foxe's *Actes and Monuments*.

martyrs' peasantry and lack of formal education as reason enough to deny them the crown of martyrdom, the most famous images from the *Actes and Monuments* are of the three so-called Oxford Martyrs: Hugh Latimer, a fellow of Clare College at Cambridge; Nicholas Ridley, the bishop of London; and, of course, Thomas Cranmer—Mary's archnemesis and the former archbishop of Canterbury.

A woodcut that first appeared in the 1563 edition depicts the burning of Latimer and Ridley, but Cranmer is hidden up in the top corner, observing the proceedings from the place of his continued imprisonment (see fig. 24). In the image, Cranmer prays that the

FIGURE 24. "A table describing the burning of Bishop Ridley and Father Latimer at Oxford" from the first English-language edition of John Foxe's *Actes and Monuments*, 1563.

Lord will strengthen his two friends in their time of need. His own case had been referred to Rome, but he would have his opportunity to become a martyr soon enough.

Meanwhile, Latimer and Ridley are shown chained together, their backs against a stake. As bundles of dried twigs are stacked around them, Richard Smith, the first Regius Professor of Divinity at Oxford, stands on a nearby dais and offers a sermon, urging them to repent. As if they needed any reminding about the gravity of their situation, Smith adapts (in Latin) Paul's words in 1 Corinthians: "If I give my body to be burned, but do not have love, I gain nothing." The biblical passage—nowadays as clichéd a choice for weddings as Pachelbel's Canon in D—was overshadowed by Latimer's words to Ridley, which are not written on the image but do form part of their martyrdom narrative: "Be of good comfort, Master Ridley," Foxe records Latimer as saying, "and play the man! We shall this day light such a candle in England, by God's grace, as I trust shall never be put out." Latimer's exhortation was fitting. He died quickly, but according to scores of onlookers the fire did not burn evenly around the two men. Ridley suffered a slow, smoldering death: "Lord have mercy on me!" he is said to have shouted. "I cannot burn!"

Exactly what Latimer said to Ridley by way of encouragement can never be known for sure. What is known is that his words changed with successive tellings of the tale. "Play the man" does not appear in the first English edition of Foxe's book but does show up later. In fact, this phrase repeats a line that Foxe would have seen before. According to Eusebius, a heavenly voice spoke the same words to Polycarp of Smyrna before he was bound to the stake at the order of a Roman proconsul: "Be strong, Polycarp, and play the man!" The similarity of Latimer's words to Ridley as recorded by Foxe, who knew his Eusebius and his Polycarp well, was no coincidence.

The woodcut image of Cranmer's death, which happened five months later, in March 1556, is just as iconic. The pope had given three English clerics—all Catholics, of course—the authority to decide the former archbishop's fate. Unsurprisingly, they found Cranmer guilty of heresy. But instead of being led straight to the stake, Cranmer was allowed to repent. He formally rejected his embrace of Lutheran theology, declared the pope the supreme arbiter of all matters theological, and received sacramental absolution for his sins against God and church. This should have spared his life, but it did nothing to resolve Mary's personal feud against him. Cranmer was still slated to burn.

Before he was executed, Cranmer was permitted to give a speech at the University Church of Saint Mary the Virgin on Oxford's High Street. In his remarks, which were prepared and vetted in advance, he was supposed to publicly reiterate his sins and beg forgiveness for his role in leading England astray. This is not what happened at the church. Knowing he could not save his life no matter how much he repented, Cranmer renounced his earlier recantation of Lutheranism, condemned the pope as the Antichrist, and vowed that when he was led to the stake he would put his right hand into the flames before the rest of him burned. It was the hand that had signed his confession. He was dragged from the pulpit before he could say anything more. In Foxe's book, the image of Cranmer at the stake depicts an old man with a "long and thick" beard doing just as he said: holding out his right hand above the flames as a first offering to God.

From a historical perspective, perhaps the most fascinating thing about the stories and images in Foxe's book is that so few of the basic facts about his martyrs are in doubt. Elements from Eusebius creep in, and Foxe is undoubtedly guilty of anti-Catholic polemic, but many of the narratives he presents are independently attested in multiple other sources. In Cranmer's case, a letter by a Catholic who witnessed the archbishop's death still survives. What struck this man the most was Cranmer's tranquility as the flames rose around him, a courageous resolve that the writer had trouble squaring with what, in his view, was Cranmer's "evell" reason for dying.

The images of Foxe's martyrs and their accompanying stories were incredibly effective for the Protestant cause. Mary's reign was short (just five years), but the size of Foxe's book and the scores of its editions, expansions, and abridgments—including several during Foxe's lifetime—would seem to suggest that many thousands of Protestants were ablaze for decades in England. In fact, Mary burned fewer than three hundred men and women over a three-year period of persecution: not an insignificant number, but not a calamitous disaster. Undoubtedly, the images of these burnings in Foxe's book had an outsize effect, profoundly affecting English history in ways that neither Foxe nor Day could have possibly anticipated. "If the influence of the *Actes and Monuments* was confined solely to the impact of these pictures," Evenden and Freeman conclude, "the work would still rank as one of the most important books printed in early modern England."

Catholics, such as the English Jesuit Persons, were acutely aware of the power of Foxe's images to transform historical narratives and shape public opinion. In his polemical rebuttal of Foxe's grand history of English Christianity, Persons makes specific reference to the "fair pictures" and "painted pageants" of the *Actes and Monuments,* saying that they "hath done more hurt alone to simple souls in our country, by infecting and poisoning them unawares . . . than many other [of] the most pestilent books together."

But martyrdom and history go two ways. The English College in Rome, a Jesuit institution at which Persons served as the rector, was itself notorious as a "seminary of the martyrs." The Catholic young men who were educated there had to take an oath that they would return to England to preach the "true" faith after their studies in Rome. This was a great personal risk. The chapel of the college, named for San Tomasso di Canterbury, served as a daily reminder of what lay in store.

In the early 1580s, thirty-four frescoes were painted on the walls of San Tomasso di Canterbury. They were lost two centuries later when the church was destroyed during Napoleon's occupation of Rome, but detailed engravings survive. One group of images traced the missionary and martyrological history of England through a pictographic story based on *The Golden Legend*. A second group was more contemporary, depicting recent martyrs like Thomas More and all the monks and anchorites who were killed when Henry emptied the monasteries. Linking Christian past to Christian present, the series of paintings in the English College in Rome concluded with the execution of Richard Thirkeld, an alumnus who was killed in York on May 29, 1583. He died the same year the frescoes were painted.

8   *The Legends of the Dead*

"In the month of October in the year of our Lord 1347," begins Michele da Piazza, a Franciscan friar from Catania, at the foot of Sicily's volcanic Mount Etna, "twelve Genoese galleys" put in at the port of Messina. This alone was not worrisome: merchant galleys were then ubiquitous in the harbors of the Mediterranean world. Thanks to their low freeboard and dozens of oarsmen, they were the merchant's vessel of choice. Galleys could navigate close to shore with minimal concern for current or wind, even in the perilous Strait of Messina. Genoese mariners, in any case, were accustomed to the narrow waterway, since it was the quickest point of passage for sailors returning home from the east to their powerful city-state up the shin and out on the knee of the Italian peninsula's boot.

The fleet about which Piazza writes had come from far-off Caffa, in Crimea. The Mongols dominated most of the land around the Black Sea in the middle of the fourteenth century, save the coast nearest to Constantinople, but the Golden Horde had carved out enclaves for others for the purpose of trade. Caffa was the Genoese jewel. As the bustling center of commerce along the Black Sea's northern shore, it was an exceedingly lucrative colony for Genoa and an outpost that connected central Asia to the British Isles via maritime networks that crossed the Mediterranean basin and extended beyond the Strait of Gibraltar into the open Atlantic. But the interconnectedness of global trade in the late Middle Ages came with a price. In addition to delivering commodities like grain, furs, and slaves, the sailors "brought with them a plague that they carried down to the very marrow of their bones, so that if anyone so much as spoke to them," Piazza writes with concern, "he was infected with a mortal sickness which brought on an immediate death."

The pestilential cargo soon spread. By the next month, November 1347, all of Sicily was afflicted. Piazza laments that his own city of Catania was "consigned to oblivion." By January 1348, the disease had jumped to the Italian mainland. Throughout the rest of that year, it was absorbed farther inland from dozens of other Mediterranean ports, making its way up roads and rivers into much of Spain, France, and the Balkans. By 1349, Germany and eastern Europe, the Low Countries and the British Isles, even parts of Scandinavia were awash with the plague. Two years later, once the wrath had largely run its course, up to half the population of Europe was dead. Though some revisionist historians writing in recent decades have argued that both the virulence and the extreme infectiousness of whatever caused the Black Death do not square with what we know of the plague, "no other disease," as John Aberth puts it in his documentary history of the period, "seems to fit the recorded symptoms and mortality patterns of the Black Death better."

Plague is a bacterial disease. According to Piazza, it spread quickly among those whom the Genoese sailors encountered in Messina. The highly lethal pneumonic variety of plague can be spread through the air from person to person, but bubonic plague is more common, and it is transmitted only by carriers other than people.

Ship rats were on the Genoese galleys that brought the plague to Messina; they no doubt infested the sailors' cargo of grain. Still smaller stowaways were the fleas carried on the rats carried by the galleys. And carried inside some of those fleas was the ultimate cause of the plague, a bacillus not isolated and identified as the killer of millions until the end of the nineteenth century: *Yersinia pestis*. A bloom of this bacteria inside a flea blocks its digestive tract, preventing the insect from feeding on blood. Starved of its only food, an infected flea will become desperate and start jumping from rat to rat—or human to human—nipping any warm body it can find in its hopeless quest for a meal. With each draw of blood the flea is unable to swallow, it barfs bacteria back into its host.

For a human bitten by an infected flea in an era before the aid of antibiotics, the effects were horrific. A red-ringed boil formed at the location of the bite. This was usually accompanied by fever, chills, headache, and nausea. Soon the bacterial invaders would proliferate in the lymphatic system. Within two or three days of exposure, the lymph node nearest the bite would swell into a large and painful bubo, giving the name to this variety of plague. Such "glandular swellings," Piazza says, are unmistakable markers of infection, growing first "to the size of a nut," then as large as "a goose egg." Late medieval and Renaissance depictions of those afflicted by the bubonic plague often show infected individuals trying to ease the pressure on their swollen masses. Those with a cervical bubo, on the neck, tilt their head to one side; those with an axillary bubo, under an armpit, lift a hand high. If a flea had bitten somewhere on the lower extremities, as was most common, then an inguinal or femoral bubo would swell in the groin. Severe vomiting and diarrhea joined the growth of the bubo, leading many medieval observers to comment on the foul breath and rancid sweat of plague victims—and the great thirst resulting from their rapid dehydration.

As the plague toxins spread from the swollen lymph node and attacked tissues and organs, a sufferer's heart rate quickened. During this dramatic final stage of infection, dark splotches from subcutaneous bleeding could appear on the skin, leading Piazza to explain the condition as the disease "putrefying the humors."

This remark, echoed in greater detail by every fourteenth-century physician, indicates just how far medieval doctors were from understanding the cause of the plague and how best to treat and prevent it. The humoral theory of disease, an evolving product of the school of Hippocrates, originated in the fifth century BC. Still fashionable during the Black Death, nearly two thousand years later, it holds that health is fundamentally a matter of balance. Health can be maintained only if the body's four humors—blood, phlegm, and black and yellow bile—are kept in a state of equilibrium. Illness results when any one humor outbalances the others. To keep the humoral scales steady, regular addition and subtraction were required. Medieval medical treatises speak at length about the importance of moderating everything from food, sleep, and exercise to wine, sex, and the emotions. To maintain proper balance in food, the characteristics on one side of the scale had to be weighed against those on the other: too many hot and wet foods, for instance, needed negation with a diet of cool and dry fare. Purging a buildup of humors through bloodletting was another common way of reestablishing balance, but as Piazza explains, if dark splotches appeared on the skin of a plague sufferer, then it was already too late for a remedy. The putrefying humors compelled the body "to spit up blood," a sure sign that it was rotting. At this stage, treatment was palliative or, as doctors, priests, and family members fled in fear, not offered at all. Hands and feet went gangrenous, organs started to fail, and the delirious patient soon slipped into a coma, followed by death.

As if by miracle, some plague victims survived. Fatality rates are difficult to determine with any certainty at a remove of so many centuries and seem to have varied by city and region, but roughly two of every three people who were infected with bubonic plague during the Black Death died from the disease, usually within just three to five days of the first onset of symptoms. Those who caught the pneumonic plague had almost no hope of recovery. Nor did those afflicted with the rare and universally lethal septicemic plague, which poisoned the blood and could cause a descent from health to sickness to death in less than a day.

Piazza understood that contact with infected individuals was treacherous. Simply speaking with one of those Genoese mariners brought "an immediate death," he says. Others believed that just being *looked* at by someone stricken with the plague was enough to transmit the disease. Along with many other fourteenth-century medical doctors, Guy de Chauliac—a Frenchman who authored an influential treatise on surgery and served as the pope's personal physician—subscribed to the ancient, Aristotelian theory of vision, which holds that sight is an ethereal form of touch. According to this idea, the "aerial spirit" emitted by the eyes of those infected with plague stretched out and transmitted it to all on whom they gazed.

Not everyone trained in the medical arts endorsed the same theories about the cause and spread of the plague, but there was general agreement that a corruption of the air, some sort of putrid miasma, was the most central concern. Relying again on Hippocratic wisdom, especially as it was interpreted by the famous doctor's most important later acolyte, the second-century AD Greek physician known as Galen, most medieval practitioners believed that the body absorbs the *pneuma*, the air or "vital spirit," from the atmosphere. Gentile da Foligno, an Umbrian physician who studied and lectured at the University of Bologna and became one of the most renowned analysts of the Black Death before succumbing to it himself in 1348, wrote that an intake of corrupt air results in "poisonous matter" settling around the heart and the lungs. The poisonous matter is then further spread by the infected, whose rotting bodies contribute to the corruption of the air.

Others pointed to the changing air itself as the cause of the plague, beyond just the effluvia of the sick and the dead. Such was the view of several doctors at the University of Paris, one of the most important centers of academic medicine in the late Middle Ages. In a treatise titled *Concerning the Particular and Near Cause,* these physicians write that unburied or unburned dead bodies were at least partly responsible for the air's corruption but that the miasma more widely afflicting the world was "spread and multiplied by frequent gusts of thick, wild, and southerly winds." These winds, they said, must have stirred up poisonous vapors arising from unknown lakes and distant valleys.

If, as most presumed, it was poisoned air that brought the plague, then there were some things that cities could do about it: streets could be scrubbed with water and bonfires of aromatic wood burned in central squares. Individual citizens could cleanse the air in their own environment as a treatment for the plague or, even better, as a preventative. Gentile suggests lighting a fire in the home or bringing in any sort of fragrant plant. Ingesting "leeks and holy water" might help too, he says, and for those who can find it, a paste of "Armenian bole," a clay rich in iron oxide, should be combined with "aloe, myrrh, and saffron." This remedy, Gentile assures his anxious readers, is often prescribed by doctors "north of the Alps."

For the wealthy, the most popular antidote was theriac, a concoction of dozens of ingredients. Recipes for its manufacture varied depending on regional custom and the flair of the local apothecary, but it was usually made from some combination of honey, cinnamon, fermented herbs, lemongrass, mineral salts, opium, and—key to its effectiveness—viper's flesh. Expensive and evocative in its list of ingredients, theriac was a treacle still being sold in ceramic urns well into the nineteenth century. (No one tell Gwyneth Paltrow.)

The importance of fresh air and heady aromas was an equally common refrain among Europe's Muslim physicians. From the city of Almería on the southern coast of Spain, we hear from the poet-physician Abu Ja'far Ahmad ibn Khatima, whose *Description and Remedy for Escaping the Plague* was published in February 1349. Just as steeped as his Christian counterparts in the theories of Hippocrates and Galen, Ibn Khatima also warns against those hot and wild southerly winds. Live in a north-facing house, he says, and fill it with the flowers of plants "such as myrtle and oriental poplars." For maximum effect, he advises his readers to anoint themselves with "cool fragrances" and inhale the scents of lemons and violets as often as possible. Burning sandalwood is another good idea, particularly if it has been "mixed with a little aloe steeped in rose water."

Unfortunately, as a physician from northern Spain, a professor at the University of Lleida, warns in a treatise published in Catalan just six months after the Genoese galleys sailed into Messina, the pneumatic miasma can enter the body through portals other than the nose. In his *Regimen of Protection against Epidemics,* Jacme d'Agramont urges against "habitual bathing" during periods of plague, explaining that hot baths open "the pores of the body" to the corrupting influence of foul air on the humors. Though d'Agramont's warning against over-frequent bathing is clearly specific to times of epidemic disease, that such an influential doctor would tell his readers not to bathe too much helps us understand the origin of the myth that medieval Europeans never washed.

According to the Parisian physicians, hot baths were especially dangerous for those whose bodies already erred toward being too hot and wet and thus more susceptible to decay. By contrast, they say, those who practice moderation in all things and "have bodies that are dry and free from impurities" will undoubtedly be "more resistant to the pestilence." D'Agramont concurs with his colleagues but, in line with his prohibition on daily bathing, counsels a more ascetic approach to the production of bodily heat: total abstinence "from carnal intercourse" when disease is rampant. The excessive heat, moisture, and emotion stirred up by sex are always threats to the body, but an imbalance can prove fatal when the air is corrupt.

Just as hot winds, hot baths, and hot sex can lead to an overheated body, so can hot foods—not on account of their temperature or spiciness but rather their more amorphous inherent qualities. Ibn Khatima declares that one should not eat "anything which could produce heat" during times of plague, singling out "rice bran or bran of millet" as among the most dangerous, since they "cause headaches and excite the bodily humors."

Food is also a concern for Gentile da Foligno. In his *Casebook against the Pestilence,* published in 1348 before his death, he maintains that "fine food and drink" are effective in warding off the plague. He speaks as a seasoned gourmand. One should opt for "fowl, chicken, and starlings," he says, or else choose from a menu of "gelded cows and lactating goats." Fish, however, "is to be avoided," as is lettuce— especially if it has been left out for too long. As an accompaniment to the platters of meat, he recommends crusty breads and "select wines." The latter, he cautions, must be used not toward the end of drunkenness but only "so that men may live in good cheer as they give vent to their fear." D'Agramont likewise stresses the importance of enjoying life so that anxious imaginings do not give way to dread, which itself can cause illness, he says. Ibn Khatima agrees. Find "serenity, relaxation, and hope," he urges his readers, not in meat and wine but in reading the Qur'an—or if not the holy book, then at least uplifting volumes "on history, humor, and romance."

The advice of all these enlightened physicians to seek out cooling smells and good food, books, and wine—in short, to keep calm and carry on in the face of the plague—may have been offered as antidotes to panic and ways of circumventing the supposed miasma coursing through the air, but it failed to account for what had brought the corruption in the first place. Taking the opposite tack from our investigation that winnowed from galley to rat to flea to bacterium, the medical faculty at the University of Paris expanded outward and upward in their search for the disease's ultimate cause. The vapors stirred up by those southerly winds came from "rottenness imprisoned in the inner parts of the earth," which is released, they surmised, "whenever there are earthquakes." Konrad of Megenberg, who studied and taught at the University of Paris, said that distant earthquakes had released noxious fumes that left schools of dead fish rotting on the seashore and acres of countryside covered in a biblical accumulation of dust, frogs, and snakes.

Yet according to the Parisian physicians, there was an even more distant cause of the plague: an ominous alignment in the zodiac. As evidence, they pointed to the "vapor trails and flare-ups" of passing comets. These were worrisome signs. At precisely 1:00 PM on March 20, 1345, they said, Mars, Saturn, and Jupiter had aligned in Aquarius, resulting in "the ruinous corruption of the air that is all around us." Aristotle had warned that this might happen. So had Saint Albert Magnus, who wrote in his thirteenth-century treatise *Concerning the Causes and Properties of the Elements* that when there is a conjunction of the major planets, it "brings about a great pestilence in the air," a contagion compounded if it occurs "under a hot and humid sign" like Aquarius. During the vernal equinox of 1345, the University of Paris doctors explained, "Jupiter, being hot and wet, drew up evil vapors from the earth, but Mars, since it is immoderately dry and hot, then ignited the risen vapors, and therefore there were many lightning flashes, sparks, and pestiferous vapors throughout the atmosphere." These were among the strange "flare-ups" that many had seen.

Reflecting on planetary conjunctions may have helped philosophically inclined physicians make intellectual sense of all the death around them, but neither astrological omens nor Gentile's good glass of wine were of much use in quelling the fears of the masses. Giovanni Boccaccio, one of the most prominent literary figures of the early Italian Renaissance, was in his midthirties when the plague struck Florence, locking down the shops and churches of his city and prompting those who could to pack their bags and flee for Tuscan cottages. "Some say it was heavenly bodies" that brought the plague, Boccaccio writes in the introduction to his *Decameron,* but tell that to those who had to drag corpses from "their houses and put them down by the front doors, where anyone passing by, especially in the morning, could have seen them by the thousands." As Boccaccio and many others wrote, there were not enough living to bury the dead. Nor was there any place to put them. "When all the graves were full," Boccaccio explains, "enormous trenches were dug in the cemeteries of the churches, into which the new arrivals were put by the hundreds, stowed layer upon layer like merchandise in ships."

Francesco Petrarch, another important humanist of the early Italian Renaissance, wrote of "empty houses, derelict cities, ruined estates, fields strewn with cadavers." Worst of all for Petrarch, who lost his wife, his son, and countless friends to the plague, was the "horrible and vast solitude encompassing the whole world." He could make new friends, he said, but where—and with whom? In 1367, twenty years after the start of the Black Death, Petrarch wrote to one of his old friends, the archbishop of Genoa. In a heartrending account of his loss, Petrarch concedes that his solitude has lessened somewhat with the passing of time and the slow return to some semblance of normal, but he laments that his loneliness has never really gone away. Nor had the plague. The Black Death was the worst outbreak of plague in human history, but the pest had come before and it would come yet again, returning in wave after wave. It would, Petrarch says, seem to recede, but then it would return and sorrow would again wash over those who had briefly known happiness. The constant recurrence of disease must be a sign of divine anger, he writes to the archbishop, and if only humanity's crimes would wane maybe God's punishment would grow milder too.

Boccaccio acknowledged the same: although some thought the cause was planets, others said it was God. The Parisian physicians, who had convinced themselves with their Hippocratic and Aristotelian explanations, also admitted that they "should not neglect to mention that an epidemic always proceeds from the divine will." Others, like Piazza, put it more bluntly: those Genoese galleys that had fled Caffa for Messina were vainly trying to escape "our Lord's wrath." It had descended upon them "for their misdeeds."

It would have come as no surprise to most that God was the cause of the plague. In a cosmos orchestrated by the omnipotent, epidemics— and everything else—always originate from "the divine will" that the Parisian physicians had mentioned. Many of the doctors in Paris would have known a story about God's willing slaughter during a much earlier outbreak of disease. It was told (or rather, *retold*) by Jacopo de Voragine, a Dominican friar and the bishop of Genoa.

Jacopo died in Genoa in 1298, half a century before his city's most notorious mariners sailed into Messina, but his *Legenda Sanctorum,* or *Readings of the Saints,* was widely known even by then. This extensive compilation of saints' lore, affectionately dubbed *The Golden Legend,* seems to have been intended as a reference work for preachers. As an avid scourer of ancient hagiographical sources, Jacopo distilled scores of earlier stories about the saints, most of them early Christian martyrs, into a manageable format that could be mined for material to be used in sermons preached about them on their feast days. Arranged according to the calendar, Jacopo's collection of readings begins on Saint Andrew's Day, November 30, which is the start of both Advent and the liturgical year.

As Sherry Reames explains in her history of *The Golden Legend,* it is almost impossible to overstate this book's popularity. It was a cultural institution for centuries: for a time, even better known and more accessible to most than the Bible. William Caxton, the first printer in England, published a translation of *The Golden Legend* in 1483, and during the thirty years between 1470 and 1500, which saw four editions of that translation, at least 150 other editions, Reames estimates, appeared on the Continent. The latter ranged from Jacopo's original Latin to translations in any number of vernacular languages, including Italian, French, Dutch, Bohemian, and both High and Low German.

Like every other tale in *The Golden Legend,* the plague story that Jacopo retells there draws upon the accounts of earlier authors. According to his sources, the Tiber had yet again breached its banks and flooded the city of Rome near the onset of winter in AD 589. Jacopo reports that the river had coughed up drowned serpents and dragons. By January 590, the reptiles' rotting bodies had poisoned the air and summoned a plague called "*inguinaria* because it causes a swelling in the groin."

At the time, Pelagius II was the pope. Once it became clear that Rome's outbreak was serious, he dispatched an envoy—a popular, middle-aged deacon named Gregory—to acquire some relics. Maybe an influx of bones could help bring an end to the plague? As a long-time papal ambassador, Gregory was accustomed to being sent on such missions. Pelagius needed to maintain good relations with other important cities, churches, and clerics, and his emissaries brought back important news from afar. When Gregory was sent to Constantinople some years earlier, he learned of the Byzantine tradition of carrying an icon of the Theotokos, the Mother of God, in procession to protect the city from harm. (Centuries later, Constantinople would acquire the Image of Edessa and deploy that miraculous depiction of Christ to similar ends.) But the people of Rome were upset when they discovered that Pelagius had sent their beloved Gregory away during a time of such need. As the plague continued to slay thousands, like a rain of "arrows coming from heaven," they insisted that the pope recall Gregory from his mission at once. Soon after he did, one of those arrows of God struck Pelagius. Since the church "could not be without a head," Jacopo explains, the people "unanimously elected Gregory to be their bishop, although he made every effort to dissuade them."

Pope Gregory, later Saint Gregory the Great, turned to what he had learned in the east. He organized citywide prayers and then a massive procession around Rome led by an image of Mary. It was said that this painting of the Virgin had been made by Saint Luke, who, Jacopo writes with approval, "was not only a physician but a distinguished painter." When the evangelist's image was hoisted into the air and processed around the city, "the poisonous uncleanness" fled at once, as if repelled by the blessed woman herself. Instead of the foulness that had hung in the air, there was "a wonderful serenity and purity." And it was through the clearing air that Gregory had a vision: a winged angel above Hadrian's mausoleum near Vatican Hill. It was perched there, resting, "wiping a bloody sword." Gregory took the vision as a sign. With the sheathing of his messenger's sword, God had finally brought an end to Rome's plague.

Jacopo's retelling of this story about Pope Gregory and the procession of the miracle-working image of Mary predates the Black Death, but like the suggested causes of that plague, it maintains a fundamental tension between two competing explanations. The proximate cause was the rottenness of the air, fouled by decaying serpents and dragons, but the ultimate, if more distant, cause of the plague was the sword of an angel and the arrows of God. Professors of medicine may have spent hours researching southerly winds, the belching of earthquakes, and Mars's ignition of Jupiter's vapors, but even they had to admit that plagues came and went capriciously, at

FIGURE 25. *Madonna of Mercy* by Benedetto Bonfigli, 1464. Church of San Francesco al Prato, Perugia. Scala / Art Resource, New York.

the whim of an angry God. When theriac and lemons proved useless, Christians knew where to hide—under the cloak of the Virgin (see fig. 25).

One of the earliest attempts to appease God's anger during the Black Death was a resuscitation of the penitent movement, which arose with new vigor in Austria and Hungary near the end of 1348 and moved into Germany the following spring. It seems to have coincided with several anti-Jewish pogroms. While some Christians held themselves accountable for the descent of the plague, others turned on Jews.

According to several medieval observers, the penitents who roamed central Europe in the mid-fourteenth century were a mob of ignorant men. Because new recruits pledged themselves to the cult for just thirty-three days (in honor of Jesus's thirty-three years), they were never lacking in fervor. For just over a month, pledges to the fraternity swore to live as wandering vagrants and not bathe or shave or have sex.

The best account of the penitent movement, or at least the most acerbic and witty, comes from Heinrich of Herford, a Dominican friar who derided its followers as uneducated buffoons. In his *Book of Memorable Matters*, from the early 1350s, Heinrich says that the penitents tromped across the land "without any order, as if this could have occurred to them." After crossing "fields and open country," they would come to a town. There they would march "down the street in procession," mumbling their hymns under wide-brimmed hats or the white hoods they pulled low over their "sad and downcast eyes." Upon entering the village church, the penitents locked the doors behind them and stripped to the waist. Then each man assumed the position.

Heinrich defines the term by which the penitents were known: "They were called the flagellants on account of the flagella . . . with which they were seen to do penance." These flagella were wooden rods "from which hung down three cords tied with great knots on their ends." Bound within each knot "were two pieces of iron sharpened to a point" and arranged in the shape of a cross. "With these flagella they beat and whipped their naked bodies" with such intensity that blood poured down their backs, sullied their robes, and "spattered the walls nearby" (see plate 11). Occasionally, Heinrich concludes, "the iron points became so embedded in the flesh" that it took more than one tug to extract them.

The flagellants were a flash in the pan. The pope suppressed the movement only a year after they began braiding their knots, and Heinrich likens the white-robed men to ghosts in the night, "nocturnal phantoms" who disappeared "just as suddenly as they had come." Still, these zealots were on to something. With their whip-scarred backs and bloodied flagella, the penitents embodied a powerful cultural conclusion: taking a few painful blows, even if they were self-inflicted, might be a way of thwarting a lethal one from God. And if this was the case, then maybe God's anger could be satisfied if his darts were absorbed by somebody else. Somebody already riddled with arrows. Somebody like Saint Sebastian.

The idea of God as both the dispenser of arrows and the shield protecting against them has a long biblical history. The "arrows of the Almighty" poison the hapless Job, but the "fortress" of the Most High is a refuge from "the arrow that flies by day" and "the pestilence that stalks in the darkness." The paradox of these two competing notions can be theologically resolved by acknowledging that everything proceeds "from the divine will," as the Parisian physicians put it. Less abstractly, it is embodied in the saints and martyrs of God. In the aftermath of the Black Death, Sebastian became the lightning rod for God's anger—a second Christ who drew the bolts of the Father away from plague-stricken cities to ground the arrows of the Almighty in his own flesh.

In an altarpiece erected after yet another wave of the plague swept across Florence in the early 1370s, Giovanni del Biondo presents Sebastian bound to a stake, studded with arrows, and placidly staring into the middle distance as an angel delivers a palm branch and crown—the symbols of the martyr's victory (see plate 12). Substitute nails and a crossbar for the arrows and Sebastian is Jesus, the shield and sacrifice of his people.

A century later, the Netherlandish painter Josse Lieferinxe envisioned a heavenly Sebastian kneeling on a cloud before God, pleading on behalf the people below (see plate 13). Beneath God and Sebastian but above a distant cityscape, a good and a bad angel square off in midair. Two more pairs of opposites are stationed below: mourners line the street across from several clerics who chant the burial rites of the dead, and in the foreground we see two gravediggers about to layer a white-shrouded corpse upon another that is already in a hole in the ground. To the concern of the red-hatted gravedigger, who grasps the uninterred corpse by its knees, his colleague, who had presumably been holding its shoulders, flails backward on the pavement as if struck by a dart. On the fallen man's neck, tilted to relieve the building pressure, we can just make out the swell of a cervical bubo.

Why did Sebastian become a plague saint? What was it in his story that made *him* the chosen protector of cities during times of plague? That he was shot with arrows makes some sense as an explanation, but it also seems insufficient. His arrows, after all, were not metaphorical darts.

According to the ancient story told about Sebastian, the soldier-martyr was killed near the end of the third century. His cult must have developed quickly, at least within a few decades, because he was already important enough by the middle of the fourth century to be included in the *Depositio martyrum,* the list of martyrs' burials in the illustrated codex-calendar known as the *Chronograph of 354.* The *Chronograph* says that Sebastian was interred in Rome's catacombs near the Via Appia on January 20. For at least the next two centuries his cult remained localized mostly in Rome, and late in the sixth century, during Gregory's papacy, Sebastian was proclaimed Rome's third patron saint, behind only the city's two martyred apostles, Peter and Paul. The basilica near Sebastian's tomb, later rededicated to him, eventually became one of the seven traditional pilgrimage churches of Rome—among those visited on the walking circuit devised by Saint Philip Neri in the 1550s as a way of remembering the ancient martyrs who had been buried in the catacombs.

Other than the calendrical memorial of 354 that notes Sebastian's name and the place and date of his burial, no source (at least none that survives) mentions him until a sermon delivered by Ambrose in the late 380s, a century after Sebastian was martyred. The bishop of Milan quoted from the Psalms to praise the faithful martyr for not swerving from his testimony, but that was about as much as he said on the subject. What else Ambrose might have known about the former soldier we cannot say, but it could not have included the epic *passio* written about Sebastian, because that text was not composed until several decades after Ambrose's death.

It is surprising that we can say when Sebastian's story was written. Most early Christian martyrdom narratives, including the one about Sebastian, are undated and anonymous; as a result, we rarely have a firm sense of when, where, or by whom they were composed. While we can often narrow the range of dates and possible places via internal clues or later quotations by identifiable others, unmasking an anonymous author is rather more difficult. In Sebastian's case, it is only thanks to the recent detective work of the French scholar Cécile Lanéry that we now know his *passio* was written in Rome, circa 440, by a man called Arnobius the Younger. This author was an

African monk who lived above Rome's catacombs in a monastery dedicated to Sebastian.

Arnobius's story about Sebastian's death is extravagantly verbose, the longest martyrdom narrative to survive from late ancient Rome, and it includes a cast of characters extensive enough to rival that of a Russian novel. Many in the tale end up dying as martyrs before Sebastian meets a similar end, and the details of their deaths account for much of the story's length. We read extended speeches from several of them, either praising the truth of Christianity or lamenting the perils of paganism. Such manufactured oratory in defense of the faith is common in martyrdom narratives—which veer into evangelical territory frequently enough that this is a recognizable hallmark of the genre. Arnobius was a master rhetorician, anonymously inspiring later writers and their derivative stories about martyred popes, slain eunuchs, and a woman forced into prostitution only to find her virtue defended by a snarling lion.

Though Ambrose claimed Sebastian as a son of Milan, from what Arnobius tells us he was only educated there: originally, he was from Narbonne, a town on the French Mediterranean coast near Montpellier. Arnobius also provides us with a detail now known to most: Sebastian served Diocletian as an officer in the emperor's Praetorian Guard. Because of his proximity to the most notorious persecutor of Christians, Sebastian had to hide his faith, but he visited Christians held under house arrest to encourage them to remain steadfast in their convictions.

According to Arnobius, Sebastian worked several miracles while still alive, curing a man with gout and loosening the tongue of a woman who had not spoken in years. After getting wind of these wonders, a Roman nobleman sought baptism as a treatment for his arthritis, but Arnobius tells us that the sincerity of his conversion was in doubt, since he maintained a prized collection of objects used for making astrological predictions, which were housed in a glass-domed room. Unaware of how handy the man's instruments would have been for later epidemiologists at the University of Paris, Sebastian forced him to smash his idols before being allowed to enter the healing waters of baptism. After all were shattered, the man, his sons, and more than a thousand of their slaves became Christians. Then, Arnobius says, the slaves were freed. Later in the narrative, some of the converts from this story are killed: one is stoned, another drowned in the Tiber. Those who try to recover the martyrs' bodies are themselves drowned in Rome's river.

Eventually, Sebastian's faith (long an open secret) became known to Diocletian. Arnobius goes out of his way to mention that after facing his would-be executioners, Sebastian was so riddled with arrows that he looked like a porcupine. Giovanni del Biondo seems to have been one of only a few artists of the Italian Renaissance to appreciate this narrative detail; others, with their token two or three arrows, focused their efforts on the muscled male nude or the martyr's disinterested gaze. But as we already know, Sebastian did not die as a porcupine. A woman named Irene, later a saint herself, extracted the arrows from his flesh and nursed him back to health. Only later, after publicly haranguing the emperor, was Sebastian clubbed to death and thrown into a sewer. Another woman, Saint Lucina, recovered his body after Sebastian appeared to her in a vision and told where to fish it out from the muck. According to tradition, the saint who was martyred twice was buried again too—near where the church of San Sebastiano ad Catacumbas still stands today.

Nothing in Arnobius's story pertains to the plague. But at the time of the Black Death, nearly a thousand years after Sebastian was killed, few would have known the old monk's account anyway. The widely known version, of course, was Jacopo's summary in *The Golden Legend*. His distillation of Sebastian's martyrdom draws upon the ancient story by Arnobius but uses other material too—including sources that describe some of Sebastian's posthumous miracles.

The work from which Jacopo borrowed that later proved key to Sebastian's transformation into a plague saint is the eighth-century *History of the Lombards* by Paul the Deacon. In a story focused on the Lombard capital of Pavia, just south of Milan, Paul recounts how Sebastian's relics ended an outbreak of plague. Two angels, he says—one good, the other bad—took nightly strolls together through the city's streets to announce the daily case count, intoning the names of the dead. Finally, Paul explains, a local man had a vision with clear instructions for how to end this angelic slaughter: if just a few of Sebastian's bones were taken from Rome's catacombs and reinterred in a Pavian church dedicated to Saint Peter, the plague would be over.

The translation of Sebastian's relics did put a stop to Pavia's plague, but the story of the man's vision—as Sheila Barker explains in her study of how Sebastian became a plague saint—seems to have been cover for using the martyr's bones for economic and political gain. On the economic front, moving the relics of one important Roman saint to a church already dedicated to another immediately created a new roadside attraction for pilgrims taking the popular Via Francigena route through Pavia on their way to or from Rome. Politically speaking, the distribution of Sebastian's relics helped cement the alliance between Rome and the powerful Lombard Kingdom, which was centered in Pavia.

Clearly borrowing from *The Golden Legend*, Giovanni del Biondo's Florentine altarpiece demonstrates how the ancient martyr became an intercessor for medieval cities afflicted with plague. The central and largest panel depicts Sebastian the Porcupine enduring his first martyrdom with arrows, while the triptych's smaller side panels tell the rest the story (see fig. 26). One shows Sebastian being clubbed to death and thrown in the sewer; in another we see Lucina retrieving the saint's body to bury him in the catacombs. This much we know from Arnobius. But the lower left panel offers something

FIGURE 26. *The Martyrdom of Saint Sebastian* by Giovanni del Biondo, 1380. Opera del Duomo Museum, Florence. Scala / Art Resource, New York. See plate 12 for just the central panel.

new, something Arnobius never mentioned: a dark angel brooding over a city of corpses. As in the scene painted by Lieferinxe a century after the Florentine altarpiece's creation, two gravediggers lay a white-shrouded corpse in the ground while other people implore a haloed Sebastian to come to the city's aid. In both artworks, the city is Pavia. By combining Sebastian's ancient martyrdom with his medieval miracles, Jacopo updated the saint's story for *The Golden Legend* and forever changed who Sebastian was and how he is remembered and venerated.

Only one other person ever rivaled Sebastian as a protector of cities afflicted with plague, but "few saints of the Middle Ages," as a French historian from Montpellier once said about him, "have generated as much controversy." He is known as Saint Roch, or San Rocco in Italian, and the controversy begins with the rather central question of his very existence. According to one account of Roch's life, he died in the 1320s, a quarter century before the start of the Black Death, but there is no solid evidence for any cult dedicated to him until more than a century *after* the great plague. In the early 1700s, the Jesuit scholar who edited three (now lost) Latin manuscripts about Roch put his apprehensions as gingerly as he could: "Some facts of his life," he wrote, knowing his words were inflammatory, "are transmitted to us not without some doubts as to their certainty."

Two fifteenth-century versions of Roch's life say that before he was born his parents were wealthy but childless. When his mother-to-be prayed that her womb might bear fruit, she heard the voice of an angel saying that God had granted her request for a son. Predictably, Roch was born with a sign of his sanctity: a cruciform birthmark on his chest. Clearly, he was destined for greatness. Even as an infant, the saintly Roch was so conscientious of others that he could sense when his mother was fasting and (as was said about Saint Nicholas) would nurse just once on those days, to spare her body more burden. Once Roch had grown into a boy of twelve or thirteen, his dying father instructed him to devote the rest of his life to serving the sick and the poor. Several years later, after Roch's mother died, the lanky young man sold what remained of his parents' property and distributed his money to the poor. Then he set out on foot as a pilgrim for Rome.

Along the way, following the Via Francigena south through the Italian Peninsula, Roch got word of a plague ravaging the city of Acquapendente, between Rome and Florence. With no concern for his own well-being, he hurried to the city's hospital. The doctors there initially declined the aid of the uninvited foreigner, but when they saw the pilgrim's fervor, they allowed him to help. Roch worked tirelessly on behalf of the sick, and his fame as a wonder-worker spread like wildfire when he drove the plague from Acquapendente just by making the sign of the cross. Eventually, Roch's pilgrimage brought him to Rome, where he spent several years helping the poor. He was in Piacenza, though, in the north of Italy, on his way home to Montpellier, when an angel appeared and told him that he had been struck with the "deadly dart" of the plague.

Far from bemoaning his affliction, Roch "gave thanks to God" for deeming him worthy to suffer like Christ and the martyrs. Always concerned for others ahead of himself, Roch left the hospital in Piacenza where he was being cared for so that the groans provoked by his illness would not be a disturbance. Believing that the man languishing outside the hospital was insane or at least a risk to public health, so exposed as he was, the people of Piacenza drove this anonymous pilgrim from their city, knowing nothing of his reputation for holiness. After traveling some distance beyond Piacenza's walls, Roch dragged himself into a grove, where he again thanked God for his trials. The delirious and dehydrated saint gathered sticks and branches to build himself a crude shelter, then prayed to find water. A spring arose right before the door of his hut.

Meanwhile, a pious noble named Gotthard, whose country estate outside Piacenza was near Roch's grove, was increasingly puzzled by the strange new behavior of one of his hunting dogs. Though the dog was well fed, it had started snatching rolls from Gotthard's dining table and running off with them into the woods. After yet another instance of thievery, Gotthard followed his dog and discovered that it had been delivering the stolen bread to a plague-stricken man in a hut. Roch saw the dog's master approach and shouted at him to stay back, for fear of contaminating him with the plague.

Gotthard turned for home but soon regretted abandoning someone so sick and alone and so returned to live a life of asceticism with the man of the woods. Roch was still recovering, but he remained an example of Christian piety and became a spiritual mentor to Gotthard. He urged the wealthy noble to renounce his property, distribute his money to the poor, and join the saints of God who beg for their bread in Jesus's name. When Gotthard accepted Roch's counsel and embraced Lady Poverty, the other nobles of Piacenza rejected their former friend, declaring his new ways disgraceful for someone wellborn. But as Roch predicted, those who denied Gotthard alms were struck with the plague. Luckily for them, Roch was merciful. Making the sign of the cross, he cured Piacenza, just as he had Acquapendente.

After Roch's own health was finally restored, he left Piacenza to continue on home. Unfortunately, his route to Montpellier took him through a region at war, and he was arrested on suspicion of being a spy. Ironically, the local lord who had Roch jailed was the saint's uncle, but the ever-humble servant of God—unrecognizable after so many years on the road—chose not to reveal who he was. Instead, he spent five years in prison, anonymously imitating the captivity of the earliest Christian martyrs.

By the time one of Roch's guards came to appreciate the imprisoned man's holiness, it was too late. Roch's health was failing, and death was drawing near. An angel appeared in his cell and asked if he had any last requests. Yet again, Roch could think only of others. He begged the angel to spare the lives of all the sick and afflicted who remembered him in the name of Jesus. Then he breathed his last and died.

Those who came for Roch's body knew at once that they were in the presence of a saint. His corpse was resting in placid repose, miraculously illuminated in the dark of the prison, and beneath the holy man's head was another surprise: a luminous tablet engraved with gold letters. The inscription was Roch's request of the angel: let any who suffer from plague call out the name Roch and thus "escape that most violent contagion." With his name now revealed, those preparing his body found the cross on his chest and confirmed that the prisoner was indeed Montpellier's lost son.

Roch was not shot with arrows or clubbed to death and tossed in the sewer, but he did suffer like Sebastian (see fig. 27). He welcomed the plague's "deadly dart," thanked God for his stint in the wilderness on the outskirts of Piacenza, and used his imprisonment as an opportunity to imitate the endurance of the saints. Confraternities devoted to Roch called him the saintly pilgrim, and that is how he is always depicted: as a traveler carrying a staff and a bag, the iconic scallop shell of Saint James often pinned to his hat or his cloak. The more important iconographic feature by which Roch can be identified, other than the diminutive hunting dog usually lurking at his feet, is not his cruciform birthmark but his inguinal bubo. Usually, Roch is seen lifting his tunic to point out the mark of the plague. In the interest of modesty, it has somehow descended from his groin to his thigh.

Roch's cult began to flourish just as the age of print was getting under way, so it is fitting that hand-colored printed images of him and Sebastian, the two great protectors against epidemic disease, were mass-produced as talismanic "plague sheets" (see fig. 28). These little paper amulets, many no larger than a business card, were rolled up and kept close to the body or else plastered to a door of the home. The block capitals running down and over the cross in the

FIGURE 27. *The Virgin and Child on the Lap of Saint Anne, with Saint Roch and Saint Sebastian* by Giovanni Jacopo Caraglio, c. 1517–24. Metropolitan Museum of Art, New York.

FIGURE 28. The holy cross, surrounded by Saint Sebastian, Saint John Nep-
omuk, and Saint Roch, and (*above*) the appearance of the Trinity, serving as an
amulet against plagues, witchcraft, etc. Wellcome Collection, London.

middle of many served as acrostic reminders, abbreviations of prayers to ward off the plague. Plague sheets were common enough even before the close of the fifteenth century that some art historians have surmised that the thin strip of paper protruding from the fold of the gravedigger's cap in Lieferinxe's painting of Sebastian interceding for Pavia must be a plague sheet tucked away for protection (see plate 13).

All the accoutrements of Roch's cult—the plague sheets, the confraternities, the churches named in his honor, the celebration of his feast on August 16—belie (or perhaps prove?) the fact that sainthood was a significantly more bureaucratic process by the late fifteenth century. In fact, a more investigative approach to sanctity appeared as early as the thirteenth century, well before the Council of Trent and the Counter-Reformation. No longer were a few miracle stories and some localized veneration sufficient for sainthood. By Roch's era, confirming a saint had become expensive and time consuming, involving the deposition of witnesses and the production of notarized dossiers that could run to the hundreds of pages. This meant that beginning in the late Middle Ages, most new saints were wealthy nobles or bishops or else members of religious orders whose promoters could afford to invest in the canonization process. Rarely was a quasi-mythological layman like Roch, an anonymous servant of the sick and the poor, added to the rolls of the saints. Cesare Baronio included Roch in his late sixteenth-century revision of the *Roman Martyrology*, but there is no evidence that Roch was ever officially canonized. It seems that he was one of the few in this period who were recognized not by bureaucracy but by popular fervor.

There is no one year to which we can point as the time when the miracle-laden past began to dissolve into the more skeptical present, but the study of saints, like the process for canonizing them, has—slowly—changed. *The Golden Legend,* long the dominant source for the saints, eventually fell out of favor. From the early 1600s until about 1850 (when antiquarian interest in the text revived), there seems to have been just a single printing of *The Golden Legend* in Europe—and it was in the original Latin. *The Golden Legend* was still known and read in the early seventeenth century, but its jumble of ancient and medieval sources, its brew of fact, fiction, and fable, made it a source more of consternation than of delight for early modern scholars who were advocating what they regarded as a more scientific approach to the saints.

Héribert Rosweyde, a young Jesuit philosophy professor in Flanders, had a deep knowledge of the lives of the saints and medieval collections like *The Golden Legend* but believed that such traditional hagiographical sources—with their miracle stories, extended speeches in defense of Christianity, and anecdotes about cross-shaped birthmarks—had shrouded the "historical figure" of the saint in an opaque veil of pious rhetoric. So when his Jesuit superior visited him in 1603, Rosweyde asked for what all professors still covet today: time off for research.

Four sabbatical years later, Rosweyde's efforts to identify what he considered the authentic historical material about the saints resulted in a preliminary sketch for still more research: a slim book called *Fasti sanctorum,* or "Calendar of the saints." Arranged around the calendar and the lives that Rosweyde could find in the manuscript libraries of what is now Belgium, the *Fasti* outlines a phenomenally ambitious, eighteen-volume project to critically analyze the stories of more than thirteen hundred saints. Ultimately, Rosweyde hoped to publish twelve volumes, one per month, on the saints of the year; three for the feasts of Christ and the Virgin; another dedicated to surveying ancient and medieval martyrologies, like those compiled by Bede and Usuard; and a final two of glossaries and indexes for the previous sixteen. Cardinal Robert Bellarmine, notorious for his later involvement in the Galileo affair, was incredulous when he got wind of this plan and quickly totted up the labor and expense it would have to involve. "Does this man," Bellarmine roared of Rosweyde, "think that he will live for two hundred years?!"

Rosweyde died from the plague in 1629, apparently after acquiring the disease during his ministrations at the bedside of another victim and long before he was anywhere close to two hundred years old or finished with his work on the saints. Another Jesuit, Jean Bolland, was subsequently tasked with reviewing his late colleague's papers to see if the spiraling project might ever make it into print. Like Rosweyde before him, but clearly not Bellarmine, Bolland failed to appreciate the immensity of the task and just how saturated medieval piety was with the saints. Not content with limiting his survey to the local libraries in the Southern Netherlands, Bolland expanded Rosweyde's plan and confidently declared that he would collect material about all the saints who had ever been venerated by the church, wherever manuscripts about them might be found.

Bolland's two most famous collaborators, Godfrey Henschen and Daniel van Papenbroek, were soon dispatched on the first of many *voyages littéraires* in search of saints' lives. Their pilgrimages from the Low Countries through Germany, the Alps, Italy, and France were quests not for bones but for texts—whatever works might have been stowed on the shelves of any monastery, palace, or civic archive that their letters of passage would allow them to enter. Henschen and Van Papenbroek copied, or had copied for them, scores of texts for later consultation. On the side, they conducted a voluminous correspondence with the librarians of Europe. According to Henschen, Van Papenbroek never tired of the seemingly endless hunt for more manuscripts: he was so devoted to his task that he feared "losing a quarter of an hour."

In 1643, fourteen years after Rosweyde's death, the circle of scholars who—in honor of Bolland—had come to be known as the

Bollandists finally published the first two folio volumes of the *Acta Sanctorum*. The title page is a visual explanation of their work: the saints are hidden in a cave behind a curtain, but the two pillars of the Bollandist venture, erudition and truth, defeat the ravages of time (see fig. 29). Critical hagiography, the image declares, will eventually triumph and record volume after volume of stories on saints.

The first two volumes of the *Acta Sanctorum* cover only the saints of January. Bolland himself wrote the entry on Sebastian, whose feast day is January 20. He attributes the martyr's *passio* to Ambrose, not Arnobius. Slowly, over many more years, volumes on the saints of other months were published by Bolland's heirs (and heirs of heirs). As David Knowles said about them, the Jesuits of the Southern Netherlands had unwittingly organized "the first great enterprise of co-operative scholarship in the modern world."

The most famous Bollandist in recent memory—known especially for his work on the ancient calendars of the saints—was a French Jesuit, Hippolyte Delehaye, who died in 1941 after a long scholarly career. Though his methodologies are now regarded as rather old fashioned, anyone who seriously studies the stories of saints knows his name. In one of his most widely read works, published in English translation as *The Legends of the Saints,* Delehaye begins by acknowledging that what he calls "scientific hagiography" has "had a somewhat disturbing effect" on "religious-minded people who regard with equal veneration not only the saints themselves but everything associated with them." He wants his readers to understand that there is a crucial distinction to be made between a saint and a legend *about* a saint. He is not "attacking the saint himself" when he suggests that an ancient hagiographer may have failed as an objective historian—he is merely attacking literary falsehoods.

Delehaye regarded his approach to the saints as a sober-minded sorting-through of ancient and medieval documents, a neutral analysis of hagiographical sources to determine their historical value.

ACTA SANCTORVM
Quotquot toto orbe coluntur, vel à Catholicis Scriptoribus celebrantur,
Quæ ex Latinis & Græcis aliarumque gentium antiquis monumentis
collegit, digessit, Notis illustrauit
IOANNES BOLLANDVS,
SOCIETATIS IESV THEOLOGVS,
Seruatâ primigeniâ Scriptorum phrasi.
OPERAM ET STVDIVM CONTVLIT
GODEFRIDVS HENSCHENIVS
EIVSDEM SOCIET. THEOLOGVS.
Prodit nunc duobus Tomis
IANVARIVS,
in quo MCLXX. nominatorum Sanctorum,
& aliorum innumerabilium memoria,
vel res gestæ illustrantur.
Cæteri menses ex ordine subsequentur

ERVDITIO.   VERITAS.

ANTVERPIÆ, APVD IOANNEM MEVRSIVM. ANNO M. DC. XLIII.

FIGURE 29. Abraham van Diepenbeeck's title page for the January volume of
the *Acta Sanctorum*, 1643.

Somehow, he hoped to peel back the layers of rhetoric veiling the saints to uncover "the simple narratives of heroic days, written, as it were, with pens dipped in the blood of the martyrs, the naïve histories," Delehaye lovingly calls them, "sweet with the perfume of true piety, in which eye-witnesses relate the trials of virgins and of ascetics." These straightforward and spartan accounts by those who saw the saints killed "deserve our fullest admiration and respect."

But just how are we to distinguish between rhetoric and reality? According to Delehaye, the key is knowing how to identify literary genres. Fables, for instance, are imaginary stories of the likes of Aesop's offerings. Myths, like those of ancient Greece, explain natural phenomena with recourse to the gods. Tales are moralistic sorts of stories that begin, "Once upon a time," and have no connection to real people or places. Romances are yet another kind of imaginary composition: they start with the real but soon soar off to become far-fetched, epic accounts. Then there are legends. This is the most difficult genre for scientific hagiography, because its stories are based in reality, are not overtly implausible, and are rooted in long-standing traditions at the heart of the church. Fortunately, Delehaye says, legends have a tell that gives them away: their sameness. Truly historical documents offer the reader "the most remarkable variations of detail," according to Delehaye, but legends of the saints are generic, "nothing but a mass of repetitions."

Recall the glowing crucifix between the stag's antlers in the tale of Saint Eustace. The same apparition, Delehaye writes, materializes in the stories of two other saintly hunters: Saint Hubert and Saint Meniful. Meanwhile, accounts of miraculous letters that descend from the heavens and images of Jesus "not made by human hands" borrow from similar legends about the Greek gods. As for those tales about "some object flung into the sea and recovered from the belly of a fish," well, they just repeat what we already know from Herodotus. In assuming the name and dress of a man, Saint Pelagia, Saint

Eugenia, and half a dozen other sainted virgins rehearse the common "adventures of a pious woman hiding herself in a monastery." For a small fee, confident locals will lead Holy Land pilgrims to "the precise spot where David composed his psalms, the rock smitten by Moses, the cave that sheltered Elijah." Footprints "of Adam and Abraham" somehow remain "in the hollows of rocks." Above all else, readers of legends about the saints must beware the hagiographers who "profess to have discovered engraved tablets," thus repeating a ridiculous theme "already familiar to the novelists of antiquity."

According to Delehaye, medieval collectors of hagiographical stories, including illustrious compilers like Jacopo, were especially taken by legendary anecdotes. Jacopo had "copious materials" at his disposal, he says, but "deliberately neglected" the respectable, historical sorts of sources in favor of repetitive ones with "more marvelous features." Read and reiterated again and again, the "marvelous" became accepted as fact. Similarly, many of those who have long remained on the church's roster of saints are there, Delehaye insists, only because an ancient authority happened to write about them. Just think of "the pious personages" in Saint Gregory's *Dialogues* who, because the pope mentioned them, "took their places among the saints of the Latin Church." Likewise, many of "the hermits of whom Theodoret wrote" were "incorporated in the annals of the Greek Church" before they had even died. In more recent centuries, saints have been invented by "erroneous interpretations of inscriptions, of carved monuments and of other antiquities." Would-be archaeologists like Antonio Bosio "imagined they had discovered bodies of saints" in the Roman catacombs even though they stopped before bones at which, Delehaye says, "the pilgrims of ancient days never dreamt of making a halt."

In so many stories of saints, Delehaye laments, "the historic element" has been "reduced to an infinitesimal quality," to perhaps nothing more than "the name of the saint, the existence of his shrine, and the date of his feast." Such minimal information might be enough to preserve the saint, but according to Delehaye it is a tragedy for historians, since "the one and only principle" useful for classifying ancient and medieval hagiographical documents is "the degree of truth and historic value they possess."

For Delehaye, there are only three categories of reliable historical sources about the saints. At the top of the list are "the official reports of the interrogation of the martyrs." Next come the testimonies "of eye-witnesses, and others worthy of confidence, or of well-informed contemporaries recording the testimonies of other eye-witnesses." Third on the list are the stories from those who rely on but freely recast the accounts of either of the first two kinds of sources.

One might wonder how many supposedly historical texts remain after Delehaye's scalpel has cut out the fables, myths, tales, romances, and legends. "Unhappily," he concedes, "the list is far from long." Roman interrogation reports *would* be immensely valuable— had any such documents been preserved untouched. Even the most celebrated among them, "we have reluctantly to admit," suffer from the reworking of later hands. At most, Delehaye says, we can rely on the writings of Ignatius of Antioch (and perhaps just the *Letter to the Romans,* which is "among the pearls" of the bishop's collection of letters) and the stories preserved by Eusebius about Polycarp and the martyrs of Lyon and Vienne. There is also the Syriac translation of Eusebius's *Martyrs of Palestine,* of course, which is "an oral and contemporary testimony" offered "without the intervention of any written sources."

So where does Delehaye's exceedingly short list of reliable sources leave the hundreds and hundreds of other stories about the saints? Few Bollandists looked kindly on *The Golden Legend,* Jacopo's blender of sources, even though, as Delehaye sympathetically puts it, this work "is so accurately representative of the hagiographic labours of the Middle Ages." Delehaye understood that a thirteenth-century collection of saints by a bishop who was hoping to inspire and edify the masses cannot "be judged according to the standards of historical criticism." The saints about whom Jacopo wrote are "God's friends," Delehaye says, and represent "what is greatest on earth." With their names and bones honored by princes and paupers alike, the saints "are human creatures lifted up above matter and above the miseries of our little world." Examples of virtue "in a superhuman degree," they "urge Christians" onward to embody "the spirit of the Gospel."

Though Jacopo's stories might tease a "tolerant smile" from Delehaye's lips, even he—that inveterate critic of fiction and fable—ultimately has to concede that the historical value of a saint's legend may not matter that much. "Legend, like all poetry," we must conclude, can sometimes "claim a higher degree of truth."

Postscript

According to Plato's account of a conversation between Socrates and his friends on the day of the philosopher's death in Athens in 399 BC, Socrates insisted that philosophy, when truly pursued, is nothing but the study of "dying and being dead." Philosophy is an embodied practice of shedding the body: a slow prying free of each nail that rivets the soul to the body whenever the body embraces an enjoyable pleasure or rejects an unwelcome pain. Death is the final unzipping, the ultimate sundering of body and soul. The soul will persist in some realm of shadows, but the body it leaves behind is a husk. This is why Socrates refuses to answer his friends when they ask what arrangements should be made for his funeral. How to dispose of his body is not for him to decide—burn it, bury it, whatever is easiest—because his body is not him, and after he dies it will no longer be his. Several decades later, Diogenes the Cynic left behind similar and characteristically theatrical instructions for the disposal of his own corpse: toss it over the city walls, he said. Let the wild animals eat it.

The Christians of antiquity who were deeply influenced by these earlier Greek philosophers agreed with Socrates on his first point: the true philosopher (now reconfigured as the zealous lover of Wisdom, who is the Word made flesh) must be an attentive student of dying. At the top of the class were the apostles and martyrs, the saints who imitated the suffering of their Master and used their bodies to testify that those who truly pursue him will be persecuted and killed for the sake of his name.

A vivid reminder of the centrality of this lesson is behind a door in Rome that is usually sealed shut with cement. The Porta Santa, or "Holy Door," of Saint Peter's Basilica is cracked open just a few times each century, during special Jubilee Years, and inside it—just beyond a statue of Jesus and Mary—is the Chapel of Saint Sebastian. Sebastian's arrow wounds, the nails of the crucifixion again and again, remind the Christian viewer that the love of wisdom is the practice of dying. Closer to the Porta Santa is another reminder: Michelangelo's *Pietà*.

This statue of the dead Christ just taken down from the cross lovingly captures Mary's immense sorrow over the death of her son (see plate 14). Jesus is almost enveloped by his mother's lap, draped as he is in her billowing folds. She, in turn, looks impossibly young to be the mother of someone who was killed in his thirties. But Michelangelo's youthful presentation of Mary is no mistake. (Sculptors, it hardly needs mentioning, are acutely attentive to bodies.) Mary's youth is an intentional commentary on her incorruptible purity. But Michelangelo's Jesus is incorrupt too. Though he has been whipped, mocked, spat on, crowned with thorns, nailed hand and foot to a cross, left to hang in the sun, and then rammed through with a lance to make sure he was dead, the marks of all this trauma are nearly invisible. Only a small divot on the back of his hand is noticeable. Even then, the eye is drawn more to his fingers, which are gently, if lifelessly, caught on a fold.

After Jesus was brought down from his cross late in the day—he died at the ninth hour, according to Mark—there was no time before the start of the Sabbath to wash and anoint his body for burial: the long night when no one can work begins at sunset. So he was laid in a borrowed tomb with a stone and a sentry blocking its exit.

The moment of Jesus's entombment in the hard afternoon light is common enough in Christian art, but depictions of his body *in* the tomb—cold, dead, and alone—are rather more rare. Perhaps the most unnervingly realistic vision is Hans Holbein the Younger's *Body of the Dead Christ in the Tomb,* which he painted just a quarter century after Michelangelo completed the *Pietà* (see plate 15). Holbein lived in Basel at the time, and his model was a corpse fished from the Rhine. A body—eyes and mouth agape—lies on a slab, the linen folds covering it thin and rough compared to those that swathe Mary's lap. Above the burial niche, an engraved mantel declares that this is the body of Jesus of Nazareth, the King of the Jews. This is not the incorrupt body of the *Pietà.* Its fingers reach beyond the slab, already shaded in tones of green, black, and gray. This is not the Friday of dying. It is the Saturday of being dead.

Fyodor Dostoyevsky saw *The Body of the Dead Christ in the Tomb* when he traveled through Basel on his honeymoon in the mid-1860s. Many of the Russian novelist's stories raise questions that intentionally challenge his Orthodox Christianity, and *The Idiot* (published two years after his honeymoon) is no exception. In one scene, the novel's protagonist is stunned when he sees a reproduction of Holbein's work hanging above a door. "That painting!" he gasps. "Some people might lose their faith by looking at that painting!" According to a diary kept by Dostoyevsky's wife, that was her husband's reaction in Basel.

For Christians, the Saturday of being dead is a temporary interlude, a tomb not borrowed for long. The Friday of dying may be the model to follow, but the Sunday of resurrection is the cornerstone of faith. Paul is unwavering about this. If the resurrection did not happen, then faith is in vain, he says, and all those who have died in Christ are, quite simply, *dead.* The promise of resurrection in the Christian tradition is a promise of reunification of body and soul: a promise that the soul will rejoin a transformed and glorified body, but a body nonetheless. According to Matthew, this happened immediately. Tombs opened at the moment of Jesus's death, and the "bodies of the saints who had fallen asleep were raised." Soon Jesus's tomb was empty too. Only his linen wrappings remained.

The paschal troparion, a hymn repeated endlessly on Easter Sunday in Orthodox churches, claims that Christ trampled upon Death. And by his death, so the troparion goes, he gave "life to those who are in the tomb." Death has no sting. The dead are not dead. In the Chora Church's fourteenth-century fresco of the *Anastasis* (literally, "Standing up"), Christ smashes the sealed doors that had kept all those who died before him enclosed in their tombs. Broken locks and hinges scatter across the ground as he grasps the newly reanimated Adam and Eve by their wrists and hauls them up from their graves (see plate 16). By implication, all of humanity is hauled along with them.

No longer is the body a barrier, just a weight to be shed; no longer is there any barrier between the Land of the Living and the Land of the Dead.

Acknowledgments

I am grateful to many people for their help with this book. Eric Schmidt, my editor at University of California Press, first realized its potential for a wider audience and was followed by two anonymous readers for the press who saw early versions of several chapters and my overly ambitious proposal. At a later stage, two more anonymous readers offered many helpful suggestions for revision, which included ways to save me from several errors and omissions. I take full responsibility for all errors that are still in the text and the omissions that aren't. Three colleagues at the University of Toronto (Bart Scott, Kevin Coleman, and Farzi Hemmasi) and two longtime friends from Byzantine lands (Mary Kerby and Andrew Ciferni, O. Praem.) were overly generous with their time and encouragement and kindly read all or parts of the manuscript. Alex Gooding provided invaluable help in sourcing the images for the inside of this book, while Paul Davis kindly let me use his "Life & Death" linocut for its cover. Special thanks are due to Juliana Froggatt, the reigning champ of copy editors.

Though *Cult of the Dead* may have begun with a serendipitous find at the Monkey's Paw bookshop in Toronto, its real genesis was decades ago—first in South Bend with my teachers Cornelius O'Boyle, Robin Darling Young, and Brian Daley, SJ, and then in Durham with Liz Clark and Luk Van Rompay. Liz died of cancer just weeks before I submitted the final manuscript, and her last words to me (spoken not so sotto voce over Zoom with a foamy glass of Heineken in her hand) were "How do I end this call?" I will be forever indebted to Liz for all she did to mentor me. The same is true for my dear friend Luk: I owe him enormously for all he has done and all he continues to do. Luk read the manuscript of this book word for word, as he has everything I have published, but what he doesn't know is that I always misitalicize a single comma in whatever I give him just to see if he'll catch it. He never lets me down.

I am most thankful to my parents, Mary Gus and Richard Smith, and my in-laws Shelley Hamel and Norm Fost, for being interested in my work even when it's not very interesting. My love for Maggie Fost—always the Mary to my Martha—and our children, Arlo and Frances, is immeasurable. The blood sacrifice of this book is that I could not have completed it without time I will never get back to spend with them.

The final nod of gratitude goes to Gabe Radford, who happily spent more time hearing, reading, and texting about *Cult of the Dead* than any friendship should demand. Thank you, Third Horn.

Notes for Further Reading

Following in the footsteps of the many ancient historians and hagiographers discussed in this book, I have tried—with undoubtedly less erudition and skill—to
gather a magpie's collection of stories and scholarship and then distill some of it
into an entertaining narrative for a general reader. In line with this approach, the
comments provided here are not bread crumbs for scholars but "Notes for Further Reading" for a nonspecialist audience. At the same time, they do credit the
publications upon which I have relied in constructing my own narrative history of
Christianity.

Although not all the works mentioned here will appeal to the general reader,
I have highlighted those that are likely to be the most accessible and interesting.
For a full list of sources consulted in the research for this book, including English
translations of the primary texts I used, see the bibliography. Finally, note that all
biblical passages in this book, apart from those embedded in the quotations of
others, are drawn from the New Revised Standard Version (NRSV).

1. The First of the Dead

Some of the more important recent-ish scholarly books about early Christian
martyrdom include Glen Bowersock's *Martyrdom and Rome,* Daniel Boyarin's
Dying for God, Elizabeth Castelli's *Martyrdom and Memory* (especially noteworthy for the intriguing ways in which it deals with questions of cultural memory),
and three publications by Candida Moss. In *The Myth of Persecution,* a trade book
written for a general audience, Moss explains why we cannot rely on even the very
earliest stories about the martyrs to draw historical conclusions about the plight

of Jesus's followers in the pre-Constantinian Roman Empire. In *The Other Christs,* she explores ancient Christians' understanding of martyrdom as an imitation of Christ. For those interested in a thoroughgoing, academic introduction to the study of martyrdom in early Christianity, the place to start is Moss's *Ancient Christian Martyrdom.* Its introduction summarizes much of the scholarship in the field (up to its 2012 publication date), while its first chapter situates early Christian notions of martyrdom within their Jewish and Greco-Roman religious and cultural contexts. For an overview of Christian martyrdom narratives in Syriac, which tend to be neglected in most studies of martyrdom in late antiquity, see "A Guide to the Persian Martyr Acts" in Sebastian Brock's *The History of the Holy Mar Ma'in.*

For an engaging account of Rome's patron saints, see David Eastman's *The Many Deaths of Peter and Paul.* Tom Bissell's *Apostle* is a lighter read that deftly weaves history together with biblical studies and travel writing to reflect on the various traditions about what became of the men closest to Jesus and where they are supposedly buried. Sean McDowell's *The Fate of the Apostles* helpfully collects and summarizes many of these stories about the deaths of the apostles, but readers should beware that in analyzing them McDowell often takes an apologetic point of view inconsistent with most scholarly approaches to these texts.

Readers eager for an in-depth analysis of the passion narratives in the Gospels should consult Raymond Brown's two-volume commentary, *The Death of the Messiah.* For a summary of how the Gospel of Luke presents Jesus as a philosopher-martyr, see Greg Sterling's "*Mors philosophi.*" And for Luke's presentation of Stephen in his second scriptural volume, the Acts of the Apostles, see Shelly Matthews's innovative study *Perfect Martyr.* The clearest account of biblical scholarship on Stephen and the early Christian creation of his cult is François Bovon's "The Dossier on Stephen, the First Martyr." Meanwhile, Elizabeth Clark's "Claims on the Bones of Saint Stephen" explains the role of the first martyr's relics in the imperial politicking of the early fifth century.

2. The Names of the Dead

Two excellent introductions to Saint Gregory the Great are *Gregory the Great and His World* by R. A. Markus and, more recently, *Gregory the Great* by George Demacopoulos. Éric Rebillard offers a useful overview of collectors and collections of martyrdom narratives in the introduction to his *Greek and Latin Narratives about the Ancient Martyrs,* which briefly discusses Gregory's letter to Eulogius, explaining the pope's ignorance of Eusebius's collection of the "martyrdoms of the ancients" as a likely result of his having read the *Ecclesiastical History* in a Latin translation that somehow failed to include references to that work of Eusebius's.

One of the best studies of Diocletian, Constantine, Eusebius, and the place of Christianity in the late Roman world remains *Constantine and Eusebius* by Timothy Barnes. As accompaniments, see Jeremy Schott's wonderful new translation of Eusebius's *Ecclesiastical History* and Michael Hollerich's *Making Christian History*, which not only introduces the reader to Eusebius's project but also explains how his work was continued and received over the centuries. For those really interested in Eusebius, add in William Cureton's English translation of the Syriac translation of the *Martyrs of Palestine*. For the full story of Polycarp's martyrdom and Eusebius's comments about the martyrs of Lyon and Vienne, intrepid readers should consult Rebillard's *Greek and Latin Narratives*. Two other useful studies of Eusebius's *Ecclesiastical History* are James Corke-Webster's *Eusebius and Empire* and David DeVore's "Greek Historiography, Roman Society, Christian Empire." This dissertation by DeVore is especially helpful for understanding how Eusebius upends traditional Greek history writing (with its focus on military valor) through a celebration of the martyrs. For more on the transmission of Syriac Christian martyrdom literature, Sozomen's knowledge of Syriac sources, and the situation of Christians in late ancient Mesopotamia, see my own *Constantine and the Captive Christians of Persia*. For Clifford Geertz's line about culture being "the stories we tell ourselves about ourselves," see his classic work *The Interpretation of Cultures*. Maya Lin's remarks come from her winning entry, now in the Library of Congress, in the 1981 design competition for the Vietnam Veterans Memorial.

William Wright's late nineteenth-century *Catalogue of the Syriac Manuscripts in the British Museum*, which is out of copyright and available online, quotes from Miss Platt's diary (pp. xi–xvii) and offers additional notes on her expedition with her stepfather to the Monastery of the Syrians. Hugh Evelyn White's *The Monasteries of the Wâdi 'n Natrûn,* also out of copyright and available online, further elaborates on the monastery's history (pp. 455–57). For Cureton's report about the ancient colophon, see his introduction to *The Festal Letters of Athanasius* (pp. xv–xxvi), which is reproduced in his out-of-print and hard-to-find *An Ancient Colophon*. Sebastian Brock's "Without Mushê of Nisibis, Where Would We Be?" briefly surveys Moses of Nisibis's travels to Mesopotamia and the abbot's manuscript acquisitions while he was delayed at the tax office in Baghdad. Brock and Lucas Van Rompay discuss some of the more recently discovered Syriac fragments in their *Catalogue of the Syriac Manuscripts and Fragments in the Library of Deir al-Surian*. For a delightful general account of medieval manuscripts and their manufacture, see Mary Wellesley's *The Gilded Page*.

3. The Remains of the Dead

For an introduction to the art of the Sainte-Chapelle and to King Louis IX, see *Art and Crusade in the Age of Saint Louis* by Daniel Weiss. On the development and spread of Saint Louis's cult, see Cecilia Gaposchkin's *The Making of Saint Louis*, and for the classic study of Louis himself—written in French and translated into English—see Jacques Le Goff's *Saint Louis*. Though the literature on relics and other human remains is vast, a brilliant (and enjoyably meandering) starting point on the cultural importance of dead bodies is Thomas Laqueur's *The Work of the Dead*. More specifically on relics, reliquaries, and relic veneration in the Middle Ages is Charles Freeman's highly engaging *Holy Bones, Holy Dust*. With an even narrower focus, mainly on objects, is the richly illustrated edited collection *Treasures of Heaven*. Within this volume, see Arnold Angenendt's "Relics and Their Veneration," Martina Bagnoli's "The Stuff of Heaven" (more focused on reliquaries and the concerns of some clerics, such as Bernard of Clairvaux, with their opulence), Holger Klein's "Sacred Things and Holy Bodies" (which addresses relic collecting), and Derek Krueger's "The Religion of Relics in Late Antiquity and Byzantium." Published elsewhere, John Wortley's "The Origins of Christian Veneration of Body-Parts" is another helpful starting point.

On the fourth-century development of a Christian "holy" land, see Robert Wilken's *The Land Called Holy*. John Wilkinson's *Jerusalem Pilgrims before the Crusades*, originally published in the late 1970s and since reprinted, remains an important investigation into travel and pilgrimage itineraries in late antiquity and the early Middle Ages.

Saint Jerome writes about Rome changing its address to the shrines beyond the city walls in his *Letter* 107, but for a groundbreaking study of private devotion to saints and relics not centered on public tombs and shrines, see *Private Worship, Public Values, and Religious Change in Late Antiquity* by Kim Bowes. Undoubtedly, the most important contribution to the study of saints' cults is Peter Brown's *The Cult of the Saints*. For saints' relics in an architectural context, including their placement in altars, see Anne Marie Yasin's *Saints and Church Spaces in the Late Antique Mediterranean*. Also helpful in this regard is Éric Palazzo's "Relics, Liturgical Space, and the Theology of the Church." Patrick Geary discusses the practice of punishing nonworking relics in his "Humiliation of Saints."

It is Geary's *Furta Sacra* on which I relied for the stories about relic thefts in the Middle Ages. For the extensive olfactory connections between saints and holiness, see Susan Ashbrook Harvey's fabulous contribution *Scenting Salvation*. Bagnoli's "The Stuff of Heaven" refers to debates over the commodification of relics within the context of a broader discussion about the medieval relic cult and the manufacture of reliquaries. For the quote from Red Smith on the zealous collection of dirt at Ebbets Field and an intriguing analysis of baseball memorabilia and Major League Baseball's authentication process more generally, see Stephen Andon's "Authenticity at the Right Price," on which I relied for my account of these issues. The official MLB website also details its authentication process, while the description of the pendant fashioned from a New York Mets game-used baseball comes from the website of the retailer Tokens and Icons.

Klein's "Sacred Relics and Imperial Ceremonies at the Great Palace of Constantinople" describes the Byzantine emperor's relic collection in the Pharos Church and explains the reciprocal duty to protect that is shared between Christ and the emperor. Meanwhile, Otto Meinardus, in "A Study of the Relics of Saints of the Greek Church," calculates the number of saints' shrines and relics in Constantinople.

For Anne Catherine Emmerich's visions and her influence on Mel Gibson's *The Passion of the Christ,* see "Between God and Gibson" by Andrew Weeks. Mark Guscin's *The Image of Edessa* tracks the Sudarium of Oviedo's journey from Jerusalem to Spain, while Ewa Kuryluk's *Veronica and Her Cloth* provides a useful history of this veil. Dante refers to the Croatian pilgrim who travels to Rome just to see "the Veronica" in canto 31 of the *Paradiso.* On the Abgar-Jesus correspondence, see book 1 of Eusebius's *Ecclesiastical History* and a study of this supposed exchange in James Corke-Webster's "A Man for the Times." Though the history of the Abgar legend—including references to it in works other than Eusebius's *Ecclesiastical History*—is convoluted, the clearest overview is Averil Cameron's "The History of the Image of Edessa." For the Syriac sources, see Han J. W. Drijvers's "The Image of Edessa in the Syriac Tradition." Guscin's *The Image of Edessa* deals with the Byzantine versions of the legend after the image arrived in Constantinople. For the supposed connection between the Mandylion and the Shroud of Turin, see Andrea Nicolotti's *From the Mandylion of Edessa to the Shroud of Turin.* And for John Calvin's skepticism about the shroud's authenticity, see his *Treatise on Relics* from 1543.

A good study of the interest of "Western" Christians in "Eastern" relics is Klein's "Eastern Objects and Western Desires." On the diversion of the Fourth Crusade to Constantinople and the sacking of that city by Christians, see Thomas Madden's "The Venetian Version of the Fourth Crusade" and David Perry's *Sacred Plunder.*

4. The Feasts of the Dead

For an environmental and cultural history of Caribbean hurricanes, including the impact of San Felipe Segundo on Puerto Rico, see Stuart Schwartz's *Sea of Storms*. Though focused more on Guadeloupe than on Haiti, Laurent Dubois's *A Colony of Citizens* is an excellent study of slavery and revolution in the French Caribbean. For the use of the Bible in polemical arguments both for and against slavery in nineteenth-century America, look no further than Jeremy Schipper's *Denmark Vesey's Bible*. Denmark Vesey, a former slave, was put on trial in Charleston, South Carolina, for plotting a revolt, and he drew upon the Bible—including the book of Exodus—to justify his actions. Vesey was hanged in Charleston in 1822, nearly thirty years before James Henley Thornwell preached his sermon, *The Rights and Duties of Masters*, in the same city. For slavery in the ancient Mediterranean, see Kyle Harper's *Slavery in the Late Roman World* and Jennifer Glancy's *Slavery in Early Christianity*, which insightfully considers the places of Christian slaves and slaveholders in the early church's institutional development. On the *Apostolic Constitutions* and the many other early Christian books that circulated as works by those who had no hand in writing them, see Bart Ehrman's *Forgery and Counterforgery*.

The theme of the Christian virgin who refuses to marry and is then tortured or martyred is common in early Christian literature. For the tale about Saint Eugenia, see *The Roman Martyrs* by Michael Lapidge. For Eugenia's attempt to disguise herself as a monk, see the final chapter of Kristi Upson-Saia's *Early Christian Dress*, which considers the relative frequency of cross-dressing in early Christian stories about female saints. "Caribbean" martyrs like Eustatius (who is often elided with Hubert, the other major patron saint of hunters), along with Martin, Vincent, Philip, Ursula, Lucy, and others, all have their stories told in Jacopo de Voragine's *The Golden Legend*, accessible in English via the two-volume translation by William Granger Ryan.

For Martin and Sulpicius Severus, see Clare Stancliffe's *St. Martin and His Hagiographer*. Martin Walsh discusses the agrarian economy and November folk traditions about Saint Martin in "Medieval English *Martinmesse*." What Walsh refers to as "grotesque" in Bruegel's depictions of Saint Martin's charity is the theme of his "*Martín y Muchos Pobres*." More expansively on this topic is Margaret Sullivan's *Bruegel's Peasants*. Finally, for the slaughter of geese and other animals in Ireland on Saint Martin's Day, see Bill Mag Fhloinn's *Blood Rite*.

To the best of my knowledge, no full English translation of the *Chronograph of 354* exists (at least not in print), but for a study of the *Chronograph* and its place in the mid-fourth-century Roman world, see Michele Salzman's *On Roman Time*. More narrowly focused is "The Chronograph of 354" by R. W. Burgess. Though Salzman's *On Roman Time* contains plenty of images, readers of French may want to consult Henri Stern's *Le calendrier de 354* for an analysis of the *Chronograph*'s illustrations.

For early Christian sermons on martyrs, see *'Let Us Die That We May Live'* by Johan Leemans et al. I relied on Peter Brown's "Enjoying the Saints in Late Antiquity" for some of my comments about Augustine's interest in martyrs and for his translation of Augustine's quote about all those eagerly hurrying to hold festival at "that holy place." See chapter 20 of Theodoret of Cyrrhus's *Religious History* for the ascetic who boasted of maintaining his virginity despite attending the celebrations of many martyrs' feasts.

One of the most interesting and readable introductions to Roman calendars (and calendars and time reckoning in general) is Arno Borst's *The Ordering of Time*. I have also benefited from *Mapping Time* by E. G. Richards. For a daily accompaniment, see *The Oxford Companion to the Year* by Bonnie Blackburn and Leofranc Holford-Strevens, which is at once a survey of the complexity of calendars across many cultures and a day-by-day calendar filled with folkloric anecdotes about each day of the year. Borst addresses the general science and importance of correctly calculating the date of Easter, but for more on the *computus* and the emergence of the AD system, see *Anno Domini* by Georges Declercq and *The Easter Computus and the Origins of the Christian Era* by Alden Mosshammer. Mosshammer explains that Dionysius relied on Julius Africanus, a Christian historian of the late second and early third centuries, to calculate Jesus's age when he died and the year of the crucifixion—which thereby provided the year of his birth.

For the Venerable Bede's investigations into time reckoning and the annual cycle of saints' feasts, see Máirín MacCarron's *Bede and Time* and two earlier contributions by Alan Thacker: "Bede and History" and "Bede and His Martyrology." Many of the fundamental studies of Frankish martyr calendars (i.e., those of Usuard and others) are rather dated at this point, but, given the paucity of more recent studies, see John McCulloh's "Historical Martyrologies in the Benedictine Cultural Tradition," Henri Quentin's *Les martyrologes historiques du Moyen Âge*, Jacques Dubois's *Les martyrologes du Moyen Âge latin*, and (in translation from the original German) Heinrich Kellner's *Heortology*. On the short-lived French Republican calendar, see Matthew Shaw's *Time and the French Revolution*.

5. The Living Dead

Two general works on medieval anchorites in England that are now decades old but remain useful are R. M. Clay's *The Hermits and Anchorites of England* and

F. D. S. Darwin's *English Medieval Recluse.* For more recent studies, see Roberta Gil-christ's *Contemplation and Action* and E. A. Jones's *Hermits and Anchorites in England.* For a wonderfully transportive twenty-five-minute audio introduction that begins inside the anchorhold at Saint Anne's Church in Lewes and describes parts of the enclosure liturgy, Mary Wellesley's "This Place Is Pryson," a podcast from the *London Review of Books,* is not to be missed. On the pontifical manuscripts that outline the enclosure rite, see Jones's "Rites of Enclosure." (The relevant biblical readings for the liturgy are Isaiah 26:20–27:3 and Luke 10:38–42.) On the construction of anchorholds, see *Hermits and Recluses in English Society* by Tom Licence. For the recluses' patrons and patronage more generally, see Ann Warren's *Anchorites and Their Patrons in Medieval England.* The comment about the anchorhold not becoming a schoolhouse, post office, bank, or newspaper comes from the helpful introduction to the *Ancrene Wisse* by Robert Hasenfratz, the editor of a recent edition. Though Robyn Cadwallader's *The Anchoress* is a fictional account of a medieval recluse, it is both beautifully written and steeped in historical research.

The apostle Paul talks about being baptized into death and putting "to death the deeds of the body" in several places in his Letter to the Romans (and elsewhere). For an exhaustive study of the history, theology, liturgy, and architecture of baptism in the first five centuries of the Christian era, see Everett Ferguson's *Baptism in the Early Church.* For Anthony's episode with the demons at the tombs, see Athanasius of Alexandria's *Life of Anthony,* and for an excellent survey of demons and monks in Egypt, which includes accounts of Anthony, Evagrius, and the other desert fathers, see David Brakke's *Demons and the Making of the Monk.* For the words of the desert fathers themselves, see *The Sayings of the Desert Fathers.* The classic general study of the holy man in this period, which includes a discussion of Simeon the Stylite, is Peter Brown's "The Rise and Function of the Holy Man in Late Antiquity." The remark about the necessity of "enclosure as a way to starve the searching virus of bodies to inhabit" comes from an article by Keeanga-Yamahtta Taylor in the March 30, 2020, issue of the *New Yorker.*

Teresa Shaw's *The Burden of the Flesh* is a good general introduction to ascetic fasting in early Christianity. Despite its self-indulgent length, which is typical of Jerome, his *Letter* 22, to Eustochium, is worth reading in its entirety, especially for an understanding of the great extent to which early Christian ascetic thinking influenced the author of the *Ancrene Wisse.* Neil Adkin's *Jerome on Virginity* is a superb commentary on this letter. For a briefer study of ascetic desire in Jerome's work, see Patricia Cox Miller's "The Blazing Body." Meanwhile, Miller's "Is There a Harlot in This Text?" addresses the lives of the so-called holy harlots, as does Virginia Burrus's *The Sex Lives of Saints.* For English translations of the three major harlot *Lives* (of Maria, Mary of Egypt, and Pelagia), see Benedicta Ward's *Harlots of the Desert.* On gender and trans identities and sexual shaming in ancient and medieval sources, see Roland Betancourt's *Byzantine Intersectionality.* For the architecture and archaeology of the monasteries that Mary of Egypt may have encountered in her desert peregrinations, see Yizhar Hirschfeld's *The Judean Desert Monasteries in the Byzantine Period.* Cyril of Scythopolis discusses many of these places and the men who inhabited them in his *Lives of the Monks of Palestine.* Though its geographic focus is outside Palestine, Daniel Caner's *Wandering, Begging Monks* is a fabulous study of wandering ascetics in late antiquity, while Peter Mena's *Place and Identity in the Lives of Antony, Paul, and Mary of Egypt* offers a more theoretically informed account of Mary of Egypt (and other Egyptian ascetics) through a conceptual analysis of the desert as borderland. I am grateful to Hieromonk Silouan Justiniano of the Monastery of Saint Dionysios the Areopagite for kindly granting me permission to reproduce his beautiful icon of Saint Mary of Egypt and Saint Zosimas.

For a line-by-line commentary on the infancy narratives in Matthew and Luke, with hundreds of pages of background and analysis that are still accessible to nonspecialists, see Raymond Brown's *The Birth of the Messiah.* More generally on Mary's place in late antiquity is Stephen Shoemaker's *Mary in Early Christian Faith and Devotion.* The jarring fourth chapter of Jennifer Glancy's *Corporal Knowledge* examines some of the earliest Christian sources on Mary in childbirth, demonstrating the multiple ways in which her body and her virginity were imagined and understood. David Hunter's *Marriage and Sexuality in Early Christian Sources* is a good compendium of the topics indicated by its title, while "Negotiating the Nativity in Late Antiquity," a dissertation by Rami Tannous (my former graduate student at the University of Toronto), explores the intersection between apocryphal Christian sources like the *Protoevangelium of James* and Syriac homilies on Mary and the birth of Jesus—and then goes on to consider the influence of such literature on the Qur'an's presentation of Mary. For the Byzantine mosaics at the Chora Church, see Robert Ousterhout's "The Virgin of the Chora."

6. The Miracles of the Dead

For *The Canterbury Tales* and all things Chaucerian, see *The Riverside Chaucer,* edited by Larry Benson. For medieval exempla in general, see Jacques Le Goff's "L''exemplum' médiéval."

Brouria Bitton-Ashkelony's *Encountering the Sacred* considers the often conflicting attitudes toward pilgrimage held by Christian theologians in late antiquity, while John Wilkinson's *Jerusalem Pilgrims before the Crusades* offers a good general survey of Holy Land pilgrimage in late antiquity. See also Blake Leyerle's perceptive article "Landscape as Cartography in Early Christian Pilgrimage Narratives." Andrew Jacobs's translation of the Piacenza Pilgrim's *Itinerary* is available in full online. William Melczer's *The Pilgrim's Guide to Santiago de Compostela* is useful for not only its English translation of the *Peregrinatio Compostellana* but also its commentary on the text and its general introduction to the development of Saint James's cult and its central importance for medieval pilgrims.

For pilgrimage during the time of Thomas Becket, see Diana Webb's *Pilgrimage in Medieval England*. Robert Bartlett discusses pilgrimage churches (including Canterbury Cathedral) in an entire section of his monumental study of saints and martyrs, *Why Can the Dead Do Such Great Things?* One of best and most engagingly readable accounts of popular beliefs and cults in medieval England is Ronald Finucane's *Miracles and Pilgrims*, which I reference several times in chapter 6. It is Finucane who refers to the wax ships, body parts, and candles at Becket's shrine and attempts to explain how medieval pilgrims understood cures—and thus miracles. More theoretically on the topic is Benedicta Ward's *Miracles and the Medieval Mind*. A superb and beautifully illustrated book that ranges across medieval medicine, miracles, art, literature, folklore, and other topics is Jack Hartnell's *Medieval Bodies*. On the ubiquitous mass-produced souvenirs collected by pilgrims, see the revised edition of Gary Vikan's *Byzantine Pilgrimage Art* and Brian Spencer's *Pilgrim Souvenirs and Secular Badges*.

Theodoret's account of Simeon the Stylite is translated by Robert Doran in *The Lives of Simeon Stylites*. Augustine writes of the miracle in Milan in the ninth book of his *Confessions* and the twenty-second (and final) book of *The City of God*. It is there at the end of *The City of God* that he discusses the miracles attributed to Saint Stephen's relics and tells the miracle stories summarized in this chapter. Peter Brown's *Augustine of Hippo,* though first published in the 1960s, remains the most engaging starting place for anyone interested in Augustine's life and thought. For Gregory the Great's perspective on martyrs, miracles, and relics, see Matthew Dal Santo's *Debating the Saints' Cults in the Age of Gregory the Great*. For the stories about Peter the Hermit and Macedonius, see R. M. Price's translation of Theodoret's *Religious History,* which also offers an introduction to Theodoret and his work. More broadly on late antique visual piety and pilgrimage to "living saints" in Egypt is Georgia Frank's *The Memory of the Eyes.*

A good English translation of Caesarius of Heisterbach's *Dialogue on Miracles,* by H. von E. Scott and C. C. Swinton Bland, is out of print and available online. On Caesarius's oral sources, see Brian Patrick McGuire's "Friends and Tales in the Cloister," and for a series of essays on Caesarius and his miracle book, see *The Art of Cistercian Persuasion in the Middle Ages and Beyond*, edited by Victoria Smirnova, Marie Anne Polo de Beaulieu, and Jacques Berlioz.

Anne Duggan's *Thomas Becket* is a good place to begin for a survey of the saint's reputation from the twelfth century to the present, while Kay Brainerd Slocum's *The Cult of Thomas Becket* covers how historians have studied him, from his earliest biographers to modern scholars. See also Michael Staunton's *Thomas Becket and His Biographers*. The most comprehensive account of the miracle collections produced at Canterbury in the late twelfth century is *Wonderful to Relate* by Rachel Koopmans. It is Koopmans's work on which I relied for most of the material in this chapter about Benedict of Peterborough and William of Canterbury. For Canterbury Cathedral's windows, see Madeline Caviness's *The Windows of Christ Church Cathedral Canterbury*, M.A. Michael's *Stained Glass of Canterbury Cathedral*, and the opening of Paul Binski's *Becket's Crown*.

7. The War for the Dead

The material on Saint Leontius and the *cavatori* at the beginning of this chapter draws on *Heavenly Bodies* by Paul Koudounaris, a book that includes many of his wonderful photographs of the bejeweled "catacomb saints" (including Saint Leontius at Muri Abbey) that were sent north of the Alps in the early modern period. On the topic of catacomb saints more generally, see Trevor Johnson's "Holy Fabrications." For a sweeping survey of the Roman catacombs that covers more than a millennium, see "The History of the Roman Catacombs from the Era of Constantine to the Renaissance" by Irina Oryshkevich.

Fundamental to this chapter is the work of Simon Ditchfield, specifically his publications on Saint Philip Neri and his circle. On Neri in the catacombs, see Ditchfield's "Text before Trowel" (focused on Antonio Bosio and his *Roma sotterranea*) and *Liturgy, Sanctity and History in Tridentine Italy*. Also useful are Ditchfield's "An Early Christian School of Sanctity in Tridentine Rome" and Martine Gosselin's "The Congregation of the Oratorians and the Origins of Christian Archaeology." Jerome's recollection of exploring "the tombs of the apostles and martyrs" comes from his *Commentary on Ezekiel* as discussed and translated by Robert Bartlett in the opening chapter of his *Why Can the Dead Do Such Great Things?* On Counter-Reformation sanctity, see Peter Burke's "How to Be a Counter-Reformation Saint" and "Images as Evidence in Seventeenth-Century Europe." On the centralization and bureaucratization of the saints in early modern Catholicism, see Ditchfield's *Liturgy, Sanctity and History* and "An Early Christian School," particularly with respect to the creation of the Sacred Congregation of Rites and Ceremonies in 1588 and, slightly earlier, the approval of the second decree of the twenty-fifth meeting of the Council of Trent, which declared that no new miracles or relics were to be acknowledged without a bishop's approval.

Giuseppe Antonio Guazelli's "Cesare Baronio and the Roman Catholic Vision of the Early Church" is a useful introduction to Baronio's scholarship that focuses on both the cardinal himself and the post-Tridentine church's keen interest in the cultic practices of the early Christians. In the same edited volume with Guazelli's chapter, two very readable surveys of Catholic and Protestant interests in church history are Anthony Grafton's "Church History in Early Modern Europe" and Euan Cameron's "Primitivism, Patristics, and Polemic in Protestant Visions of Early Christianity." More comprehensively on these topics is *Historical Method and Confessional Identity in the Era of the Reformation* by Irena Backus. There is relatively little scholarship on Gallonio, and Opher Mansour's "Not Torments, but Delights" and Jetze Touber's *Law, Medicine, and Engineering in the Cult of the Saints in Counter-Reformation Rome* are the most useful. On Charles Carrington and the publication of the English version of Gallonio's *Treatise on the Instruments of Martyrdom,* see the comments of Virginia Burrus in "Torture, Truth, and the Witnessing Body." Finally, far and away the best overview of Christian martyrdom in early modern Europe (including a survey of Catholic, Protestant, and Anabaptist discourses on martyrdom) is Brad Gregory's *Salvation at Stake.*

On the making of John Foxe's *Actes and Monuments,* see Elizabeth Evenden and Thomas Freeman's *Religion and the Book in Early Modern England,* which discusses everything from the price of paper in sixteenth-century Europe to the work of the pressmen and the relationship between Foxe and his printer, John Day. For Foxe as a historical narrator, especially one who was deeply indebted to Eusebius, see Gregory's *Salvation at Stake,* Evenden and Freeman's *Religion and the Book,* and Susannah Brietz Monta's *Martyrdom and Literature in Early Modern England.* Evenden and Freeman also discuss the oral histories that were delivered to Foxe and Day. On Day's decision to include a calendar of martyrs in Foxe's book, see Thomas Freeman's "The Power of Polemic," and for Catholic criticism of Foxe's calendar, see O. T. Hargrave's "Bloody Mary's Victims." On Robert Persons, the Jesuit critic of Foxe, see Freeman's "The Power of Polemic," Anne Dillon's *The Construction of Martyrdom in the English Catholic Community,* and Victor Houliston's *Catholic Resistance in Elizabethan England.* On the importance of the images in the *Actes and Monuments,* see Evenden and Freeman's *Religion and the Book,* Gregory's *Salvation at Stake,* and Tessa Watt's *Cheap Print and Popular Piety.* Watt also addresses the rural English wills through which copies of Foxe's book were passed from one generation to the next. For the deaths of Cranmer, Latimer, and

Ridley, see *The Oxford Martyrs* by David Loades, and for the Catholic letter writer who witnessed Cranmer's execution, see Monta's *Martyrdom and Literature*. Diarmaid MacCullouch's excellent biography *Thomas Cranmer* is not to be missed. More broadly on religious change in fifteenth- and sixteenth-century England is Eamon Duffy's *The Stripping of the Altars*.

The frescoes of both ancient and contemporary martyrs at the English College in Rome are considered by Richard Williams in his "Ancient Bodies and Contested Identities in the English College Martyrdom Cycle" and by Dillon in her *Construction of Martyrdom in the English Catholic Community*. Alexandra Herz's "Imitators of Christ" discusses other martyr cycles in sixteenth-century Rome.

8. The Legends of the Dead

The brief quotation of Boccaccio's *Decameron* comes from the translation by Wayne Rebhorn, while those of Petrarch and the fourteenth-century chroniclers and medical doctors who wrote about the plague are from John Aberth's illuminating collection *The Black Death*. In addition to a readable introduction to the plague, Aberth's book offers a well-curated and topically organized series of chapters with clear translations of the documentary evidence. His selections include material on the origin of the plague, the suggestions of medical professionals for its prevention and treatment, and commentaries on the social and religious impact of the Black Death. For a study of medical instruction at the University of Paris between 1250 and 1400, see Cornelius O'Boyle's *The Art of Medicine*. One of the more notable publications from a revisionist historian of the Black Death is Samuel Cohn's *The Black Death Transformed*. More generally on the social repercussions of the plague and other epidemics are Frank Snowden's *Epidemics and Society,* which came out in the fall of 2019, just months before the emergence of the novel coronavirus, and Kyle Harper's *Plagues upon the Earth,* which appeared in the fall of 2021 and situates COVID-19 within a broader examination of disease and human history.

My quotations of Heinrich of Herford also come from Aberth's volume; for more on the flagellants, see John Henderson's "The Flagellant Movement and Flagellant Confraternities in Central Italy." Though it focuses on the twelfth century, Robert Chazan's *Medieval Stereotypes and Modern Antisemitism* provides useful background for understanding some of the anti-Semitism that arose in response to the Black Death.

Quotations of Jacopo de Voragine come from William Granger Ryan's two-volume translation of *The Golden Legend*. For studies of this text and its history, see The "Legenda Aurea" by Sherry Reames, The Talents of Jacopo da Varagine by Steven Epstein, La légende dorée by Alain Boureau, and Jacques Le Goff's In Search of Sacred Time.

For the artistic response to the Black Death that relied on Jacopo's narrative in The Golden Legend to transform Sebastian into the protector of cities afflicted with epidemic disease, see Sheila Barker's "The Making of a Plague Saint." On Josse Lieferinxe's painting of Sebastian interceding for Pavia and the artist's related images, see Melissa Katz's "Preventative Medicine." More broadly on Christian art in the aftermath of the Black Death are Christine Boeckl's Images of Plague and Pestilence, Louise Marshall's "Manipulating the Sacred," and Peter Mitchell's "The Politics of Morbidity."

For a translation and study of Arnobius the Younger's passio of Sebastian, see The Roman Martyrs by Michael Lapidge. Specifically on the identification of Arnobius as the author of the passio is "Arnobe le Jeune et la Passion de Sébastien" by Cécile Lanéry. For the fifteenth-century accounts of Saint Roch, see Irene Vaslef's "The Role of St. Roch as a Plague Saint." On the historiographical difficulties with Roch, see "Le problème de saint Roch" by Augustin Fliche. Don Skemer's Binding Words is a fascinating study of textual amulets in the Middle Ages. For the transformation of canonization practices, see the important work by André Vauchez Sainthood in the Later Middle Ages.

Simon Ditchfield briefly discusses the hiatus in publishing The Golden Legend from the early seventeenth century until the middle of the nineteenth, as well as Cardinal Bellarmine's reservations about Rosweyde's plans, in his Liturgy, Sanctity and History in Tridentine Italy. See also Ditchfield's "What Was Sacred History?" and the chapter on the Bollandists in Great Historical Enterprises by David Knowles. Éric Rebillard mentions some of the concerns about "scientific" approaches to hagiography in the introduction to his Early Martyr Narratives. In addition to Hippolyte Delehaye's The Legends of the Saints—whose main points I summarize in this chapter—his The Work of the Bollandists through Three Centuries exists in English translation, and it provides a good survey of the scholarly work on which his own is built. That said, Knowles's briefer account of the Bollandists is likely to be of more interest to the general reader. Out of print and available online are Delehaye's Les origines du culte des martyrs and Les passions des martyrs et les genres littéraires. In The Legends of the Saints, he stops short of excluding the historical admissibility of "the Persian martyrs," saying that without further investigation into the relevant Syriac sources "it would be premature to pronounce on the original form and consequently also on the documentary value of these narratives." For some general remarks in this direction, see the introduction to my

The Martyrdom and History of Blessed Simeon bar Ṣabbaʿe. As I argue, all martyrdom narratives from late antiquity are wonderfully precious from a literary and even historical perspective, but to read them for their "documentary value," as if they provided hard evidence for real events, would be to fundamentally misunderstand their nature. I discuss this further in my *Constantine and the Captive Christians of Persia.*

Bibliography

Ancient and Medieval Sources in English Translation

Acts of Paul and Thecla. Translated by J. K. Eliott in *The Apocryphal New Testament: A Collection of Apocryphal Christian Literature in an English Translation*. Oxford: Oxford University Press, 1993.

Aelred of Rievaulx. *Rule of Life for a Recluse*. Translated by Mary Paul Macpherson in *Treatises and Pastoral Prayer*, edited by D. Knowles, 41–102. Kalamazoo, MI: Cistercian Publications, 1971.

Ambrose of Milan. *Letter* 22. Translated by H. Walford in *The Letters of St. Ambrose, Bishop of Milan*. Oxford: James Parker, 1881.

Ancrene Wisse. Translated by Bella Millett in *Ancrene Wisse: A Guide for Anchoresses—a Translation Based on Cambridge, Corpus Christi College, MS 402*. Exeter: University of Exeter Press, 2009.

Apostolic Constitutions. Translated by James Donaldson in *Ante-Nicene Fathers*, vol. 7, edited by A. Roberts, Donaldson, and A. Cleveland Coxe. Buffalo: Christian Literature, 1886.

Athanasius of Alexandria. *Life of Anthony*. Translated by Robert C. Gregg in *Athanasius: The Life of Antony and the Letter to Marcellinus*. Mahwah, NJ: Paulist, 1980.

Augustine. *The City of God*. Translated by R. W. Dyson in *Augustine: The City of God against the Pagans*. Cambridge: Cambridge University Press, 1998.

———. *Confessions*. Translated by Henry Chadwick in *Saint Augustine: Confessions*. Oxford: Oxford University Press, 2008.

Bede. *Ecclesiastical History of the English People*. Translated by Leo Sherley-Price in *Bede: Ecclesiastical History of the English People*. New York: Penguin, 1991.

———. *On the Reckoning of Time*. Translated by Faith Wallis in *Bede: The Reckoning of Time*. Liverpool: Liverpool University Press, 1999.

Benedict. *Rule of Saint Benedict*. Translated by Terrence G. Kardong in *Benedict's Rule: A Translation and Commentary*. Collegeville, MN: Liturgical Press, 1996.

Boccaccio, Giovanni. *The Decameron*. Translated and edited by Wayne A. Rebhorn. New York: Norton, 2015.

The Book of Steps. Translated by Robert A. Kitchen and Martien F. G. Parmentier in *The Book of Steps: The Syriac "Liber Graduum."* Kalamazoo, MI: Cistercian Publications, 2004.

Caesarius of Heisterbach. *Dialogus miraculorum*. Translated by H. von E. Scott and C. C. Swinton Bland in *The Dialogue on Miracles: Caesarius of Heisterbach (1220–1235)*. 2 vols. New York: Harcourt, Brace, 1929.

Calvin, John. *A Treatise on Relics*. Translated by Valerian Krasinski. Edinburgh: Johnstone, Hunter, 1870.

Chaucer, Geoffrey. *The Canterbury Tales*. In *The Riverside Chaucer,* edited by Larry D. Benson. Oxford: Oxford University Press, 2008.

Cyril of Scythopolis. *Lives of the Monks of Palestine*. Translated by R. M. Price in *Cyril of Scythopolis: The Lives of the Monks of Palestine*. Kalamazoo, MI: Cistercian Publications, 1991.

Dante Alighieri. *Paradiso*. Translated by Robert Hollander and Jean Hollander. New York: Anchor Books, 2007.

Egeria. *Itinerary*. Translated by Anne McGowan and Paul F. Bradshaw in *The Pilgrimage of Egeria: A New Translation of the "Itinerarium Egeriae" with Introduction and Commentary*. Collegeville, MN: Liturgical Press, 2018.

Eusebius of Caesarea. *Ecclesiastical History*. Translated by Jeremy M. Schott in *The History of the Church: A New Translation*. Berkeley: University of California Press, 2019.

———. *Martyrs of Palestine*. Translated by William Cureton in *History of the Martyrs in Palestine, by Eusebius, Bishop of Caesarea, Discovered in a Very Antient [sic] Syriac Manuscript*. London: Williams and Norgate, 1861.

Gallonio, Antonio. *Treatise on the Instruments of Martyrdom*. Rome: A. e G. Donangeli, 1591. Translated by A. R. Allinson in *Tortures and Torments of the Christian Martyrs*. London: printed for the subscribers, 1903.

Goscelin of Saint-Bertin. *Book of Consolation*. Translated by Monika Otter in *Goscelin of St. Bertin: Book of Encouragement and Consolation (Liber Confortatorius)*. Cambridge: Cambridge University Press, 2004.

Gregory of Nyssa. *Life of Macrina*. Translated by Kevin Corrigan in *The Life of Saint Macrina by Gregory, Bishop of Nyssa*. Eugene, OR: Wipf and Stock, 2001.

Gregory the Great. *Dialogues*. Translated by Odo John Zimmerman. Fathers of the Church, vol. 39. Washington, DC: Catholic University of America Press, 1959.

———. *Letters*. Translated by John R. C. Martyn in *The Letters of Gregory the Great*. 3 vols. Toronto: Pontifical Institute of Medieval Studies, 2004.

Ignatius of Antioch, *Letter to the Romans*. Translated by William R. Schoedel in *Ignatius of Antioch: A Commentary on the Letters of Ignatius of Antioch*. Philadelphia: Fortress, 1985.

Jacopo de Voragine. *The Golden Legend*. Translated by William Granger Ryan in *The Golden Legend: Readings on the Saints*. 2 vols. Princeton: Princeton University Press, 1993.

Jerome. *Letter 22, to Eustochium*. Translated by F. A. Wright in *Jerome: Select Letters*, 52–159. Cambridge, MA: Harvard University Press, 1933.

———. *Letter 107, to Laeta*. Translated by F. A. Wright in *Jerome: Select Letters*, 338–69. Cambridge, MA: Harvard University Press, 1933.

Life of Maria the Harlot. Translated by Benedicta Ward in *Harlots of the Desert: A Study of Repentance in Early Monastic Sources*, 92–101. Kalamazoo, MI: Cistercian Publications, 1987.

Life of Saint Mary of Egypt. Translated by Benedicta Ward in *Harlots of the Desert: A Study of Repentance in Early Monastic Sources*, 35–56. Kalamazoo, MI: Cistercian Publications, 1987.

Life of Saint Pelagia the Harlot. Translated by Benedicta Ward in *Harlots of the Desert: A Study of Repentance in Early Monastic Sources*, 66–75. Kalamazoo, MI: Cistercian Publications, 1987.

The Martyrdom and History of Blessed Simeon bar Ṣabba'e. Translated by Kyle Smith. Piscataway, NJ: Gorgias, 2014.

Peregrinatio Compostellana. Translated by William Melczer in *The Pilgrim's Guide to Santiago de Compostela*. New York: Italica, 1993.

Piacenza Pilgrim. *Itinerary*. Translated by Andrew S. Jacobs at "The Piacenza Pilgrim." http://andrewjacobs.org/translations/piacenzapilgrim.html.

Plato. *Phaedo*. Translated by Alex Long in *Plato: Meno and Phaedo*, edited by David Sedley and Long. Cambridge: Cambridge University Press, 2010.

Protoevangelium of James. Translated by George T. Zervos in *The Protoevangelium of James: Greek Text, English Translation, Critical Introduction*, vol. 1. London: T&T Clark, 2019.

The Sayings of the Desert Fathers. Translated by Benedicta Ward in *The Sayings of the Desert Fathers: The Alphabetical Collection*. Kalamazoo, MI: Cistercian Publications, 1987.

Sozomen. *Ecclesiastical History.* Translated by Edward Walford in *The Ecclesiastical History of Sozomen, Comprising a History of the Church, from* A.D. 324 *to* A.D. 440. London: Henry G. Bohn, 1885.

Theodoret of Cyrrhus. *Life of Simeon the Stylite.* Translated by Robert Doran in *The Lives of Simeon Stylites.* Kalamazoo, MI: Cistercian Publications, 1992.

———. *Religious History.* Translated by R. M. Price in *Theodoret of Cyrrhus: A History of the Monks of Syria.* Kalamazoo, MI: Cistercian Publications, 1985.

Modern Sources

Aberth, John. *The Black Death: The Great Mortality of 1348–1350, A Brief History with Documents.* New York: Palgrave MacMillan, 2005.

Achermann, Hansjakob. *Die Katakombenheiligen und ihre Translationem in der schweizerischen Quart des Bistums Konstanz.* Stans, Switzerland: Historischer Verein Nidwalden, 1979.

Adkin, Neil. *Jerome on Virginity: A Commentary on the "Libellus de virginitate servanda" (Letter 22).* Cambridge: Francis Cairns, 2003.

Andon, Stephen. "Authenticity at the Right Price: The Development and Implications of Commodified Sports Memorabilia." *Quadrivium: A Journal of Multidisciplinary Scholarship* 5, no. 1 (2013): art. 2.

Angenendt, Arnold. "Relics and Their Veneration." In *Treasures of Heaven: Saints, Relics, and Devotion in Medieval Europe,* edited by M. Bagnoli, H. A. Klein, C. G. Mann, and J. Robinson, 19–28. London: British Museum Press, 2010.

Ariès, Philippe. *Western Attitudes toward Death from the Middle Ages to the Present.* Translated by P. M. Ranum. Baltimore: Johns Hopkins University Press, 1974.

Backus, Irena. *Historical Method and Confessional Identity in the Era of the Reformation (1378–1615).* Leiden: Brill, 2003.

Bagnoli, Martina. "The Stuff of Heaven: Materials and Craftsmanship in Medieval Reliquaries." In *Treasures of Heaven: Saints, Relics, and Devotion in Medieval Europe,* edited by M. Bagnoli, H. A. Klein, C. G. Mann, and J. Robinson, 137–47. London: British Museum Press, 2010.

Barker, Sheila. "The Making of a Plague Saint: Saint Sebastian's Imagery and Cult before the Counter-Reformation." In *Piety and Plague from Byzantium to the Baroque,* edited by F. Mormando and T. Worcester, 90–131. Kirksville, MO: Truman State University Press, 2007.

Barnes, Timothy D. *Constantine and Eusebius.* Cambridge, MA: Harvard University Press, 1984.

Bartlett, Robert. *Why Can the Dead Do Such Great Things? Saints and Worshippers from the Martyrs to the Reformation.* Princeton: Princeton University Press, 2013.

Baynes, Norman H. "The Supernatural Defenders of Constantinople." *Analecta Bollandiana* 67 (1949): 165–77.

Beck, Brian E. " 'Imitatio Christi' and the Lucan Passion Narrative." In *Suffering and Martyrdom in the New Testament,* edited by W. Horbury and B. McNeil, 28–47. Cambridge: Cambridge University Press, 1981.

Betancourt, Roland. *Byzantine Intersectionality: Sexuality, Gender, and Race in the Middle Ages.* Princeton: Princeton University Press, 2020.

Binski, Paul. *Becket's Crown: Art and Imagination in Gothic England, 1170–1300.* New Haven: Yale University Press, 2004.

Bissell, Tom. *Apostle: Travels among the Tombs of the Twelve.* New York: Vintage, 2016.

Bitton-Ashkelony, Brouria. *Encountering the Sacred: The Debate on Christian Pilgrimage in Late Antiquity.* Berkeley: University of California Press, 2005.

Blackburn, Bonnie, and Leofranc Holford-Strevens. *The Oxford Companion to the Year: An Exploration of Calendar Customs and Time-Reckoning.* Oxford: Oxford University Press, 1999.

Boeckl, Christine M. *Images of Plague and Pestilence: Iconography and Iconology.* Kirksville, MO: Truman State University Press, 2000.

Borst, Arno. *The Ordering of Time: From the Ancient Computus to the Modern Computer.* Chicago: University of Chicago Press, 1994.

Boureau, Alain. *La légende dorée: Le système narratif de Jacques de Voragine (†1298).* Paris: Cerf, 1984.

Bovon, François. "The Dossier on Stephen, the First Martyr." *Harvard Theological Review* 96 (2003): 279–315.

Bowersock, Glen W. *Martyrdom and Rome.* Cambridge: Cambridge University Press, 1995.

Bowes, Kim. *Private Worship, Public Values, and Religious Change in Late Antiquity.* Cambridge: Cambridge University Press, 2008.

Boyarin, Daniel. *Dying for God: Martyrdom and the Making of Christianity and Judaism.* Stanford: Stanford University Press, 1999.

Bozóky, Edina. *La politique des reliques de Constantin à Saint Louis: Protection collective et légitimation du pouvoir.* Paris: Beauchesne, 2006.

Brakke, David. *Demons and the Making of the Monk: Spiritual Combat in Early Christianity.* Cambridge, MA: Harvard University Press, 2006.

Branner, Robert. "The *Grande Châsse* of the Sainte-Chapelle." *Gazette des Beaux-Arts* 77 (1971): 6–18.

——. "The Painted Medallions in the Sainte-Chapelle in Paris." *Transactions of the American Philosophical Society* 58 (1968): 1–42.

Brock, Sebastian P. *The History of the Holy Mar Maʿin, with a Guide to the Persian Martyr Acts.* Piscataway, NJ: Gorgias, 2009.

——. "Without Mushê of Nisibis, Where Would We Be? Some Reflections on the Transmission of Syriac Literature." *Journal of Eastern Christian Studies* 56, nos. 1–4 (2004): 15–24.

Brock, Sebastian P., and Lucas Van Rompay. *Catalogue of the Syriac Manuscripts and Fragments in the Library of Deir al-Surian, Wadi al-Natrun (Egypt).* Leuven: Peeters, 2014.

Brown, Peter. *Augustine of Hippo: A Biography.* Berkeley: University of California Press, 1969.

——. *The Cult of the Saints: Its Rise and Function in Latin Christianity.* Chicago: University of Chicago Press, 1981.

——. "Enjoying the Saints in Late Antiquity." *Essays in Medieval Studies* 9 (2000): 1–24.

——. "The Rise and Function of the Holy Man in Late Antiquity." *Journal of Roman Studies* 61 (1971): 80–101.

Brown, Raymond E. *The Birth of the Messiah: A Commentary on the Infancy Narratives in the Gospels of Matthew and Luke.* Updated ed. New Haven: Yale University Press, 1999.

——. *The Death of the Messiah: From Gethsemane to the Grave (A Commentary on the Passion Narratives in the Four Gospels).* 2 vols. New York: Doubleday, 1994.

Burgess, R. W. "The Chronograph of 354: Its Manuscripts, Contents, and History." *Journal of Late Antiquity* 5 (2012): 345–96.

Burke, Peter. "How to Be a Counter-Reformation Saint." In *Religion and Society in Early Modern Europe, 1500–1800*, edited by K. Von Greyerz, 44–55. London: George Allen and Unwin, 1984.

——. "Images as Evidence in Seventeenth-Century Europe." *Journal of the History of Ideas* 64 (2003): 273–96.

——. *Popular Culture in Early Modern Europe.* New York: Harper and Row, 1978.

Burrus, Virginia. *The Sex Lives of Saints: An Erotics of Ancient Hagiography.* Philadelphia: University of Pennsylvania Press, 2004.

———. "Torture, Truth, and the Witnessing Body: Reading Christian Martyrdom with Page duBois." *Biblical Interpretation* 25 (2017): 5–18.

Cadwallader, Robyn. *The Anchoress.* New York: Sarah Crichton/FSG, 2015.

Cameron, Averil. "The History of the Image of Edessa: The Telling of the
Story." In *Okeanos: Essays Presented to Ihor Ševčenko on His Sixtieth Birthday,*
edited by C. Mango and O. Pritsak, 80–94. Cambridge, MA: Harvard
University Press, 1984.

Cameron, Euan. "Primitivism, Patristics, and Polemic in Protestant Visions of
Early Christianity." In *Sacred History: Uses of the Christian Past in the
Renaissance World,* edited by K. Van Liere, S. Ditchfield, and H. Louthan,
27–51. Oxford: Oxford University Press, 2012.

Caner, Daniel. *Wandering, Begging Monks: Spiritual Authority and the Promotion
of Monasticism in Late Antiquity.* Berkeley: University of California Press,
2002.

Castelli, Elizabeth A. *Martyrdom and Memory: Early Christian Culture Making.*
New York: Columbia University Press, 2004.

Caviness, Madeline H. *The Windows of Christ Church Cathedral Canterbury.*
London: Oxford University Press, 1981.

Chazan, Robert. *Medieval Stereotypes and Modern Antisemitism.* Berkeley:
University of California Press, 1997.

Clark, Elizabeth A. "Claims on the Bones of Saint Stephen: The Partisans of
Melania and Eudocia." *Church History* 51 (1982): 141–56.

Clay, R. M. *The Hermits and Anchorites of England.* London: Methuen, 1914.

Cohen, Meredith. "An Indulgence for the Visitor: The Public at the Sainte-
Chapelle of Paris." *Speculum: A Journal of Medieval Studies* 83 (2008): 840–83.

Cohn, Samuel K. *The Black Death Transformed: Disease and Culture in Early
Renaissance Europe.* London: Bloomsbury, 2003.

Corke-Webster, James. *Eusebius and Empire: Constructing Church and Rome
in the "Ecclesiastical History."* Cambridge: Cambridge University Press,
2019.

———. "A Man for the Times: Jesus and the Abgar Correspondence in Eusebius
of Caesarea's *Ecclesiastical History.*" *Harvard Theological Review* 110 (2017):
563–87.

Cureton, William. *An Ancient Colophon: A Memoir by William Cureton.* Edited by
J. F. Coakley. Oxford: Jericho, 1999.

Dal Santo, Matthew. *Debating the Saints' Cults in the Age of Gregory the Great.*
Oxford: Oxford University Press, 2012.

Darwin, F. D. S. *English Medieval Recluse.* London: SPCK, 1944.

Declercq, Georges. *Anno Domini: The Origins of the Christian Era.* Turnhout: Brepols, 2000.

Delehaye, Hippolyte. *The Legends of the Saints: An Introduction to Hagiography.* Translated by V. M. Crawford. New York: Longmans, 1907.

———. *Les origines du culte des martyrs.* Brussels: Bureaux de la société des Bollandistes, 1912.

———. *Les passions des martyrs et les genres littéraires.* Brussels: Bureaux de la société des Bollandistes, 1921.

———. *The Work of the Bollandists through Three Centuries, 1615–1915.* Translated from the French. Princeton: Princeton University Press, 1922.

Demacopoulos, George E. *Gregory the Great: Ascetic, Pastor, and First Man of Rome.* Notre Dame, IN: University of Notre Dame Press, 2015.

DeVore, David J. "Greek Historiography, Roman Society, Christian Empire: The *Ecclesiastical History* of Eusebius of Caesarea." PhD diss., University of California, Berkeley, 2013.

Dibelius, Martin. *From Tradition to Gospel.* New York: Charles Scribner's Sons, 1935.

Dillon, Anne. *The Construction of Martyrdom in the English Catholic Community, 1535–1603.* London: Ashgate, 2002.

Ditchfield, Simon. "An Early Christian School of Sanctity in Tridentine Rome." In *Christianity and Community in the West: Essays for John Bossy,* edited by Ditchfield, 183–205. Aldershot: Ashgate, 2001.

———. *Liturgy, Sanctity and History in Tridentine Italy: Pietro Maria Campi and the Preservation of the Particular.* Cambridge: Cambridge University Press, 2002.

———. "Text before Trowel: Antonio Bosio's *Roma sotterranea* Revisited." In *The Church Retrospective,* edited by R. N. Swanson, 343–60. Woodbridge, Suffolk: Boydell, 1997.

———. "What Was Sacred History? (Mostly Roman) Catholic Uses of the Past after Trent." In *Sacred History: Uses of the Christian Past in the Renaissance World,* edited by K. Van Liere, S. Ditchfield, and H. Louthan, 72–97. Oxford: Oxford University Press, 2012.

Dostoyevsky, Fyodor. *The Idiot.* Translated by David McDuff. New York: Penguin, 2004.

Drijvers, Han J. W. "The Image of Edessa in the Syriac Tradition." In *The Holy Face and the Paradox of Representation,* edited by H. L. Kessler and G. Wolf, 13–31. Bologna: Nuova Alfa, 1998.

Dubois, Jacques. *Les martyrologes du Moyen Âge latin.* Turnhout: Brepols, 1978.

Dubois, Laurent. *A Colony of Citizens: Revolution and Slave Emancipation in the French Caribbean, 1787–1804.* Chapel Hill: University of North Carolina Press, 2004.

Duffy, Eamon. *The Stripping of the Altars: Traditional Religion in England, 1400–1580.* New Haven: Yale University Press, 1992.

Duggan, Anne. *Thomas Becket.* London: Bloomsbury, 2004.

Durand, Jannic, and Bernard Flusin, eds. *Byzance et les reliques du Christ.* Leuven: Peeters, 2004.

Durand, Jannic, and Marie-Pierre Laffitte, eds. *Le trésor de la Sainte-Chapelle.* Paris: Musée du Louvre, 2001.

Eagleman, David. *Sum: Forty Tales from the Afterlives.* New York: Penguin, 2010.

Eastman, David L. *The Ancient Martyrdom Accounts of Peter and Paul.* Atlanta: SBL, 2015.

———. *The Many Deaths of Peter and Paul.* Oxford: Oxford University Press, 2019.

———. *Paul the Martyr: The Cult of the Apostle in the Latin West.* Atlanta: SBL, 2011.

Ehrman, Bart D. *Forgery and Counterforgery: The Use of Literary Deceit in Early Christian Polemics.* Oxford: Oxford University Press, 2012.

Emmerich, Anne Catherine. *The Dolorous Passion of Our Lord Jesus Christ: From the Meditations of Anne Catherine Emmerich.* Edited by Clemens Brentano. London: Burns and Lambert, 1862.

Epstein, Steven A. *The Talents of Jacopo da Varagine: A Genoese Mind in Medieval Europe.* Ithaca, NY: Cornell University Press, 2016.

Evelyn White, Hugh G. *The Monasteries of the Wâdi 'n Natrûn, Part II: The History of the Monasteries of Nitria and of Scetis.* Edited by W. Hauser. Publications of the Metropolitan Museum of Art Egyptian Expedition 7. New York: Metropolitan Museum of Art, 1932.

Evenden, Elizabeth, and Thomas S. Freeman. *Religion and the Book in Early Modern England: The Making of Foxe's 'Book of Martyrs.'* Cambridge: Cambridge University Press, 2014.

Ferguson, Everett. *Baptism in the Early Church: History, Theology, and Liturgy in the First Five Centuries.* Grand Rapids: W. B. Eerdmans, 2009.

Finucane, Ronald C. *Miracles and Pilgrims: Popular Beliefs in Medieval England.* New York: St. Martin's, 1995.

Fliche, Augustin. "Le problème de saint Roch." *Analecta Bollandiana* 68 (1950): 353–61.

Frank, Georgia. *The Memory of the Eyes: Pilgrims to Living Saints in Christian Late Antiquity.* Berkeley: University of California Press, 2000.

Freeman, Charles. *Holy Bones, Holy Dust: How Relics Shaped the History of Medieval Europe*. New Haven: Yale University Press, 2011.

Freeman, Thomas S. "The Power of Polemic: Catholic Responses to the Calendar in Foxe's 'Book of Martyrs.'" *Journal of Ecclesiastical History* 61 (2010): 475–95.

Gaposchkin, M. Cecilia. *The Making of Saint Louis: Kingship, Sanctity, and Crusade in the Later Middle Ages*. Ithaca, NY: Cornell University Press, 2008.

Geary, Patrick J. *Furta Sacra: Thefts of Relics in the Central Middle Ages*. Princeton: Princeton University Press, 1990.

———. "Humiliation of Saints." In *Saints and Their Cults: Studies in Religious Sociology, Folklore, and History*, edited by S. Wilson, 123–40. Cambridge: Cambridge University Press, 1983.

———. "Sacred Commodities: The Circulation of Medieval Relics." In *The Social Life of Things: Commodities in Cultural Perspective*, edited by A. Appadurai, 169–91. Cambridge: Cambridge University Press, 1986.

Geertz, Clifford. *The Interpretation of Cultures*. New York: Basic Books, 1973.

Gilchrist, Roberta. *Contemplation and Action: The Other Monasticism*. London: Leicester University Press, 1995.

Glancy, Jennifer. *Corporal Knowledge: Early Christian Bodies*. Oxford: Oxford University Press, 2010.

———. *Slavery in Early Christianity*. Oxford: Oxford University Press, 2002.

Gosselin, Martine. "The Congregation of the Oratorians and the Origins of Christian Archaeology: A Reappraisal." *Revue d'histoire ecclésiastique* 104 (2009): 471–93.

Grabar, André. *Martyrium: Recherches sur le culte des reliques et l'art chrétien antique*. 2 vols. Paris: Collège de France, 1943–46.

Grafton, Anthony. "Church History in Early Modern Europe: Tradition and Innovation." In *Sacred History: Uses of the Christian Past in the Renaissance World*, edited by K. Van Liere, S. Ditchfield, and H. Louthan, 3–26. Oxford: Oxford University Press, 2012.

Gregory, Brad S. *Salvation at Stake: Christian Martyrdom in Early Modern Europe*. Cambridge, MA: Harvard University Press, 1999.

Grig, Lucy. *Making Martyrs in Late Antiquity*. London: Duckworth, 2004.

Guazelli, Giuseppe Antonio. "Cesare Baronio and the Roman Catholic Vision of the Early Church." In *Sacred History: Uses of the Christian Past in the Renaissance World*, edited by K. Van Liere, S. Ditchfield, and H. Louthan, 52–71. Oxford: Oxford University Press, 2012.

Guscin, Mark. *The History of the Sudarium of Oviedo: How it Came from Jerusalem to Spain in the Seventh Century A.D.* Lewiston: Edwin Mellen, 2004.

———. *The Image of Edessa.* Leiden: Brill, 2009.

Hahn, Cynthia. *Strange Beauty: Issues in the Making of Reliquaries from the Fourth Century to 1204.* University Park: Penn State University Press, 2012.

Hargrave, O. T. "Bloody Mary's Victims: The Iconography of John Foxe's Book of Martyrs." *Historical Magazine of the Protestant Episcopal Church* 51 (1982): 7–21.

Harper, Kyle. *Plagues upon the Earth: Disease and the Course of Human History.* Princeton: Princeton University Press, 2021.

———. *Slavery in the Late Roman World, A.D. 275–425.* Cambridge: Cambridge University Press, 2011.

Hartnell, Jack. *Medieval Bodies: Life, Death and Art in the Middle Ages.* London: Wellcome Collection, 2018.

Harvey, Susan Ashbrook. *Scenting Salvation: Ancient Christianity and the Olfactory Imagination.* Berkeley: University of California Press, 2006.

Hasenfratz, Robert. Introduction to *Ancrene Wisse,* edited by Hasenfratz, 1–58. Kalamazoo, MI: Medieval Institute Publications, 2000.

Head, Thomas. *Hagiography and the Cult of the Saints: The Diocese of Orléans, 800–1200.* Cambridge: Cambridge University Press, 1990.

Henderson, John. "The Flagellant Movement and Flagellant Confraternities in Central Italy, 1260–1400." In *Religious Motivation: Biographical and Sociological Problems for the Church Historian,* edited by D. Baker, 147–60. Oxford: Basil Blackwell, 1978.

Herz, Alexandra. "Imitators of Christ: The Martyr-Cycles of Late Sixteenth-Century Rome Seen in Context." *Storia dell'arte* 62 (1988): 53–70.

Hillerbrand, Hans J. *The Division of Christendom: Christianity in the Sixteenth Century.* Louisville, KY: Westminster John Knox Press, 2007.

Hirschfeld, Yizhar. *The Judean Desert Monasteries in the Byzantine Period.* New Haven: Yale University Press, 1992.

Hollerich, Michael J. *Making Christian History: Eusebius of Caesarea and His Readers.* Oakland: University of California Press, 2021.

Houliston, Victor. *Catholic Resistance in Elizabethan England: Robert Persons's Jesuit Polemic, 1580–1610.* London: Routledge, 2007.

Hunter, David. *Marriage and Sexuality in Early Christian Sources.* Minneapolis: Fortress, 2018.

Johnson, Trevor. "Holy Fabrications: The Catacomb Saints and the Counter-Reformation in Bavaria." *Journal of Ecclesiastical History* 47 (1996): 274–97.

Jones, E. A. *Hermits and Anchorites in England, 1200–1550.* Manchester: Manchester University Press, 2019.

———. "Rites of Enclosure: The English *Ordines* for the Enclosing of Anchorites, S. XII–S. XVI." *Traditio* 67 (2012): 145–234.

Katz, Melissa R. "Preventative Medicine: Josse Lieferinxe's *Retable Altar of St. Sebastian* as a Defense against Plague in 15th Century Provence." *Interfaces* 26 (2006–7): 59–82.

Kazantzakis, Nikos. *The Last Temptation of Christ.* Translated by Peter A. Bien. New York: Simon and Schuster, 1960.

Kellner, K. A. Heinrich. *Heortology: A History of the Christian Festivals from Their Origin to the Present Day.* London: Kegan Paul, 1908.

Klein, Holger A. "Eastern Objects and Western Desires: Relics and Reliquaries between Byzantium and the West." *Dumbarton Oaks Papers* 58 (2004): 283–314.

———. "Sacred Relics and Imperial Ceremonies at the Great Palace of Constantinople." In *Visualisierungen von Herrschaft: Frühmittelalterliche Residenzen— Gestalt und Zeremoniell,* Byzas 5, edited by F. A. Bauer, 79–99. Istanbul: Ege Yayınları: 2006.

———. "Sacred Things and Holy Bodies: Collecting Relics from Late Antiquity to the Early Renaissance." In *Treasures of Heaven: Saints, Relics, and Devotion in Medieval Europe,* edited by M. Bagnoli, H. A. Klein, C. G. Mann, and J. Robinson, 55–67. London: British Museum Press, 2010.

Kloppenborg, John S. "*Exitus clari viri:* The Death of Jesus in Luke." *Toronto Journal of Theology* 8 (1992): 106–20.

Knowles, David. *Great Historical Enterprises: Problems in Monastic History.* London: Nelson and Sons, 1963.

Koopmans, Rachel. *Wonderful to Relate: Miracle Stories and Miracle Collecting in High Medieval England.* Philadelphia: University of Pennsylvania Press, 2011.

Koudounaris, Paul. *Heavenly Bodies: Cult Treasures and Spectacular Saints from the Catacombs.* London: Thames and Hudson, 2013.

Krueger, Derek. "The Religion of Relics in Late Antiquity and Byzantium." In *Treasures of Heaven: Saints, Relics, and Devotion in Medieval Europe,* edited by M. Bagnoli, H. A. Klein, C. G. Mann, and J. Robinson, 5–17. London: British Museum Press, 2010.

Kuryluk, Ewa. *Veronica and Her Cloth: History, Symbolism and Structure of a "True" Image.* Oxford: Oxford University Press, 1991.

Lanéry, Cécile. "Arnobe le Jeune et la Passion de Sébastien (*BHL* 7543)." *Revue des études augustiniennes et patristiques* 53 (2007): 267–93.

Lapidge, Michael. *The Roman Martyrs: Introduction, Translations, and Commentary.* Oxford: Oxford University Press, 2018.

Laqueur, Thomas W. *The Work of the Dead: A Cultural History of Mortal Remains.* Princeton: Princeton University Press, 2015.

Leemans, Johan, Wendy Mayer, Pauline Allen, and Boudewijn Dehandschutter. *'Let Us Die That We May Live': Greek Homilies on Christian Martyrs from Asia Minor, Palestine and Syria (c. A.D. 350–A.D. 450).* New York: Routledge, 2003.

Le Goff, Jacques. *In Search of Sacred Time: Jacobus de Voragine and "The Golden Legend."* Translated by L. G. Cochrane. Princeton: Princeton University Press, 2014.

———. "L'‘exemplum' médiéval." In *L' "exemplum,"* by C. Brémond, Le Goff, and J.-C. Schmitt, 15–107. Turnhout: Brepols, 1982.

———. *Saint Louis.* Translated by G. E. Gollrad. Notre Dame, IN: University of Notre Dame Press, 1996.

Lewis, Nicola Denzey. *The Early Modern Invention of Late Antique Rome.* Cambridge: Cambridge University Press, 2020.

Leyerle, Blake. "Landscape as Cartography in Early Christian Pilgrimage Narratives." *Journal of the American Academy of Religion* 64 (1996): 119–43.

Licence, Tom. *Hermits and Recluses in English Society: 950–1200.* Oxford: Oxford University Press, 2011.

Limberis, Vasiliki M. *Architects of Piety: The Cappadocian Fathers and the Cult of the Martyrs.* Oxford: Oxford University Press, 2011.

Loades, David M. *The Oxford Martyrs.* London: Batsford, 1970.

Lorinc, John, Michael McClelland, Ellen Scheinberg, and Tatum Taylor, eds. *The Ward: The Life and Loss of Toronto's First Immigrant Neighbourhood.* Toronto: Coach House, 2015.

MacCarron, Máirín. *Bede and Time: Computus, Theology and History in the Early Medieval World.* London: Routledge, 2020.

MacCulloch, Diarmaid. *Thomas Cranmer: A Life.* New Haven: Yale University Press, 1996.

Machielsen, Jan. "Heretical Saints and Textual Discernment: The Polemical Origins of the *Acta Sanctorum* (1643–1940)." In *Angels of Light? Sanctity and Discernment of Spirits in the Early Modern Period,* edited by C. Copeland and Machielsen, 103–41. Leiden: Brill, 2013.

Madden, Thomas F. "The Venetian Version of the Fourth Crusade: Memory and the Conquest of Constantinople in Medieval Venice." *Speculum: A Journal of Medieval Studies* 87 (2012): 311–44.

Mag Fhloinn, Bill. *Blood Rite: The Feast of St. Martin in Ireland*. Helsinki: Suomalainen Tiedeakatemia, 2016.

Mansour, Opher. "Not Torments, but Delights: Antonio Gallonio's *Trattato degli instrumenti di martirio* of 1591 and Its Illustrations." In *Roman Bodies: Antiquity to the Eighteenth Century*, edited by A. Hopkins and M. Wyke, 167–83. London: British School at Rome, 2005.

Markus, R. A. *Gregory the Great and His World*. Cambridge: Cambridge University Press, 1997.

———. "How on Earth Could Places Become Holy? Origins of the Christian Idea of Holy Places." *Journal of Early Christian Studies* 2 (1994): 257–71.

Marshall, Louise. "Manipulating the Sacred: Image and Plague in Renaissance Italy." *Renaissance Quarterly* 47 (1994): 485–532.

Matthews, Shelly. *Perfect Martyr: The Stoning of Stephen and the Construction of Christian Identity*. New York: Oxford University Press, 2010.

McCulloh, John M. "Historical Martyrologies in the Benedictine Cultural Tradition." In *Benedictine Culture, 750–1050*, edited by W. Lourdaux and D. Verhelst, 114–31. Leuven: Leuven University Press, 1983.

McDowell, Sean. *The Fate of the Apostles: Examining the Martyrdom Accounts of the Closest Followers of Jesus*. New York: Routledge, 2016.

McGuire, Brian Patrick. "Friends and Tales in the Cloister: Oral Sources in Caesarius of Heisterbach's *Dialogus Miraculorum*." *Analecta Cisterciensia* 36 (1980): 167–247.

Meinardus, Otto. "A Study of the Relics of Saints of the Greek Church." *Oriens Christianus* 54 (1970): 130–278.

Melczer, William. *The Pilgrim's Guide to Santiago de Compostela*. New York: Italica, 1993.

Mena, Peter. *Place and Identity in the Lives of Antony, Paul, and Mary of Egypt: Desert as Borderland*. New York: Palgrave Macmillan, 2019.

Michael, M. A. *Stained Glass of Canterbury Cathedral*. Rev. ed. London: Scala Arts, 2015.

Miller, Patricia Cox. "The Blazing Body: Ascetic Desire in Jerome's *Letter to Eustochium*." *Journal of Early Christian Studies* 1 (1993): 21–45.

———. *Dreams in Late Antiquity: Studies in the Imagination of a Culture*. Princeton: Princeton University Press, 1998.

———. "Is There a Harlot in This Text? Hagiography and the Grotesque." *Journal of Medieval and Early Modern Studies* 33 (2003): 419–35.

Mitchell, Peter. "The Politics of Morbidity: Plague Symbolism in Martyrdom and Medical Anatomy." In *The Arts of 17th-Century Science: Representations of*

the Natural World in European and North American Culture, edited by C.
Jowitt and D. Watt, 77–94. New York: Routledge, 2016.

Monta, Susannah Brietz. *Martyrdom and Literature in Early Modern England.*
Cambridge: Cambridge University Press, 2009.

Moss, Candida R. *Ancient Christian Martyrdom: Diverse Practices, Theologies, and
Traditions.* New Haven: Yale University Press, 2012.

———. "Current Trends in the Study of Early Christian Martyrdom." *Bulletin for
the Study of Religion* 41 (2012): 22–29.

———. *The Myth of Persecution: How Early Christians Invented a Story of Martyrdom.* New York: HarperCollins, 2013.

———. "On the Dating of Polycarp: Rethinking the Place of the *Martyrdom of
Polycarp* in the History of Christianity." *Early Christianity* 1 (2010): 539–74.

———. *The Other Christs: Imitating Jesus in Ancient Christian Ideologies of
Martyrdom.* Oxford: Oxford University Press, 2010.

Mosshammer, Alden A. *The Easter Computus and the Origins of the Christian Era.*
Oxford: Oxford University Press, 2008.

Nagel, Alexander. "The Afterlife of the Reliquary." In *Treasures of Heaven:
Saints, Relics, and Devotion in Medieval Europe,* edited by M. Bagnoli, H.A.
Klein, C.G. Mann, and J. Robinson, 211–22. London: British Museum Press,
2010.

Nau, François, ed. and trans. "Martyrologe du IVᵉ siècle." In *Martyrologes et
ménologes orientaux, I–XIII: Un martyrologe et douze ménologes syriaques édités
et traduits,* Patrologia Orientalis 10.1, 5–26. Paris: Firmin-Didot, 1912.

Nicolotti, Andrea. *From the Mandylion of Edessa to the Shroud of Turin: The
Metamorphosis and Manipulation of a Legend.* Leiden: Brill, 2014.

Nothaft, C. Philipp E. *Dating the Passion: The Life of Jesus and the Emergence of
Scientific Chronology (200–1600).* Leiden: Brill, 2011.

O'Boyle, Cornelius. *The Art of Medicine: Medical Teaching at the University of
Paris,* 1250–1400. Leiden: Brill, 1998.

Oryshkevich, Irina T. "The History of the Roman Catacombs from the Era of
Constantine to the Renaissance." PhD diss., Columbia University, 2003.

Ousterhout, Robert. "The Virgin of the Chora: An Image and Its Contexts." In
The Sacred Image East and West, edited by Ousterhout and L. Brubaker,
91–109. Champaign: University of Illinois Press, 1995.

Pagels, Elaine. *Revelations: Visions, Prophecy, and Politics in the Book of Revelation.* New York: Penguin, 2012.

Palazzo, Éric. "Relics, Liturgical Space, and the Theology of the Church." In
Treasures of Heaven: Saints, Relics, and Devotion in Medieval Europe, edited by

M. Bagnoli, H.A. Klein, C.G. Mann, and J. Robinson, 99–109. London: British Museum Press, 2010.

Perry, David. *Sacred Plunder: Venice and the Aftermath of the Fourth Crusade.* University Park: Penn State University Press, 2015.

Pervo, Richard I. *Dating Acts: Between the Evangelists and the Apologists.* Santa Rosa, CA: Polebridge, 2006.

Quentin, Henri. *Les martyrologes historiques du Moyen Âge.* Paris: J. Gabalda, 1908.

Reames, Sherry L. *The "Legenda Aurea": A Reexamination of Its Paradoxical History.* Madison: University of Wisconsin Press, 1985.

Rebillard, Éric. *The Early Martyr Narratives: Neither Authentic Accounts nor Forgeries.* Philadelphia: University of Pennsylvania Press, 2020.

———, ed. *Greek and Latin Narratives about the Ancient Martyrs.* Oxford: Oxford University Press, 2017.

Richards, E.G. *Mapping Time: The Calendar and Its History.* Rev. ed. Oxford: Oxford University Press, 2000.

Rudolph, Conrad. *The "Things of Greater Importance": Bernard of Clairvaux's "Apologia" and the Medieval Attitude toward Art.* Philadelphia: University of Pennsylvania Press, 1990.

Salzmann, Michele Renee. *On Roman Time: The Codex-Calendar of 354 and the Rhythms of Urban Life in Late Antiquity.* Berkeley: University of California Press, 1990.

Saxer, Victor. *Morts, martyrs, reliques en Afrique chrétienne aux premiers siècles: Les témoignages de Tertullien, Cyprien et Augustin à la lumière de l'archéologie africaine.* Paris: Beauchesne, 1980.

Schipper, Jeremy. *Denmark Vesey's Bible: The Thwarted Revolt That Put Slavery and Scripture on Trial.* Princeton: Princeton University Press, 2022.

Schwartz, Stuart B. *Sea of Storms: A History of Hurricanes in the Greater Caribbean from Columbus to Katrina.* Princeton: Princeton University Press, 2015.

Shaw, Matthew. *Time and the French Revolution: The Republican Calendar, 1789–Year XIV.* Suffolk: Boydell and Brewer, 2011.

Shaw, Teresa M. *The Burden of the Flesh: Fasting and Sexuality in Early Christianity.* Minneapolis: Fortress, 1998.

Shoemaker, Stephen J. *Mary in Early Christian Faith and Devotion.* New Haven: Yale University Press, 2016.

Sigal, Pierre-André. *L'homme et le miracle dans la France médiévale (XIe–XIIe siècle).* Paris: Cerf, 1985.

Skemer, Don C. *Binding Words: Textual Amulets in the Middle Ages.* University Park: Pennsylvania State University Press, 2006.

Slocum, Kay Brainerd. *The Cult of Thomas Becket: History and Historiography through Eight Centuries*. New York: Routledge, 2019.

Smirnova, Victoria, Marie Anne Polo de Beaulieu, and Jacques Berlioz, eds. *The Art of Cistercian Persuasion in the Middle Ages and Beyond*. Leiden: Brill, 2015.

Smith, Kyle. *Constantine and the Captive Christians of Persia: Martyrdom and Religious Identity in Late Antiquity*. Oakland: University of California Press, 2016.

Snowden, Frank M. *Epidemics and Society: From the Black Death to the Present*. New Haven: Yale University Press, 2019.

Southern, R. W. *The Making of the Middle Ages*. New Haven: Yale University Press, 1953.

Spencer, Brian. *Pilgrim Souvenirs and Secular Badges*. Suffolk: Boydell, 2010.

Stancliffe, Clare. *St. Martin and His Hagiographer: History and Miracle in Sulpicius Severus*. Oxford: Clarendon, 1983.

Staunton, Michael. *Thomas Becket and His Biographers*. Woodbridge: Boydell and Brewer, 2006.

Sterling, Greg. "*Mors philosophi:* The Death of Jesus in Luke." *Harvard Theological Review* 94 (2001): 383–402.

Stern, Henri. *Le calendrier de 354: Étude sur son texte et ses illustrations*. Paris: Imprimerie nationale, 1953.

Sullivan, Margaret A. *Bruegel's Peasants: Art and Audience in the Northern Renaissance*. Cambridge: Cambridge University Press, 1994.

Tabb, Brian J. "Is the Lucan Jesus a Martyr? A Critical Assessment of a Scholarly Consensus." *Catholic Biblical Quarterly* 77 (2015): 280–301.

——. *Suffering in Ancient Worldview: Luke, Seneca, and 4 Maccabees in Dialogue*. London: Bloomsbury, 2017.

Tannous, Rami. "Negotiating the Nativity in Late Antiquity: The Qur'ān's Rereading of Mary's Preparation for the Conception of Jesus." PhD diss., University of Toronto, 2019.

Thacker, Alan. "Bede and His Martyrology." In *Listen, O Isles, unto Me: Studies in Medieval Word and Image in Honour of Jennifer O'Reilly*, edited by E. Mullins and D. Scully, 126–41. Cork: Cork University Press, 2011.

——. "Bede and History." In *The Cambridge Companion to Bede*, edited by S. DeGregorio, 170–90. Cambridge: Cambridge University Press, 2010.

Thornwell, James Henley. *The Rights and the Duties of Masters: A Sermon Preached at the Dedication of a Church Erected in Charleston, S.C., for the Benefit and Instruction of the Coloured Population*. Charleston: Walker and James, 1850.

Touber, Jetze. *Law, Medicine, and Engineering in the Cult of the Saints in Counter-Reformation Rome: The Hagiographical Works of Antonio Gallonio, 1556–1605.* Leiden: Brill, 2014.

Twain, Mark. *The Innocents Abroad, or The New Pilgrims' Progress.* Hartford, CT: American, 1869.

Upson-Saia, Kristi. *Early Christian Dress: Gender, Virtue, and Authority.* New York: Routledge, 2014.

Van Dam, Raymond. *Saints and Their Miracles in Late Antique Gaul.* Princeton: Princeton University Press, 1993.

van Henten, Jan Willem. "The Concept of Martyrdom in Revelation." In *Die Johannesapokalypse: Kontexte—Konzepte—Rezeption / The Revelation of John: Contexts—Concepts—Reception,* edited by J. Frey, J. A. Kelhoffer, and F. Tóth, 587–618. Tübingen: Mohr Siebeck, 2010.

van Henten, Jan Willem, and Friedrich Avemarie. *Martyrdom and Noble Death: Selected Texts from Graeco-Roman, Jewish and Christian Antiquity.* London: Routledge, 2002.

Vaslef, Irene. "The Role of St. Roch as a Plague Saint: A Late Medieval Hagiographic Tradition." PhD diss., Catholic University of America, 1984.

Vauchez, André. *Sainthood in the Later Middle Ages.* Translated by J. Birrell. Cambridge: Cambridge University Press, 2005.

Verheyden, Joseph. "Pain and Glory: Some Introductory Comments on the Rhetorical Qualities and Potential of the *Martyrs of Palestine* by Eusebius of Caesarea." In *Martyrdom and Persecution in Late Antique Christianity: Festschrift Boudewijn Dehandschutter,* edited by J. Leemans, 353–91. Leuven: Peeters, 2010.

Vikan, Gary. *Byzantine Pilgrimage Art.* Rev. ed. Washington, DC: Dumbarton Oaks, 2010.

Walsh, Martin W. "*Martín y Muchos Pobres:* Grotesque Versions of the Charity of St. Martin in the Bosch and Bruegel Schools." *Essays in Medieval Studies* 14 (1997): 107–20.

———. "Medieval English *Martinmesse:* The Archaeology of a Forgotten Festival." *Folklore* 111 (2000): 231–54.

Ward, Benedicta. *Miracles and the Medieval Mind: Theory, Record and Event, 1000–1215.* Philadelphia: University of Pennsylvania Press, 1982.

Ward-Perkins, J. B. "Memoria, Martyr's Tomb and Martyr's Church." *Journal of Theological Studies* 17 (1966): 20–38.

Warren, Ann K. *Anchorites and Their Patrons in Medieval England.* Berkeley: University of California Press, 1985.

Watt, Tessa. *Cheap Print and Popular Piety, 1550–1640*. Cambridge: Cambridge University Press, 1993.

Webb, Diana. *Pilgrimage in Medieval England*. London: Bloomsbury, 2007.

Weeks, Andrew. "Between God and Gibson: German Mystical and Romantic Sources of *The Passion of the Christ*." *German Quarterly* 78 (2005): 421–40.

Weiss, Daniel. *Art and Crusade in the Age of Saint Louis*. Cambridge: Cambridge University Press, 1998.

Wellesley, Mary. *The Gilded Page: The Secret Lives of Medieval Manuscripts*. New York: Basic Books, 2021.

———. "This Place Is Pryson." *London Review of Books* 41, no. 10 (May 23, 2019): https://www.lrb.co.uk/the-paper/v41/n10/mary-wellesley/this-place-is-pryson.

Wilken, Robert L. *The Land Called Holy: Palestine in Christian History and Thought*. New Haven: Yale University Press, 1992.

Wilkinson, John. *Jerusalem Pilgrims before the Crusades*. Rev. ed. Liverpool: Liverpool University Press, 2002.

Williams, Richard L. "Ancient Bodies and Contested Identities in the English College Martyrdom Cycle, Rome." In *Roman Bodies: Antiquity to the Eighteenth Century*, edited by A. Hopkins and M. Wyke, 185–200. London: British School at Rome, 2005.

Wortley, John. "The Marian Relics at Constantinople." *Greek, Roman, and Byzantine Studies* 45 (2005): 171–87.

———. "The Origins of Christian Veneration of Body-Parts." *Revue de l'histoire des religions* 223 (2006): 5–28.

Wright, William. "An Ancient Syriac Martyrology." Pts. 1 and 2. *Journal of Sacred Literature (and Biblical Record)*, n.s. 8, no. 15 (1865): 45–56; no. 16 (1866): 423–32.

———. *Catalogue of the Syriac Manuscripts in the British Museum, Acquired since the Year 1838, Part III*. London: British Museum, 1872.

Yarrow, Simon. *Saints and Their Communities: Miracle Stories in Twelfth-Century England*. Oxford: Oxford University Press, 2006.

Yasin, Anne Marie. *Saints and Church Spaces in the Late Antique Mediterranean*. Cambridge: Cambridge University Press, 2009.

Index

Page references in italics refer to figures.

ampullae, pilgrims', 75–76, 76; popularity of, 87

anachōrein (to retreat), 139, 141

The Anastasis (Church of the Holy Saviour in the Chora), 270, plate 16

anchoresses, 139–40; bishops' approval of, 144; church support for, 143; constant prayer by, 142; as dead to world, 147; demonic combat of, 153–54; dependence on men, 144; enclosure of, 142–43, plate 4; external stimuli for, 147; following English Dissolution, 214; perils for, 150; ritual death of, 141; spiritual authority of, 144; spiritual sight of, 147; use of funeral liturgy, 140; work of prayer, 146. *See also* women, ascetic

anchorholds (recluses' cells), 140, 280; cells of, 137, 143; cost of, 143; forbidden uses for, 146; windows of, 147–48. *See also* enclosure

anchorites: English, 140, 214, 279; etymology of, 139; guidebooks for, 145–47; pontifical liturgy for, 139; ritual death of, 140–41; struggles against sexual urges, 150–51; support of, 145; vocation of, 145. *See also* asceticism, Christian

Ancrene Wisse, 145–47, 280; on defense against demons, 153–54; "inner/ outer" rules in, 146, 147; use of *Sayings of the Desert Fathers*, 151; works included in, 145

Andon, Stephen, 94

Andrew, Saint: bones of, 97; Toronto ward-namesake, 21; *X*-shaped cross of, 18

animals, miracle stories concerning, 190–92

Anna, Saint (mother of Mary), 164, 256

Anne of Cleves, marriage to Henry VIII, 214

Anonymous, Saint: relics of, 199

Anthony, Saint, of Egypt, 120, 139; daily death of, 142; demons' attack on, 151–52, 280, plate 5–6; patronage of swine and swineherds, 116; tomb dwellings of, 141, 151

Apocalypse, Seven Churches of, 46

Apostles: crucifixion of, 22; at Gethsemane, 28; holidays celebrating, 111; martyrs' deaths of, 21–22, 23, 24; miracles of, 85, 180, 184; relics of, 4, 86, 97; study of dying, 267. *See also* Acts of the Apostles

Apostolic Constitutions: composition of, 111, 112; holidays in, 109, 111–12

Arch of Titus (Rome), 25, 26–27

Aristotle: on astrological disasters, 238; theory of vision, 234, 240

Arlington National Cemetery, individuals' names at, 58

Armenians, conversion of, 55

army, Roman: purge of Christians from, 40. *See also* soldiers, Roman

Arnobius the Younger, *passio* of Saint Sebastian, 247–49, 261, 286

asceticism, Christian: of Egypt, 64; Marian theology of, 164; practice of enclosure within, 139. *See also* anchorites; enclosure; Mary of Egypt; Simeon the Stylite; women, ascetic

astrology, Christian study of, 113, 238

astronomers, Egyptian: and Julian calendar, 124–25; lunar tables of, 131

Athanasius (bishop of Alexandria), on Saint Anthony, 141–42

Athens, Laws of, 30

Augustine of Hippo, Saint: celebration of martyrs, 115, 279; at disinterment of Gervasius and Protasius, 182; on

monastic registrars of, 195–96; pilgrimage to, 172, 174–75, 194, 196; shrine of Thomas Becket, 171–72, 175, 194, plate 9; Trinity Chapel, 175, 196, plate 9. *See also* Chaucer, Geoffrey: *Canterbury Tales*; Thomas Becket

Caraglio, Giovanni Jacopo: *The Virgin and Child on the Lap of Saint Anne, with Saint Roch and Saint Sebastian*, 256

Caribbean nations: martyr names of, 105–6, 108–9, 117; tourism of, 109

Carmelite order, founding myth of, 7

Carrington, Charles: sadomasochistic publications of, xix, xx; *Treatise on the Instruments of Martyrdom*, xix–xxi

Carthage, miracles at, 182–83

Cassian of Imola, Saint: martyrdom of, xxi

catacombs, Roman, 283; art of, 199, 209; Bosio's study of, 209–10; evidence for devotional practices, 210–11; excavation of, 199–200; mistaken identifications in, 209, 264; Saint Sebastian in, 247, 249; tours of, 199–200

Cathedral Church of Saint James (Toronto), 11

cathedrals, English: *Foxe's Book of Martyrs* at, 216

Catherine of Alexandria, Saint: torture of, xxi

Catherine of Aragon (consort of Henry VIII), 212–13

Catherine wheels, *xvii*, xxi

cavatori (excavators of the catacombs), 199

Caxton, William, 241

Chadwick, Henry, 114, 115

Chapel of Saint Mary of the Pharos (Constantinople), passion relics of, 98

Chaucer, Geoffrey: *Canterbury Tales*, 2, 5, 170–71, 281; "The Pardoner's Tale," 168–71; Wife of Bath's pilgrimages, 173. *See also* Canterbury Cathedral

Chennai (India), relics of Saint Thomas in, 24

chōra (rural regions): of Bethlehem, 165; liminal space of, 141; hermits of, 139

Christianity: centrality of martyrdom to, 18; corporeality of, 79; intertwining with martyr narratives, 51; imperially sponsored, 113; inversion of Roman world, 74; justification of slavery in, 110; Marian theology of, 164; materiality of, 74; novelty in Rome, 113; spread of, 55. *See also* martyrs; Roman Catholic Church; saints

Christmas: date of, 126–28; Orthodox, 126. *See also* nativity of Jesus

Christopher, Saint: island named for, 108; in *Ghent Altarpiece*, 176, plate 8

Chronograph of 354, 112, 278; calendrical information in, 113; *Depositio martyrum* in, 247; as a model martyrology, 113; nativity of Christ in, 127–28; Roman consuls in, 128; Saint Sebastian in, 247

Church of England: on *Foxe's Book of Martyrs*, 216; schism from Rome, 5, 214. *See also* Reformation, English

Church of the Holy Sepulchre (Jerusalem), 54, 55; pilgrims' crosses at, 176; veneration of cross at, 75; Virgin Mary icon, 157, 160, 162

Cyril (bishop of Jerusalem): distribution of relics, 74; encouragement of pilgrimage, 74
Cyril of Scythopolis, on wandering monks, 156–57, 281

Dafoe, Willem, 155
D'Agramont, Jacme: *Regimen of Protection against Epidemics*, 236–37; on serenity, 237
Dalí, Salvador: *The Temptation of Saint Anthony*, 151, 152, plate 6
Dandolo, Enrico (doge of Venice), 101
Daniel of Schönau, abbott: perception of miracle, 189–90
Dante: purgatory of, 201; on Veronica's Veil, 83, 277
David, Jacques-Louis: *The Death of Socrates*, 30–31, 32–33
David, Saint, 12, 18; natural death of, 19
Day, John, 284; publication of *Foxe's Book of Martyrs*, 220, 221–23
Dead Sea Scrolls, discovery of, 156
Delehaye, Hippolyte, 286; hagiographical research of, 261, 263–66; on reliable history, 265
del Biondo, Giovanni: *The Martyrdom of Saint Sebastian*, 246, 249, 250, 251, plate 12
demons, 156; anchorholds' defense against, 146; attack on ascetics, 150–54; in Christian art, 151–52, plate 5–6; combat with anchoresses, 153–54; Jesus's exorcism of, 178; miracles concerning, 182; as temptations, 152; torment of Saint Anthony, 151–52, 280, plate 5–6
Depositio martyrum, dates of burials, 113, 247

Diepenbeeck, Abraham: *Acta Sanctorum* engraved title page, 261, 262
Diocletian, Emperor: "Great Persecution" of, 40, 42–43, 131, 275; in martyrology for November 11, 134–35; in reckoning of time, 131, 133; in Sebastian's martyrdom, 42, 248, 249
Diogenes the Cynic, on death, 267
Dionysius the Humble: coining of *anno domini* style, 131; computation of Easter, 130–31, 279
disease: natural/supernatural explanations of, 185, 187, 239; transmission by noxious air, 234–38. *See also* medicine, humoral
Ditchfield, Simon, 210, 283, 286
divine intervention: causing Black Death, 239–40, 244; Gregory the Great on, 184; nature of, 172. *See also* miracles
Dome of the Rock, 28
Dominicans, writing/use of *Golden Legend*, 5, 240
Dostoyevsky, Fyodor: on Holbein's *Body of the Dead Christ in the Tomb*, 269; *The Idiot*, 269
Duccio di Buoninsegna, *Maestà*, 166, 167
Dürer, Albrecht: *Saint Eustace*, 107

Eagleman, David: *Sum: Forty Tales from the Afterlives*, 68
the East (Persia): Christian martyrs of, 56–57, 59, 62
Easter: calculation of date, 129–33, 279; and celebration of Passover, 129–30; in Metonic cycles, 130–31
Ebbets Field (Brooklyn), relics of, 79, 93–94, 277

exempla (moral lessons): of adultery, 191; of greed, 169-70, 171
experience, social perception of, 187-88

fables (literary genre), in hagiography, 263
Fabriano, Gentile da: *The Crippled and Sick Cured at the Tomb of Saint Nicholas*, 96-97, plate 2
fasting, 119, 142, 252, 280; Jesus's, 154, 155
feast days, 278-79; anticipation of, 134; celebration of, 113-16; drunkenness at, 115, 118-19; Luther on, 203; martyrs', 105, 109, 111-12; pagan, 113
festivals, harvest: on feast of Saint Martin, 117-19, 134-35
Finucane, Ronald: on miracles, 185-86, 195, 282
flagellation, penitents', 244-45, 285, plate 11
fleas, spread of bubonic plague, 232
Florence, Black Death in, 239, 246, 251
Florus (deacon of Lyon), martyrology of, 133
Foligno, Gentile da: on Black Death, 234, 235; *Casebook against the Pestilence*, 237; on fine/dangerous foods, 237
Foxe, John: exile of, 215, 218; expulsion from Oxford, 215; as historian, 221; scholarship of, 216-17, 220; use of Eusebius, 221, 227
—*Book of Martyrs*, 6, 215-18, 284; attestations of fact in, 227; Catholic responses to, 222-23, 228; commoners in, 223-24; cost of, 220; Day's publication of 220, 221-22; dedication to Elizabeth I, 221;

distribution of, 216, 222; early Christian martyrs in, 223, 224; expansions and abridgements of, 227; first English edition, 218-19; folio format of, 221; as *Golden Legend*, 221, 222; government support of, 216, 220; historical reach of, 220; illustrations of, 222-28; influence of, 228; Latin edition of, 218; length of, 219; martyrs' images in, 223-28, 224, 225; "A most exact Table of the first ten Persecutions of the Primitive Church," 222-23, 224; popular input into, 221; second edition, 216, 220; second edition preface, 221-22; source material of, 216; "A table describing the burning of Bishop Ridley and Father Latimer at Oxford," 224-26, 225; torture in, 223, 224
Freeman, Thomas, 219, 222, 228, 284
French Revolution, calendar of, 135-36
Friday, etymology of, 128-29
furta sacra (stolen relics), rationalization of, 95, 276

Gabriel, Angel: annunciation to Mary, 163
Galen: on lustfulness of women, 149-50; on *pneuma*, 234
Galerius, Emperor: divine suffering of, 43; edict of toleration, 42-43
galleys, Genoese: in Mediterranean trade, 230; spread of plague, 231-32, 236, 240
Gallonio, Antonio: assistance to Baronio, 207; *Trattato de gli instrumenti di martirio*, xv-xxi, 207-9; Carrington's republication

indulgences, papal: Counter-Reformation reaffirmation of, 206; financing of Saint Peter's Basilica, 202; Luther on, 201–2; sale of, 170

initiation rituals: association with death, 140–41; for female recluses, 137–38

Innocentia (noblewoman of Carthage), miraculous cure of, 183–84

Irene, Saint: care of Saint Sebastian, 249

Jacob (scribe), dated manuscript of, 61, 63, 67

Jacob the Deacon, on Saint Pelagia, 161

Jacopo de Voragine: *The Golden Legend*, 4–5, 157, 229; ahistorical sources for, 265–66; Bollandists on, 265; English translation of, 241, 285; feast day arrangement of, 240; the marvelous in, 264; plague in, 240, 241, 242, 286; popularity of, 5, 221, 240, 259; preachers' use of, 240; Saint Sebastian in, 249–50, 252; on Saint Luke's portrait of Mary, 242

Jägermeister (German herbal liqueur), homage to Saint Eustace, 106

James, Saint (son of Zebedee): death of accuser, 19; martyrdom of, 19; relics of, 19; Toronto ward-namesake, 21

James the Less, Saint: stoning of, 21

jealousy, exempla of, 191

Jerome, Saint, 200; in Bethlehem, 144; on catacombs, 200, 283; *Letter 22*, 144, 153, 280; on abandonment of pagan temples in *Letter 107*, 77, 276

Jerusalem: Jewish uprising (AD 70), 25; Roman destruction of, 25, 26–27, 28; Western Wall, 28

Jesus Christ: *acheiropoiēton* (likeness) of, 83; in Acts of the Apostles, 2; age at death, 279; ascension of, 72; celebration of martyrdom, 15, 18, 24; as *Chōra tōn Zōntōn* (Land of the Living), 167; "contact" relics of, 4, 71, 72, 81; correspondence with Abgar, 99–100; date of birth, 126–29; entombment of, 268–69; female visionaries on, 85; in Gospel of John, 22, 81, 176, 177, 178; in Gospel of Luke, 2, 25, 28, 126, 127, 162–63, 178; in Gospel of Mark, 28, 178–79; in Gospel of Matthew, 2, 126, 127, 154, 162–63; grief of, 28; healing of bleeding, 84; Holy Face of, 85; *homoousios*, 54; imitation of, 1, 274; incorruptibility of, 268; intercession by, 184; in Kazantzakis's *Last Temptation of Christ*, 155; last words of, 28, 29; marriage controversy of, 155; martyrs' similarity to, 47; Michelangelo's *Pietà*, 268, plate 14; miracles of, 176–79, 184; parents of, 163–64; Paul's vision of, 35; on persecution of followers, 24–25; resurrection of, 24, 182, 269–70; as sacrificial lamb, 129; Saint Stephen's vision of, 35; in Scorsese's *Last Temptation of Christ*, 155; as second Moses, 2; as second Socrates, 2; temptation of, 154; in Veronica legends, 84. *See also* cross of Jesus; crucifixion; miracles, Jesus's; nativity of Jesus; passion of Christ

Jews, Persian: charges against Christians, 56

John (bishop of Jerusalem), 36

John, Gospel of: Lazarus in, 177–78

John, Saint: crucifixion in, 29; death of old age, 19, 21

John Chrysostom, sermons of, 114
John Paul II, Pope: beatification of
Emmerich, 85
Joseph (husband of Mary): age of, 165,
167; omen of dove for, 165; vision of
angel, 163–64
Judas Iscariot, violent death of, 21
Jude, Saint: crucifixion of, 22
Judean Desert, celibates of, 155–56;
Mar Saba Monastery in, 156, 158–59;
Mary of Egypt in, 157, 160–61; as
site of Jesus's retreat, 154
Julia Eustochium (ascetic), 144, 153,
280
Julian, Saint (bishop of Le Mans), 145
Julian of Norwich, Saint, 144–45;
Revelations of Divine Love, 145
Julian the Apostate (emperor of
Rome), 116
Justiniano, Hieromonk Silouan: Saint
Mary of Egypt Receiving the Holy
Eucharist from Saint Zosimas, plate 7

Kazantzakis, Nikos: The Last
Temptation of Christ, 154–55
kites, murderous: miraculous
punishment of, 192
Knowles, David, 261, 286
Konrad of Megenberg, on noxious
air, 238
Koopmans, Rachel, 194, 195, 196, 283

Lanéry, Cécile, 247, 286
Latimer, Hugh, 284; burning of,
224–26, 225; final words of, 226
Latin plainsong, Gregorian, 44–45
Lawrence, Saint: martyrdom of, 12–13,
15, 18, 106
legends (literary genre): in hagiography, 263, 264, 266; truth within, 266
Lent, forty days of, 154

Leonardo da Vinci: Salvator Mundi,
80; authentication of, 79; sale of,
78–79
Leontius, Saint: disinterment of, 199;
miracles of, 198, 199; skull and
bones of, 198–99, plate 10
Lieferinxe, Josse: Saint Sebastian
Interceding for the Plague Stricken,
246, 251, 258, 286, plate 13
Life of Pelagia, 161
Life of Saint Mary of Egypt, 157,
160–61
Limbourg Brothers, "The Procession
of Flagellants," 245, plate 11
Lin, Maya, 58, 275
literary titles, early modern: encapsu-
lation of contents, 218–19
logismoi (evil thoughts), 152–53; seven
deadly sins and, 154
Louis IX (king of France), 79, 276;
acquisition of passion relics, 73,
101, 103; artistic patronage of, 72;
atonement of, 103; crusade of, 72,
103; death of, 103; piety of, 71–72;
ransoming of, 103; Sainte-Chapelle
of, 69, 70, 71–72; sale of crown of
thorns to, 102
Lucian (priest), vision of Gamaliel, 36
Lucina, Saint, 249, 250, 251
Lucy of Syracuse, Saint: feast day of,
105, 111; martyrdom of, 71, 105
Luke, Gospel of: on crucifixion, 28–30;
death of Jesus, 28 in; depiction of
Jesus, 2; Jesus's miracles in, 178;
Jesus the Martyr in, 25; Mary and
Martha in, 138, 144, 147, 154; on
nativity of Jesus, 126, 127, 162–63
Luke, Saint: contribution to cult of the
dead, 25, 31; Greek-speaking
audience of, 31, 35; icon of Virgin
Mary, 242; knowledge of Greek

Luke, Saint *(continued)*
    philosophers, 30; on martyrdom of
    Stephen, 31
lunar month: length of, 121; in solar
    year, 121–22. *See also* calendar
Luther, Martin: on indulgences, 201–2;
    Roman Catholic response to,
    205–6, 211; on saints' shrines, 203.
    Works: *Depiction of the Papacy*,
    204, 205; *Ninety-Five Theses*,
    200–201, 202
Lyon, martyrs of, 49–50, 265; charges
    against, 50

Macedonius (monk), performance of
    miracle, 185
Macrina, 162; wearing of relics,
    75, 78
"Mad" Henry of Fordwich, cure of,
    197, plate 9
Magdeburg Centuries (Protestant
    annals), 207
Magi ("Three Kings"), 106, 166
magi, Zoroastrian: charges against
    Christians, 56
Maisonneuve, Paul de Chomedey de,
    12
Major League Baseball (MLB),
    authentic memorabilia of, 93–95,
    277
Mandylion. *See* Edessa, Image of
manuscripts, Syriac: in British
    Museum/Library, 59–62, 63, 67;
    curses protecting, 65; at Monastery
    of the Syrians, 65–67
Marie of Saint Peter, Sister: devotion
    to Holy Face of Jesus, 85
mariners, Genoese: spread of plague,
    230–32, 234
Mark, Gospel of: Aramaic in, 177; date
    of composition, 25; death of Jesus

in, 28; Jesus's miracles in, 178–79;
    miracles in, 177
Mark, Saint: Coptic church names, 24;
    martyrdom in Egypt, 20; relics in
    Venice, 20; theft of bones, 96;
    Toronto ward-namesake, 21
Mar Saba (Greek Orthodox Monas-
    tery), 156, 158–59
Martha (Gospel of Luke), 138, 141,
    144; *Book of Steps* on, 147; in
    Kazantzakis's *Last Temptation of
    Christ*, 154–55; in Scorsese's *Last
    Temptation of Christ*, 155
Martin of Tours, Saint: cavalry service
    of, 116, 117; clothing of beggar, 117;
    feast day of, 117–19, 134–35;
    imprisonment of, 117; island named
    for, 106; in martyrology, 134;
    Sulpicius Severus on, 116, 278;
    veneration of, 108, 116; in Bruegel's
    Wine of Saint Martin's Day, plate 3
martyr bones, 3; apostles', 86;
    attesting of persecution, 268;
    redeposit of, 87; relocation
    (translation) of, 95; of Roman
    catacombs, 199; search for, 199. *See
    also* relics
martyr cults, 81, 85, 87; bishops'
    catering to, 86–87; cultural
    reticence concerning, 77; donations
    to, 86–87; early modern, 2; effect of
    Protestant Reformation on, 217–18;
    irrationality of, 77; polytheistic, 77;
    Protestant, 2; remembrances of,
    xxi; Saint Luke's contribution to, 31;
    tomb-centered, 77
martyrdom, 273–74; Roman instru-
    ments of, 208, 209; Socrates',
    30–31, 32–33
martyrdom, Christian: acceptance of,
    30; centrality of Christianity in, 18;

84; for paralytics, 178–79; raising of Lazarus, 177–78; resurrection, 182; of spit, 177; water-into-wine, 176, 177

miracle stories: analogy to butterfly collections, 194, 196; Caesarius of Heisterbach's, 188–92; concerning animals, 190–92; oral, 194; religious men's, 187–88; of Thomas Becket, 194–97; truth of, 188; used as exempla, 191–92

Mohamed (Egyptian guide), 66

monasteries: architecture of, 281; English Dissolution of, 214; of Judean Desert, 155–56, 160; Mar Saba, 156, 158–59; ruined, 155–56

Monastery of the Syrians (Egypt): Abbasid taxation of, 64–65; Coptic Orthodox monks of, 65; European visitors to, 66–67; manuscripts of, 65–66

monasticism: bookish culture of, 190; daily life in, 119; Egyptian, 64–67; reforms of eleventh century, 139; regulation of life, 121

money, as root of all evil, 169

Mongols, Golden Horde of, 230

Monica, Saint (mother of Augustine): Ambrose's censure of, 114; feast day celebrations, 114–15

Monkey's Paw bookshop (Toronto), xv–xvi

monks: "duty to doubt," 187; of Judean Desert, 156–57; registries of, 187–88, 196

Montréal, martyrs' names in, 12

More, Thomas: beheading of, 214; burning of books, 211; communist celebration of, 212; imprisonment of, 213; martyrdom of, 211, 229; *Utopia*, 211–12

Morgan, J. P., 11

Moses (patriarch): emulation of, 142; on Mount Sinai, 154

Moses of Nisibis: appeal to Abbasid caliph, 64–65; collection of Syriac manuscripts, 65

Moss, Candida, 18, 273–74

myth (literary genre of), in hagiography, 263

names, martyrs': in Gallonio's *Trattato*, xxi; Gregory the Great on, 45; lists of, 4, 6, 19, 45–46, 59, 62, 68, 111–13; in Montréal, 12; remembrance of, 59, 68; scholarship on, 274–75; in Toronto, 11–14, 19, 20

naming: of Caribbean islands, 105–6, 108–9; of Christian martyrs, 58, 59, 62, 68; in Genesis, 58–59; of icons, 59; monastic, 59; of Saint Peter, 59; of tropical cyclones, 104–5

nativity of Jesus: calculation of, 126–29; calendar beginning with, 131; in *Chronograph of 354*, 127–28; connection with crucifixion, 129; Duccio's depiction of, 166, 167; in Gospels, 126–27, 162–63; lunar calculation of, 128; in *Protoevangelium of James*, 165–66

Neri, Philip, Saint, 283; charismatic leadership of, 207; intellectual circle of, 206–7, 209; tours of martyr sites, 199–200, 247

Nero (emperor of Rome), mark of the beast, 20

New Year, Muslim: date of, 122

Nicaea, Council of (first), 55; on date of Easter, 130; homoousian doctrine, 54

Nicholas, Saint, 252; stolen relics of, 96–97; tomb of, plate 2

Philippe de Champaigne, *Translation of the Relics of Saint Gervasius and Saint Protasius*, 88, 90–91
philosophy, as study of dying, 267
physicians, medieval: on divine anger, 240; understanding of Black Death, 233, 234–35
physicians, Muslim: on fresh air, 236
physicians, Parisian: on divine will, 245; on plague remedies, 236; on planetary conjunctions, 238
Piacenza, plague at, 253–54
Piacenza Pilgrim, 282; on ampullae, 76; measurements of, 175; on miracle of Cana, 176; on Sudarium of Oviedo, 82
Piazza, Michele da: on Black Death, 230–34, 240
piety, female: concerning agony of Jesus, 85
piety, medieval: in martyr narratives, 5
pilgrimage: in ascent from purgatory, 201; to Canterbury Cathedral, 172, 194, 196; in the *Canterbury Tales*, 5; conflicting attitudes toward, 281; dangers of, 174; etymology of, 173; guidebooks, 173–74; to Holy Land, 73, 264, 282; Luther on, 203; to martyrs' shrine, 1; in medieval economy, 175; for miracles, 174; as penance, 174; prescribed routes of, 175; to Rome, 250; to Santiago de Compostela, 173; scope of, 173; to Simeon the Stylite, 180; souvenirs from, 73, 75–76, 76, 87, 176, 282; themes from antiquity in, 264; twilight of, 172
pilgrimage churches: of Rome, 247; traffic through, 175
pilgrims: costume of, 170; donations to martyrs' cults, 86–87; equipment of, 175–76; exemption from tolls, 174; expectations of, 175; ex-voto-offerings by, 174; measuring by, 174–75; scallop shells of, 176, plate 8; in van Eyck's *Ghent Altarpiece*, 176, plate 8; vows made by, 174
plague: astrological omens on, 238; bacterial nature of, 231, 238; bubonic, 231–32; competing explanations of, 242; cosmology of, 240; of Egypt, 129; icons' protection from, 242; medieval understanding of, 242; pneumonic, 231, 234; printed talismans for, 255, 257, 258; Saint Sebastian's intercession for, 245–46, 250–52, plate 13; septicemic, 234; sexual intercourse during, 237; spread to Europe, 231; vermin's spread of, 231; waves of, 242, 244. *See also* Black Death
Plato, on death of Socrates, 30, 267
Platt, Eliza: travel diary of, 66
pogroms, anti-Jewish, 244
Polycarp (bishop of Smyrna): Eusebius on, 46–48, 226, 265; as icon of perseverance, 51; miracle of, 48; naming of, 59; parallels with Jesus, 47; rejection of emperor worship, 46, 47; relics of, 48–49; Smyrnaeans' letter on, 46–9; vision of flames, 47, 48
pontificals (liturgical books), 139, 145, plate 4
Pontius Pilate, 133; wife of, 86
Port Elizabeth (Bequia), painting of Saint Vincent at, 106, 108, 108
printing: aid to Protestant Reformation, 203, 205, 217; journalistic, 217
printing, English Elizabethan: human labor in, 219–20

Protasius, Saint: disinterment of bones, 88, 90–91, 182; miracle of, 182

Protestantism. *See* martyrs, Protestant; Reformation

Protoevangelium of James (second century), 164–66; nativity of Jesus in, 165–66

Puerto Rico, Hurricane Maria in, 104

purgatory: means of ascent from, 201, 202; papal control over, 202

quarantena, against spread of plague, 154

Quirino, Nicola, 102

Quirinus (governor of Syria), date of governorship, 127

rats, spread of bubonic plague, 232

Reames, Sherry, 241

recluses, female. *See* anchoresses; women, ascetic

reclusories, English, 140. *See also* anchorholds

Reformation: effect of printing on, 203, 205, 217; effect on saints' cults, 217–18; Roman Catholic response to, 205–6; theologians of, 202

Reformation, English, 211–12; Act of Supremacy (1534), 213–14; anti-Catholic propaganda in, 216, 218; Dissolution of the Monasteries, 214; under Edward VI, 214; literary pillars of, 6, 215–16. *See also* martyrs, Protestant

Reginald FitzUrse, murder of Becket, 194

relics: Ambrose's search for, 87–88, 182; authenticity of, 81, 87, 92–95; of baseball, 79, 93–95; church's promotion of, 74; commodification of, 277; "contact," 4, 71, 72, 81;

counterfeit, 89, 92; cult of, 75; distribution of, 74, 77; Eastern, 277; etymology of, 72; fraudulent, 81; healing power of, 81, 85, 87, 89, 97; holiness through, 75; human intersection with the holy, 79, 81; human remains and, 78; humiliation of, 89; illegally sold, 89, 92; Luther on, 203; miracles of, 74, 88; nonbodily, 78; non-Christian attitudes toward, 77; odor of, 95, 96, 276; in "The Pardoner's Tale," 171; pilgrims' viewing of, 175; portability of, 3, 37, 95; power of preservation, 75; princely collectors of, 4, 73; in private chapels, 77; protective power of, 74–75, 97–98; recovery of, 2, 87–88, 90–91, 182; role in Crusades, 73; of Saint Sebastian, 250; scholarship on, 276–77; second-hand contact, 75–76; stored near altars, 89; theft of, 89, 95–97, 276; of Thomas Becket, 194, 196; touching of, 74; ubiquity of, 78. *See also* martyr bones

relics, passion, 86, 87; of Constantinople, 97–101; Louis IX's, 73, 101, 103. *See also* crucifixion; Edessa, Image of; Shroud of Turin; Veil of Veronica

reliquaries: cosmetic purpose of, 92; opulent, 92, 93. *See also* Grande Châsse reliquary

reliquiae (remnants), 72

remains, human: revulsion at, 77, 78. *See also* martyr bones; relics

Rembrandt van Rijn, *The Stoning of Saint Stephen*, 31, 34

Remembrance Day (Veterans Day), on feast of Martin of Tours, 117

Saint Peter and Paul (Benedictine foundation, Northumbria), 131; hub of learning at, 132

Saint Peter's Basilica: Chapel of Saint Sebastian, 268; indulgences' financing of, 202; Porta Santa of, 268

saints: bureaucratization of, 206, 283; "catacomb," 199, 200, 283; divine will for, 245; existence on earth, 81; ineffective patronage of, 89; intercession with God, 180; local, 206; plague, 172, 245-46, 250-52; resurrection of, 270. *See also* feast days; hagiography; martyrs

saints, patron: of British Isles, 12; of Rome, 247, 274; of Toronto, 18

saints' cults: Counter-Reformation reorganization of, 206; development of, 38. *See also* martyr cults

Saint Vincent of Saragossa (Saint Mary's Anglican Church, Port Elizabeth), 106, 108, 108

San Felipe Segundo (hurricane), 105

San Sebastiano ad Catacumbas (Rome), 249

Santiago de Compostela: pilgrims' guidebook to, 173-74, 175; relics of Saint James at, 19

Sayings of the Desert Fathers: struggle against sexual desire in, 150; use in *Ancrene Wisse*, 151

"Scala Sancta" relic, Helena's acquisition of, 73

Scetis, Desert of: manuscripts from, 64, 66

Scorsese, Martin: *The Last Temptation of Christ*, 155

Scotland, Saint Andrew's cross flag, 18

Sebastian, Saint, 245, 256; Ambrose's praise for, 247; Arnobius's *passio* of,

247-49; birthplace of, 247; in Bolland's hagiography, 261; cult of, 246-47; curse of Diocletian, 42, 249; date of burial, 113; del Biondo's depiction of, 246, 249, 250, 251, plate 12; in *Depositio martyrum*, 247; in *The Golden Legend*, 249-50, 252; intercession for Pavia, 250, 251, 258; interment in catacombs, 247, 249; Lieferinxe's depiction of, 246, 251, plate 13; martyrdom of, 40, 41, 42, 249, 255, 261, 286; martyr's crown of, 246, plate 12; miracles of, 247-50; as patron saint of Rome, 247; as plague saint, 245-46, 250-52, plate 13; printed talismans of, 255, 257, 258; Renaissance paintings of, 40; Saint Peter's Basilica Chapel, 268; service to Diocletian, 247, 248; translation of relics, 250

sexuality, women's, 149-50

Seymour, Jane: marriage to Henry VIII, 214

shrine of the Twenty Martyrs (Hippo), miracle at, 182-83

Shroud of Turin, 4; authenticity of, 82

Sicily, spread of plague to, 231

Simeon, Bishop: martyrdom of, 56, 62

Simeon the Stylite, Saint, 151, 282; clay token depicting, 181; enclosure feat of, 142, 143; fasting by, 142; miracles of, 180; pilgrimage to, 180; residence on pillar, 180-81

Simon of Cyrene, carrying of cross, 28, 29

Simon the Zealot, Saint: crucifixion of, 22

sin: absolution of, 203; forgiveness of, 179; repentance for, 202

Thomas, Saint: disciples in India, 24; place of martyrdom, 20; Toronto ward-namesake, 21; women converts of, 20

Thomas Becket, Saint, 283; Canterbury shrine of, 171–72, 175, 194, plate 9; cult of, 194; expansion of church legal system, 193; ex-voto offerings to, 174; miracles of, 5, 171–72, 192, 194–95; miracle stories of, 194–97; murder of, 194; relationship with Henry II, 192–94; relics of, 194, 196

Thornwell, James Henley: sermon on slavery, 109–10, 278

thoughts, evil: categories of, 152–53

time, reckoning of, 119, 120–21; Bede's, 132–33; by Diocletian's reign, 131, 133

Timothy, Saint: bones of, 97

tombs, martyrs': ransacking of, 87, 88. *See also* martyrs' shrines

Toronto: martyrs' names in, 11–14, 19, 20–21; multiculturalism of, 11–12; patron saints of, 18; ward-namesakes of, 19, 20–21

torture: in *Foxe's Book of Martyrs*, 223, 224; instruments of, xvi, *xvii, xviii, xix,* 208–9; Persian methods of, 57; Roman, 6, 208, 209

Trent, Council of, 205–6, 284

Trump, Donald: far-right Catholic support for, 212

Tudor, Arthur: death of, 212

Twain, Mark, 79; *The Innocents Abroad,* 78; on ubiquity of relics, 78

Ursula, Saint: martyrdom of, 106

Usuard (Parisian monk): abridgement of Ado, 134; liturgical calendar of, 4

US Weather Bureau, 104

Valentinus (Roman senator), and *Chronograph of 354,* 112–13, 128

Van Dam, Raymond, 186

Van Eyck, Jan: "The Hermits and the Pilgrims" (*Ghent Altarpiece*), 176, plate 8

vanity, as cause of disease, 185, 187

Vatican Council, Second: liturgical modernization by, 135

Veil of Veronica, 83–86, 93, 277, plate 1; biblical connection with, 84; fame of, 83; on pilgrims' badges, 170; reliquary of, 83; vernicles (reproductions) of, 83; written record of, 84

Venice: in Fourth Crusade, 101–2; loan to Baldwin II, 102; Saint Mark's remains at, 96

Veronica: legends of, 83–84; in *Passion of the Christ,* 86. *See also* Veil of Veronica

Verulamium (St Albans), England: persecutions in, 13

Vesey, Denmark, 278

Vienne, martyrs of, 49–50; charges against, 50

Vietnam Veterans Memorial (Washington, DC), individuals' names at, 58

Viger, Denis-Benjamin, 12

Vincent, Saint: island named for, 106; martyrdom of, 12, 106; veneration of, 108

Virgin Islands, naming of, 106

Virgins of Cologne, martyrdom of, 106

virtue: learned through suffering, 192; physical health and, 179

vision: Aristotelian theory of, 234; transmission of plague through, 234